BIRTH
of a
DYNASTY

Behind the Pinstripes with the 1996 Yankees

RODALE

JOEL SHERMAN

Foreword by David Cone

Rodale books may be purchased for business or promotional use or for special sales.
For information, please write to:
Special Markets Department, Rodale Inc., 733 Third Avenue, New York, NY 10017

Printed in the United States of America
Rodale Inc. makes every effort to use acid-free ♾, recycled paper ♻.

Cover design by Andy Carpenter
Interior design by Joanna Williams

Library of Congress Cataloging-in-Publication Data
Sherman, Joel, date
    Birth of a dynasty : behind the pinstripes with the 1996 Yankees / Joel Sherman ;
foreword by David Cone.
        p.   cm.
    Includes bibliographical references and index.
    ISBN-13 978–1–59486–244–1 hardcover
    ISBN-10 1–59486–244–3 hardcover
    ISBN-13 978–1–59486–670–8 paperback
    ISBN-10 1–59486–670–8 paperback
    1. New York Yankees (Baseball team)—History.   2. World Series (Baseball) (1996)   I. Cone,
David, 1963-   II. Title.
    GV875.N4S54 2006
    796.357′64097471—dc22   2005036601

Distributed to the trade by Holtzbrinck Publishers

2   4   6   8   10   9   7   5   3   1   hardcover
2   4   6   8   10   9   7   5   3   1   paperback

*To my father, Murry, who taught me hard work, loyalty,
and baseball, and the memory of my mother, Janet, a selfless angel
in a too-often selfish world.*

Contents

Foreword

I'll never forget the look on Joe Torre's face the day we reached the World Series in the fall of 1996. The scene was the visiting clubhouse at Camden Yards in Baltimore. Just a few months earlier, Joe had lost his brother Rocco to a heart attack and another brother, Frank, was in a New York hospital, awaiting a heart transplant. Joe's emotions were evident to all of us who knew and loved him. He was dealing with both great triumph and great loss. A lifelong dream to make the Fall Classic was intersecting with his family drama.

"Coney," Joe said to me as we embraced, "we wouldn't have gotten here without you." He must have said that to every player that day, but we all knew how sincere he was. He had invested in each of us during that trying season, and we had invested in him. We knew we had become more than just a baseball team. We were a collection of human-interest stories that had captured the imagination of New York and the country. Now we were heading to the World Series.

Not only did we defeat the Atlanta Braves for the first Yankees championship since 1978, we added three more over the next four seasons. Yankee fans had waited nearly 20 years to celebrate, but in a span of 5 years, there were four ticker-tape parades culminating with a victory over the crosstown Mets in the 2000 Subway Series.

These years were as noteworthy for what happened outside the lines as for the championships. We became a family and a Yankee team that was hard to hate, even for our most traditional adversaries. These were the most incredible years of my baseball career and, I'm sure, for a lot of other players as well. I experienced the joy of championships, and I did it in association with men whom I considered brothers, such was the respect I had for how they prepared and played.

On Opening Day 1996 in Cleveland, I was set to start in sub-40-degree weather and looked over my right shoulder, and there was a young man named Derek Jeter about to start his rookie season. It was a spectacular beginning. He homered and made a tremendous over-the-head catch of a pop-up to help preserve my win. When I shook his hand after that play, he remarked how cold and clammy my right hand felt. Little did I know, but there was a small aneurysm in my right shoulder that would not be detected for 6 more weeks.

Dwight Gooden, my longtime friend from our time together as New York Mets, stepped into my rotation spot and in mid-May pitched a no-hitter. I was in a hospital that night, the same one Frank Torre would have his heart-transplant surgery in. I remember listening to the radio broadcast from my bed, trying to digest my first meal after having vein-graft surgery performed on my right shoulder, and trying to digest all that was going on just a few miles away at Yankee Stadium. I was overwhelmed by the moment. I had so much elation for Gooden, battling his way back after a drug-related suspension. And I was besieged by self-pity at not being able to experience such a great event with my teammates. I cried in my hospital bathroom in a way I had not since losing a Little League championship when I was 10 years old.

But grown men crying was a theme that would recur during the championship years for the Yankees. Even George Steinbrenner couldn't hold back the tears when receiving the championship trophy from baseball commissioner and fellow owner Bud Selig. Several players saw their fathers or someone close pass away during these years. Personal battles with cancer took the spotlight in 1998 with Darryl Strawberry, in 1999 with Joe Torre, and in 2000 with Mel Stottlemyre. We became experts in crisis management as everyone took turns helping or protecting one another, finding strength in the family we had become in 1996.

It is hard to put into words just what 1996 meant to me, so let me try someone else's: "We play today, we win today. Dat's it." That was the statement our second baseman, Mariano Duncan, made the team motto as the 1996 season progressed. It was especially fitting that year because of all the adversity and distractions that we encountered. We could have had excuses, but that was not a team for excuse making. It was a team that focused on getting a job done. True genius is sometimes measured by the ability to simplify, and Mariano's statement struck a chord throughout the organization. David Szen, the traveling secretary for the Yankees, started to include this motto at the top of every itinerary for road trips.

A lot of people have tried to define or quantify the importance of team chemistry, but this remains one of the mysteries of sport. A bonding and confidence materialized before our eyes that year because everyone bought into a team-oriented concept. You ask me how this happened, and why . . . Numerous variables came into play, but one constant I remember was, no matter who was hurt, who we were playing, or what kind of lineup we ran out there, "We play today, we win today. Dat's it." It was our rally cry. It was our soul.

Joel Sherman was there every step of the way, covering the development of those championship Yankees for the *New York Post*. I remember him as tough but fair and a relentless pursuer of the inside story. I'm confident his work ethic will translate into one of the most insightful looks at these years when we were trying to build our own dynasty, one that could stand forever against the storied past of the Yankees.

—David Cone

1 | THE PERFECT
ENDING/BEGINNING

What if Buck Showalter had known?

It was the eighth inning of Game 5 of the 1995 Division Series, and David Cone was fried. He was pitching with his heart and his head. His arm was just about gone. No major league pitcher had thrown more innings or faced more batters than Cone had during the 1995 regular season—first for the Toronto Blue Jays and now for the Yankees. He already had won Division Series Game 1 against a Seattle lineup so fierce that it had set franchise records for homers (182) and runs scored (796), despite having its regular season shortened to 145 games by labor unrest. However, to navigate land mines named Ken Griffey Jr., Edgar Martinez, Tino Martinez, and Jay Buhner in the opener, Cone had coaxed another grueling eight innings out of his 32-year-old right arm; he had dispensed another 135 high-octane pitches.

Now in a win-or-go-home Game 5 at Seattle's Kingdome, Cone had uncovered enough outs in the mighty Mariners' lineup to carry a 4–2 lead into the bottom of the eighth. But the cost was 120 pitches, the strain robbing him of a few miles per hour on his fastball, the bite on his breaking stuff, and overall precision. Yet no one was warming up in the Yankee bullpen. Not yet, anyway. The manager trusted none of his relievers.

The Kingdome shook again, the noise swelling before Cone had even thrown a pitch to initiate the bottom of the eighth. The 57,411 fans in attendance were reacting to a 6-foot, 10-inch freak of nature beginning to throw from the

1

bullpen mound down the left-field line. Over the past 7 weeks, Seattle had transformed into a baseball town. Normally at this time of year, the NFL Seahawks dominated sporting attention in the Emerald City. But earlier on this day the Seahawks had lost, 34–14, to their most heated rival, the Raiders, in Oakland, to comparatively blasé local reaction. Meanwhile, a banner at the Kingdome read, "Who said Seattle isn't a baseball town?"

No single player was more responsible for this conversion than Randy Johnson. The Mariners, 13 games behind the California Angels on August 2, had won the last 10 times Johnson started in the regular season and were 27–3 overall when he pitched. The capper was October 2, when, on 3 days' rest, Johnson still had enough heat to author a three-hit, 12-strikeout tour de force that enabled Seattle to defeat the Angels in a one-game playoff, break the deadlock atop the AL West, and advance to the playoffs for the first time in its 19-year history.

In this Division Series, Seattle also had to play from behind. The Yankees won the first two games of this best-of-five series in the Bronx. But Mariners manager Lou Piniella remembers nearly a decade later why he retained hope. "We had Randy in Game 3. The whole club trusted we would win that game and felt we would beat [Scott] Kamieniecki the next day. And then it is one game. And that is exactly what happened." Johnson won Game 3. The Yankees, with Kamieniecki unable to hold a five-run lead, lost Game 4. And that propelled this riveting Division Series to a decisive Game 5: The Yankees up 4–2 in the eighth. Randy Johnson up in the Mariner bullpen. No one up in the Yankee bullpen.

What if Buck Showalter had known?

Somehow the crowd grew louder, the noise trapped and reverberating within the Kingdome. Years later the players would remember the sound as an actual part of the game, it was so earsplitting. With one out, Cone tried to go away with a 1–0 fastball to Griffey, but the withering effect of so many pitches was obvious. The pitch tailed back over the plate—essentially a ball on a tee for a hitter as hot and great as Junior Griffey. He responded by going deep into the right-field second deck for his third homer off Cone in the series, his fifth overall. That tied Reggie Jackson for most homers in a postseason series. Jackson, in the capacity of special advisor to the Yankees, happened to be in the Kingdome to see it, watching from a private enclosed box recessed slightly down the first-base line. In the row behind him was George Steinbrenner, glowering toward the field. The Mariners were down by one. Still, no one was up in the Yankee bullpen as this homer deprived Cone of any lingering faith in his fast-ball. He threw 22 more pitches in the inning and asked the majors' most abused arm to generate just two additional fastballs.

Nevertheless, Cone followed Griffey by getting Edgar Martinez to ground out to short. Griffey might have tied Jackson's record, but signs around the Kingdome paid homage to "Señor October" in honor of Martinez, who was tor-turing Yankee pitching. In Game 4 alone, he had hit a three-run homer off of Kamieniecki to erase much of that early 5–0 Yankee lead, and he had clubbed an eighth-inning grand slam to straightaway center off John Wetteland to break a 6–6 tie, assure a Game 5, and establish in Showalter's mind that his closer was not to be trusted in this decisive matchup. But Showalter could simply have bypassed Wetteland and turned to the only reliever who had performed well in this series for the Yankees. He could have turned to his own freak of nature. Only he did not yet know that Mariano Rivera was a freak of nature.

Somebody in the ballpark did know: a 21-year-old who was present in the Kingdome on a "watch, but don't talk" basis. "A lot of people didn't know that, not just Buck," Derek Jeter recalls. "But I knew it from the minor leagues. I knew what Mariano could do."

Jeter and Rivera had played together throughout the Yankees' system, in Greensboro, Tampa, Albany, and Columbus. They had coincidentally both been optioned to Triple-A Columbus on the same day—June 11, 1995—after their first major league cups of coffee. In fact, 1995 was the pinstriped debut year not only for Jeter and Rivera but also for Andy Pettitte and Jorge Posada, which symbolized the rejuvenation of the farm system over the past decade. Rivera,

Pettitte, and Posada (on the bench as a third catcher) were all active that night of October 8, 1995. Jeter was not. By rule, he was a bystander and, by Showalter's distrustful decree, Rivera was shackled far too long from action.

In October 1995, in fact, Rivera was not even the most prized member of his own family in a Yankee uniform. That honor belonged to his cousin Ruben. It actually had been Showalter's idea to have Jeter and outfielder Ruben Rivera — the twin crown jewels of the organization — travel with the club during the post-season, partake in the pregame workouts, and sit on the bench in uniforms, though neither was active. Jeter, the sixth pick in the 1992 draft, was given a $700,000 signing bonus to forgo a scholarship to the University of Michigan and was instantly hailed as a special prospect. The Rivera cousins hadn't received either the same riches or reception.

Following the 1988 season, working as a birddog for the Kansas City Royals in his native Panama, Herb Raybourn had traveled to the seaside city of La Chorrera to watch the national tournament for the 18-to-25 age group, and he saw a scrawny shortstop playing for the Oeste team whom he noted had a nice arm, but not enough bat to consider signing.

A year later in the same tournament, Oeste's top pitcher performed so poorly that the shortstop volunteered to pitch against the San Carlos team in San Carlos. The converted shortstop pitched so well that his teammates, catcher Claudino Hernández and center fielder Emilio Gáez, tipped off a Yankee scout named Chico Heron and got the converted shortstop into a Yankee tryout camp run by Heron 2 weeks later in Panama City. Heron watched Mariano Rivera throw one time, and, he says, "his arm was so loose and the ball jumped so much that I told him to stay" the entire week of camp. On the final day, the Yankees' new director of Latin American operations watched Rivera pitch. That executive was Herb Raybourn.

Raybourn instantly recognized that this was the shortstop with the good arm. Rivera was already 20 years old, and his fastball was a pedestrian 85 to 87 mph. Latin American baseball prospects are like female tennis players; those earmarked for greatness are recognized in their teens, often in their early teens. So to Yankees executives in the States, Raybourn knew, the combination of adulthood and sub-90 velocity would mark Rivera as undesirable—particularly because it made Rivera an afterthought even on these dusty fields. No other club was interested in Rivera.

But Raybourn saw possibility. He watched just nine pitches, then told Rivera to stop. Heron figured that meant he did not like the scout's find. But it was the opposite: Raybourn had seen enough to love the fluidity of Rivera's arm, the cat-quick athleticism, and how Rivera's pitches sustained deceptive life regardless of the speed. What Raybourn appreciated most was in his imagination. Rivera was just 155 pounds. But in Raybourn's head, he was putting on weight and miles per hour. A lot could happen with better nutrition and the right training program.

What Raybourn imagined convinced him to visit Rivera's home in Puerto Caimito, a fishing town on the country's southeast coast, 40 miles east of Panama City. Rivera's father captained a shrimp boat owned by another man. As a teenager, Rivera worked 12-hour days alongside his father, who was affectionately known as Captain Mariano in the tiny village that reeked of fish. This line of work kept the Riveras in a regular tango with poverty, so when Raybourn showed up offering $2,000, Rivera quite willingly signed right there in his own living room on February 17, 1990. Raybourn knew if more teams were after Rivera, the offer would have to be $25,000, maybe even $50,000. But no one else saw what Herb Raybourn saw.

"I was surprised by everything," Rivera recalls of those frenetic few weeks. "Usually a player prepares for years. Here I was signing, and I wasn't even a pitcher."

Rivera was so appreciative that a year later, when Raybourn was back in La Chorrera to give him an award, he tipped off the Yankees executive to another local player with great skills, his 16-year-old cousin Ruben, who was making money on the side as a pearl diver. Later that day, Raybourn watched Ruben

Rivera double twice and triple for La Chorrera in the district playoffs. Raybourn held a private tryout the following afternoon for Ruben Rivera and signed him immediately for $3,500, knowing that other organizations would pursue Ruben—unlike Mariano—when word spread.

The scout's enthusiasm proved justified. While Mariano's organizational climb was slowed by elbow surgery in 1992, Ruben exhibited a power/speed combination as a center fielder that was drawing comparisons to Mickey Mantle. By the postseason of 1995—with all their personnel wearing black No. 7s on their left sleeves to honor the passing of Mantle in August—the Yankees were sure the family gem was Ruben. That was why Showalter wanted Jeter and Ruben to experience the playoffs up close, with an eye on mentally preparing them for future postseasons—postseasons Showalter would not be part of because the real jewel was still sitting in the bullpen, watching the life leave David Cone's right arm.

What if Buck Showalter had known?

As early as August 24, Showalter had begun worrying about Wetteland against the Mariners. The Yankees had lost five straight games, falling a hopeless 14½ games behind the Red Sox. Yet despite being 53–55, the Yankees were just 4½ games out of a playoff spot because this was the first year a postseason would have wild cards. Cone had won his only three starts in the Kingdome, and Showalter had decided to run with his ace as long as possible in the opener of that three-game series on August 24. The tough-minded Cone permitted a first-inning grand slam to Jay Buhner, yet persevered to throw 132 pitches, work eight innings, and hand Wetteland a 7–6 lead to protect in the ninth. Wetteland recorded two outs without harm before walking Vince Coleman, allowing a game-tying single to Joey Cora, and surrendering a winning two-run homer to Ken Griffey Jr.

In Game 1 of this Division Series, Wetteland had again taken over from Cone after eight innings, this time with a 9–4 lead, and gave up two runs and brought the tying run to the plate twice. In Game 2, he had allowed a 12th-inning homer to Griffey, but the Yankees rallied dramatically to win and carry a two-games-to-none lead westward in spite of their high-strung closer. And then, in Game 4, Wetteland was summoned in the eighth inning to maintain a 6–6 tie. He never registered an out against four batters, Edgar Martinez culminating the brutalizing sequence with his grand slam. So Showalter's faith in Wetteland expired while he remained fully invested in Cone, ragged arm and all. It was only after Cone had refused to throw a single fastball to Tino Martinez, walking the first baseman on five pitches following Griffey's homer, that Showalter finally, reluctantly, decided to warm up a reliever. But not John Wetteland.

The noise was so Led Zeppelin–on-steroids deafening inside the Kingdome that the Yankees' bullpen catcher, Glenn Sherlock, had to keep his hand on the phone at all times simply to feel the vibration because he could not hear the ring. Sherlock was instructed to begin warming Mariano Rivera. Sherlock had been Rivera's first pro manager, in 1990 in the Gulf Coast League. And although Rivera had begun his career considered, at best, a fringe prospect, Sherlock had come to adore the professionalism, competitiveness, maturity, and resoluteness Rivera radiated. Sherlock thought the quiet youngster had the stomach for a challenge, regardless of the role or atmosphere. But that had been 5 years and one elbow surgery ago against kids fresh out of the draft. This was the Seattle Mariners, on national TV for the right to advance to the AL Championship Series. So Showalter permitted Cone to soldier on.

Three sliders into an at-bat against Jay Buhner, the count was 2–1. Cone tried a fastball once more, and Buhner lashed a single perhaps the width of the baseball over the glove of leaping second baseman Randy Velarde. Cone, his black T-shirt soaked under his short-sleeved uniform, was now at 135 pitches, the same number he had used in Game 1. His last two fastballs had been mauled for a homer by Griffey and a rifled single by Buhner. Yet as Alex Diaz moved to the plate to pinch-hit for shortstop Felix Fermin, the reliever with the Yankees' best fastball remained down the right-field line, warming up.

On August 24, Joey Cora's ninth-inning single against Wetteland should have been caught by shortstop Tony Fernandez. It eluded him by an even smaller distance than Buhner's ball evaded Velarde in Game 5. An inch here or there can change history. The Mariners had entered that August 24 game 54–55, two games ahead of last-place Oakland and in third place, 11½ games behind the Angels. Just 17,592 had attended that game in the Kingdome, and it seemed possible the Mariners would record their 17th losing season in their 19-year history. But Griffey's homer off of Wetteland altered the course of a season and a franchise. The Mariners went on to win 25 of their final 36 games. The historic run spawned the phrase "Refuse to Lose" as baseball shockingly joined grunge and coffee as Seattle addictions.

The love affair came at a desperate time. On September 19, even with their baseball infatuation growing, Seattle voters narrowly defeated a referendum to fund a new Mariners ballpark. More would be needed to keep the Mariners in the Great Northwest, to motivate the public, and to develop the political groundswell necessary to build a new facility.

"Our whole franchise rested on that Game 5," remembers Alex Rodriguez, then a 20-year-old rookie who was a mere pinch-runner in that series. "If we didn't win, we were going to Tampa."

In the euphoric aftermath of the Division Series, the King County Council held a special session to approve the combination of tax increases and lottery proceeds necessary to fund what would become Safeco Field. But the state-of-the-art stadium was not the most important institution built from the happenings inside the cavernous Kingdome on October 8. From the rubble of one of the most heart-rending losses in their history, the Yankees constructed a dynasty. No one could have known it that night. No one could have recognized a Yankee season slowly ebbing toward extinction and one of the greatest runs in sports history coming to life because of this debilitating setback. No one could have foreseen that there was a 165-pound answer in the bullpen whom Showalter was afraid to use and who very probably would have rewritten the ending of Game 5 and kept Yankee history and, thus, baseball history from changing forever.

Just a week earlier, in another domed stadium, Showalter's Yankee future had seemed so certain—the Yankees had made a mad rush to the playoffs, just like Seattle. After the August 24 loss to the Mariners, matters worsened initially for the Yankees. The next night, Seattle knocked rookie Andy Pettitte out in $2^2/_3$ innings. It was easy to ignore amid the loss that Mariano Rivera had relieved Pettitte and beguiled the Mariners over $5^1/_3$ innings, allowing just two hits and one run, that coming on a homer by Edgar Martinez. The next day Randy Johnson threw a three-hitter in a 7–0 rout that sent the Yankees to an eighth straight loss. They were 53–58 and not only $5^1/_2$ games out of the wild card but behind five teams: Texas, Milwaukee, Seattle, Kansas City, and Oakland. So much had gone wrong in a year. In 1994, the Yankees had the AL's best record at the time of the season-canceling strike, and Showalter and GM Gene "Stick" Michael were being hailed for the player personnel decisions and leadership that had elevated the skill level and professionalism in the clubhouse, raising the Yankees from humiliation to contention.

The 1980s had been the Yankees' first title-less decade since the teens, and the 1990 Yankees managed first by Bucky Dent and then by Stump Merrill had produced the worst winning percentage for a Yankee team in 77 years. But Michael took over the baseball operations in August 1990 after George Steinbrenner was suspended for paying a reputed gambler named Howie Spira for damning information about Dave Winfield. Michael hired Showalter following the 1991 season to replace the uncouth Merrill. Together, Stick and Buck built something special, especially when they did not let the cancellation of a potential championship in 1994 daunt them, and instead obtained White Sox ace Jack McDowell and Expos closer John Wetteland for the 1995 season. Those acquisitions made the Yankees the darling pick to win the 1995 World Series. But the Yankees underachieved through most of the campaign, even after acquiring Cone in late July. It was not until the Yankees avoided a four-game sweep at the Kingdome by beating the Mariners on August 27 that they finally took off, going 26–7 to conclude the season.

The Yankees had entered the final weekend at Toronto's SkyDome needing to win all three games to clinch their first playoff berth in 14 years and assure the first postseason action for Don Mattingly of his 1,785-game career that began in 1982. The Yankees reached the ninth inning of the Friday night, September 29, series opener in Toronto trailing 3–0. The Blue Jays had a lefty reliever named Tony Castillo pitching, and the Yankees closed to 3–2 with one on, one out and the ninth-place hitter, righty-swinging Pat Kelly, due. The standard move was to summon a righty reliever such as Tim Crabtree or Mike Timlin. But Showalter had ordered lefty slugger Darryl Strawberry to simply grab a bat and sit on the bench in full view of Toronto manager Cito Gaston. Kelly, hitting .238 with three homers, hardly looked imposing in comparison—that is, until he pulled a 2–2 pitch inside the left-field foul pole to give the Yankees a 4–3 triumph. Showalter also manipulated his rotation on the final weekend to provide further recuperation time for McDowell, who had pitched much of the second half of the season with a muscle strain in his upper back that left a golf-ball-size knot under his right shoulder blade. It was the first missed start of his career. Riskier for Showalter was holding Cone back to be used only in case the Yankees faced elimination, or if a one-game playoff to decide the wild card was necessary that Monday. Under the best scenario, that would give Cone, who had started September 27 on 3 days' rest for the first time in 4 years, an extra day to ready for a Division Series opener Tuesday. In the worst-case scenario, Showalter was shunning two veteran stars and asking three young, homegrown starters—Andy Pettitte, Scott Kamieniecki, and Sterling Hitchcock—to save the season and perhaps his job.

Pettitte, Kamieniecki, and Hitchcock each won that weekend. Mattingly,

Donnie Baseball, pounded the artificial turf as the last out was recorded. The Yankees were in the playoffs for the first time since 1981, and Showalter's strategizing meant Cone was fresh to start Game 1. Steinbrenner entered the coaches' room after the clinching victory and those inside expected congratulations. Instead, Steinbrenner barked at the group, "If you assholes don't get to the World Series, you're all out of here." In the euphoric clubhouse, Steinbrenner put on a different show. He turned misty-eyed and told reporters that Showalter had a "sixth sense" to make the right moves and "the last 5 days, Buck was a genius. Every move he made worked out. He reminded me of Billy Martin."

The quick change of emotions was pure Steinbrenner, whose rare pleasant thoughts about an employee had the same lasting power as the concentration span of a Kool Aid–addicted child. And the Boss's mood had darkened considerably as he watched the 1995 Division Series unfold. Strawberry was reduced to a spectator, and this time the Boss found nothing brilliant about a player he had personally signed 4 months earlier being limited to a high-profile cheerleader. The teams combined to hit a then postseason series record 22 homers, and Showalter was trying to match firepower with the volcanic Mariners by stubbornly sticking with the slap-hitting left fielder Dion James, 1-for-12 in the series, because he felt Strawberry was too deficient defensively.

Further aggravating Steinbrenner was that a Seattle victory would mean a slap-in-his-face triumph for its manager, Lou Piniella, whom he had twice fired as Yankee skipper. In Game 5 at the Kingdome, Steinbrenner was joined in his private box by Yankee officials Brian Cashman, Stuart Hershon, Reggie Jackson, Tim McCleary, Gene Michael, and David Sussman. Sussman, the Yankees' executive vice president and general counsel, recalls the box feeling 4 feet by 4 feet, so overwhelming was the stress. "Some of the tension naturally existed from the deciding game and the fact that we had led the series 2–0, and that we had experienced such a long drought without being in the playoffs," Sussman says. "But most of the tension emanated from George by force of his will and character and manner. He was alternating cheering when something positive happened and directing blame at Showalter throughout the series. George kept coming to the conclusion that Showalter was a novice and that Lou has such great experience. Over and over, George kept saying, 'Buck is being outmanaged by Lou.'"

The contracts of Showalter and Michael were up at the end of the season, and their Yankee careers were now in greater peril than ever as Piniella, with a 1–0 count on Alex Diaz, sent in Alex Rodriguez to pinch-run at second for Tino Martinez. A few Yankee officials already were wondering how to replace Don Mattingly if he retired, and Martinez's .409 Division Series average was a calling card. Pitching coach Nardi Contreras and catcher Mike Stanley had visited the mound, but Cone had all but ignored them. Sure, Buhner had singled, but it meant Cone was now through the lethal 3-4-5-6 of Griffey, Edgar Martinez, Tino Martinez, and Buhner, who combined to hit .456 (41-for-90), with 9 of the 11 homers generated by Seattle in this Division Series.

Cone imagined himself a great jazz musician, capable of conjuring what worked as he went along, able by sense of feel to know what was in his repertoire that day and adjust. He was not even a teenager when he first experimented with release points and finger pressure by learning how to make Wiffle balls dart and dance away from the swings of his older brothers, Danny and Chris. That was in his backyard on St. John Avenue on the northeast side of Kansas City, dubbed Cone-dlestick Park by the family. Now, in the cacophonous Kingdome, Cone was still convincing himself that between his will, his intellect, and his capacity to play the right notes at the right time, he could steer through any danger. But what that often cost him was pitches. Cone never gave in and he never conserved, especially with runners on base, and thus he asked a body built more like a movie usher than a pro athlete to produce whatever was necessary to succeed.

The jazz musician was learning just what the price was. He did not have enough arm to challenge even Alex Diaz with a fastball, not with the tying run at second base and the series-winning run at first. So Cone, using exclusively sliders and splitters, walked a light-hitting reserve outfielder who had drawn just

13 walks all season in nearly 300 plate appearances. The bases were now loaded. A-Rod, in this series for the first time, moved to third as the tying run. Piniella called for Doug Strange to pinch-hit for Dan Wilson. Cone was at 141 pitches. Strange had not played since Game 2, which concluded memorably with Jim Leyritz's two-run, 15th-inning homer into a driving rain at Yankee Stadium at 1:22 a.m. Throughout that game and also the previous day's Game 1, Steinbrenner had inflicted himself on the series by publicly warring with the umpires and AL president Gene Budig over what he felt was a spate of calls against the Yankees.

Between Steinbrenner's hysteria, Leyritz's dramatics, and the continuing fallout from the previous day's not-guilty verdict for O.J. Simpson, the October abilities of another player were easily overlooked in Game 2. Mariano Rivera had stamped his first playoff game with $3\frac{1}{3}$ innings of five-strikeout, two-hit, no-run relief to earn the win. Strange had faced him twice in that game, popping out and whiffing. Rivera had followed that with a four-up, four-down, two-strikeout effort in Game 3, overshadowed this time by Randy Johnson's brilliance. But Gene Michael was not blinded. To this point Mariano Rivera's major league career had consisted of spot starts, long relief, and fluctuating results. Michael, however, always trusted his scout's eyes and turned to David Sussman and said, "I think we found someone here." The statement resonated years later with Sussman because "Stick is not the kind of man to make statements like that."

But Showalter did not trust his eyes. Like playing the slumping Dion James rather than turning to Strawberry, Showalter obstinately stuck to his preconceptions. In this case, he had preprogrammed himself to believe in Cone beyond his expiration pitch.

Rivera?

As a rookie manager in 1992, Showalter had once explained to a *New York Post* reporter that strikeout-to-walk ratio was a strong indicator of which pitchers were true prospects. This was a decade before Billy Beane and the *Moneyball* revolution would make such computations common. Showalter pointed only to the numbers in the Yankee media guide while covering up a name: 58 strikeouts, 7 walks in the Gulf Coast League; 123 strikeouts, 36 walks in the Sally League. "That is impressive in any league," Showalter had said. "This guy is going to make it."

The guy was Mariano Rivera.

But now, at the biggest moment of his managerial career, Showalter did not care about numbers on a stat sheet. His contract was up in 3 weeks, and Steinbrenner's praise from Toronto's SkyDome had already dissipated. If the Mariners were playing to stay in Seattle, Showalter was managing this game to stay in the only organization from which he had ever drawn a paycheck. He had toiled 7 years as a minor league player, eclipsed by a superior first base/outfield prospect named Don Mattingly. He had served 8 more years as a minor league manager or major league coach as Steinbrenner favored bigger names such as Lou Piniella. Now he was the longest-serving manager of the Steinbrenner era. But the fiery Piniella was in the Mariner dugout, making the Boss even crazier about what was transpiring.

What if Buck Showalter had known?

This was the first and only time a monstrosity called The Baseball Network televised the postseason. The Network was a joint venture of Major League Baseball, ABC, and NBC, designed to give baseball a direct share of national advertising revenue. But the concept left fans irate because telecasts were regionalized, meaning only Game 5 of the Yankee-Mariner series was available in every home in the country, and that was because it was the lone first-round game still in play. But the network had a more devastating impact on the Yankees. To simplify coverage for the fledgling operation, the Commissioner's Office had permitted the matchups for the first-ever eight-team opening round to be prearranged. So, in the AL, the wild-card winner was to face the West champion, and the winners of the East and Central were to meet.

In 1998, the majors went to a fairer system, in which the team with the best record faced the wild card, as long as those two teams were not from the same division. Had that system been in place in 1995, the wild-card Yankees would have faced the Cleveland Indians in the Division Series. And the Yankees owned the Indians. In 1994, they had gone 9–0 against Cleveland, their first undefeated record against an opponent. The Yankees broke the Indians' longest-ever home winning streak of 18 games in 1994, and they also ended Cleveland winning streaks at Jacobs Field of 8 and 14 games in 1995. All told, the Yankees were 6–2 at the 2-year-old Jake. Because of all of that, a young Indian employee named Josh Byrnes, who was in charge of video scouting, pessimistically began to assemble a report to face the Yankees in the AL Championship Series as soon as Leyritz's homer gave the Yankees a two-games-to-none lead over the Mariners. "We feared the Yankees a lot more than we feared the Red Sox [who Cleveland beat in the Division Series] or the Mariners," Byrnes says.

To further appease The Baseball Network, Major League Baseball had also approved a system whereby a five-game series would move cities just once. So the club with the home-field advantage opened with two away games before returning for as many as three home games. This also would change in 1998 to a two-two-one format. However, in 1995, because of The Baseball Network, the Yankees had to play the Mariners rather than the Indians in the first round, and Seattle had generated 23 homers and 84 runs against Yankee pitching during the regular season, the most by any opponent. And because of The Baseball Network, the Yankees had to play three straight momentum-changing games at the Kingdome, where they had performed in an unnerved fashion in going 1–6, their worst-ever regular-season record in Seattle.

Now, here they were in the third straight game at the Kingdome, the noise more ferocious than ever as Rivera and Randy Johnson both stopped their warmup activities to see Cone throw two breaking balls and two splitters to fall behind Strange 3–1. Third-base coach Sam Perlozzo and Strange met midway down the line to chat, and shortstop Tony Fernandez went to the mound to encourage Cone with a pat on the back. Cone sent a fastball down the middle and

Strange, taking all the way, saw the count run full. Now what to call as the Kingdome crushed down upon Cone and the Yankee season? Strange had just taken the fastball. He would not do that again, but could Cone risk a less-controllable off-speed pitch? Cone was at 146 pitches, his warrior mentality having taken him to this place. It was that strength of mind, as much as his devastating array of pitches, that in several weeks would motivate the start of the 1996 AL East race as the Yankees and Orioles would bid and bid and bid some more for the gutsy free agent's services.

Cone stared in for a sign from Mike Stanley. During the year, there had been plenty of scuttlebutt that Cone did not like how Stanley worked behind the plate. But in this case, pitcher and catcher were in synchronization. Both agreed that the veteran righty just did not have enough fastball for this situation. Cone envisioned throwing a split to the middle of the plate that would dive and seduce Strange into an inning-ending groundout. Coming to a set from the first-base side of the rubber, Cone delivered a pitch that by 45 feet already was knee-high and sinking rapidly toward the hitter. Strange barely lifted his front right foot in anticipation to swing, but this splitter had no tantalizing mystery, so Strange put his foot down and watched the ball bounce between him and the plate and into Stanley's mitt. Home-plate umpire Jim Evans made no signal. Cone's follow-through had taken him to the first-base side of the oval, where he doubled over in anguish, staring at the floor like a drunk waiting to vomit. Cone instantly decoded the implications; he did not need to see A-Rod actually touch home plate. All this work and all this trauma on his arm, and for what? His 147th pitch of this scintillating game and the last pitch of his draining season was ball 4. Yankees 4, Mariners 4.

Showalter finally emerged to get him. Cone walked off holding his glove in his right hand. The tunnel to the clubhouse was right in the middle of the dugout, and Cone never lifted his head or broke his stride. Cone was all about accountability, and he felt that he had let down himself, a team, and a city 3,000 miles away. The first coach to reach him for a pat on the back was Willie Randolph. The first player was not even active. Derek Jeter. Mariano Rivera was at last in the game, but no longer in position to preserve a series-clinching lead. What if Buck Showalter had known?

"At that time even I didn't know what I had," Mariano Rivera says.

Rivera had yet to develop the cutter, the pitch that would elevate him to the pantheon of all-time greats. Instead, what he had in 1995 was a crocodile-tears pitch. He unfurled from a slow, smooth delivery that relaxed hitters, a calm before the storm, and then unleashed a high fastball at 95 mph. In October 1995, hitters simply could not lay off of a pitch even Rivera conceded was "straight as an arrow," and they just as simply could not hit it.

There had been a time when the organization had stopped believing Rivera would ever generate enough fastball to be effective in the majors. Instinctively, Rivera had a fluid delivery, the quality Herb Raybourn had liked so much. But he did not know how to pitch. He developed a changeup that actually served as his out pitch through much of his minor league career. But Rivera felt he needed more—a breaking ball of some sort. So, with his rudimentary knowledge of pitching, Rivera figured that to make his slider dive more, he had to snap his wrist with even greater torque. As a result, he ended up under the scalpel of Frank Jobe, MD, on August 27, 1992, to fix nerve damage in his elbow. For the Yankees, it was the most well-timed elbow surgery in history. Less than 3 months later, Major League Baseball held its expansion draft to stock the Colorado Rockies and Florida Marlins, and the way the rules were arranged, Rivera had enough professional service time that he had to be protected, or else he was free to be drafted.

But the Yankees did not protect him because there were no certainties about his future after elbow surgery. The Yankees used their 15 protection slots to shield, among others, Mark Hutton, Domingo Jean, Sam Militello, Russ Springer, Dave Silvestri, and Gerald Williams. The Yankees lost Charlie Hayes in the first round and protected Kevin Maas, Hensley Meulens, Danny Tartabull, and Randy Velarde. They lost Carl Everett to the Marlins in the second round and pulled back Robert Eenhoorn, Steve Farr, Scott Kamieniecki, and Bobby Muñoz. The Rockies drafted catcher Brad Ausmus in the third and final round. The Yankees never protected Rivera, and neither the Marlins nor the Rockies saw reason to draft damaged goods.

During that spring training, Rivera began to rebuild arm strength by playing long toss on the backfields of Fort Lauderdale Stadium with Whitey Ford and Ron Guidry, which remains an enduring image for Showalter. Rivera's recuperation was quickened by his elite athleticism. Hoyt Wilhelm, Rivera's first minor league pitching coach, broke up the monotony of the daily routine by throwing batting practice to his pitchers, and he swore to the manager, Glenn Sherlock, that Rivera was one of the best hitters on the team. The following year at Single-A Greensboro, manager Brian Butterfield watched Rivera run down balls during batting practice and decided, "This guy is our best outfielder."

Rivera's recovery from surgery and rise through the system were mostly about makeup, however. Rivera impressed Yankee personnel with his unflappable persona and humble self-assurance. His face before, during, and after good performances and bad was harder to read than Amarillo Slim at a poker table. "I was with Mariano when he came back . . . and he is the same guy he is now," says reliever Mike DeJean, who played with Rivera in 1993 and 1994 in the Yankee system. "I never saw him get mad. I never saw him sweat. When he pitched, it was like he was acting as if he were the only guy on the field. Even then you could see the easy mechanics and how the ball just exploded out of his hand. But more than anything, you could see Mariano had quiet confidence."

By the time the 1995 season began, these attributes had enabled Rivera to work his way back to being ranked ninth best among Yankee prospects by Baseball America. His cousin, Ruben, was first, Derek Jeter was second, and Andy Pettitte was third. In late May, Mariano Rivera was summoned from Columbus, made four Yankee starts, and, with just a 90 mph fastball and skimpy secondary pitches, worked to a 10.20 ERA before his demotion. Off of that performance, and with his club hungry for an experienced starter, Michael was mulling the Detroit Tigers' trade request of David Wells for Rivera. Then, on June 26, 1995, against the Rochester Red Wings, Rivera pitched a rain-shortened, five-inning no-hitter at Columbus's Cooper Stadium in the second game of a doubleheader. "He kept pumping fastball after fastball, and they had no chance," remembers his catcher that day, Jorge Posada. But these fastballs were unique for Rivera.

"I faced Rivera as a starter in Columbus and thought he was no big deal," recalls catcher Gregg Zaun, who hit against Rivera in the minors as an Oriole farmhand. "Then he added 3 to 4 miles per hour to his fastball, and everything changed. Well, that and he moved into the role he was born to be in."

To this day, Rivera cannot offer a physical reason why his fastball suddenly soared to 96 mph and stayed consistently at 95. A religious man, Rivera calls it an act of God. The nonbeliever was Michael, who saw the reports filed from the game the following day. He called Bill Evers, the Columbus manager, to verify that the radar gun was working properly. Not satisfied, Michael phoned his friend Jerry Walker, who, as the Cardinals' director of player personnel, had been at Cooper Stadium because St. Louis also had interest in Rivera. Concerned about tipping off his competitor to his true intentions, Michael ambled through the conversation on a variety of topics before casually asking about Rivera's gun readings. Ninety-five, Walker offered. Michael hung up and told Showalter that not only were the Yankees not trading Rivera, they needed to call him back up to start.

On July 4, Rivera benefited from the glare of an afternoon game time at Comiskey Park and scripted the best of his 10 major league starts, an eight-inning shutout with 11 strikeouts against the White Sox. By early August, however, Rivera had pitched his way back to Columbus, and when he returned a few weeks later, he made just one start. The last of his career. Against the Mariners. On September 5, 1995, Cal Ripken tied Lou Gehrig's iron-man record by playing his 2,130th consecutive game, and Rivera was bombed for five runs in $4\frac{2}{3}$ innings. He was relegated to the bullpen thereafter and, as at the very onset of his professional career, was thought so little of that he was used essentially for mop-up and put on the postseason roster as the ninth pitcher on a 10-man staff. Only lefty Bob McDonald, the lone Yankee available who went unused in the Division Series, was lower on the pitching hierarchy.

Now the Yankee season was in his right hand, the world shaking around him. Mike Blowers, 21-for-50 and a .420 career hitter with the bases loaded, was the batter, the series-winning run was 90 feet away, and just farther down the line, still lurking to protect that potential lead in the ninth inning, was the intimidating Randy Johnson, the first pitcher since Bob Feller from 1938 to 1941 to lead the majors in strikeouts 4 straight years. Rivera had thus far faced 16 batters in the series, allowed two singles, permitted no runs, and struck out seven. As early as the fourth inning, with Cone's pitch count already escalating, the Mariners' bombastic play-by-play man Dave Niehaus had mentioned on KIRO radio that in the Yankee bullpen, "only one man has been effective, and that is Mariano Rivera." But Buck Showalter thought he was stealing outs with Rivera, not getting a very real gift. He failed to recognize that Rivera's calm was not a minor league pose; there simply was no tremor in his game. Rivera hissed a fastball down the middle, strike 1 to Blowers. Rivera wore long black sleeves under his uniform top, hiding the 4-inch-long red scar on the inside of his right elbow. He came with high heat again, and Blowers fouled it back. Rivera reared back one last time, his glitchless delivery manufacturing a fastball on the outside corner at the knees. The pop of the glove finally turned off the noise of the Kingdome momentarily. Blowers did not bother swinging. Why would he? It is possible that if that at-bat were still going on today, Blowers would not yet have a hit. Blowers struck out looking; the inning was over.

But what if Buck Showalter had known?

"When someone says they would never do anything different, I say bull-fucking-shit," Showalter said nearly a decade removed from his fateful decision. "I don't know what would have happened," Rivera says. "Nobody knows."

Showalter did not know that Piniella was pleading with his hitters in the Mariner dugout to make the rookie get the ball down, or else he would own you up in the strike zone. Showalter, though, was captivated by his matchup sheet.

Edgar Martinez had batted seven times against Rivera during the regular season and been retired just once, amassing five hits, including two homers and a double plus a walk. In his only encounter with Rivera in this Division Series, Martinez had one of the two singles against the righty. With a runner on second and one out in the ninth inning, Showalter decided he could not let the five-homers-in-this-series power of Ken Griffey beat him in a lefty-righty match-up. He had Pettitte warming to face Griffey but decided instead to intentionally walk Griffey and replace Rivera with McDowell, who was making his first relief appearance since 1987 for Single-A Sarasota in the Florida State League. Many Yankee players from that team say Showalter succumbed to the pressure and simply tried to mimic Piniella, who had brought Johnson out of the bullpen on a single day's rest to get out of a ninth-inning jam. But Showalter says he summoned McDowell, despite an achy shoulder, for the same reason he stuck with Cone: trust.

"I only removed him [Rivera] because of track record," Showalter says. "But if you play the 'what if' game, maybe you can say if I left him in and he fails, what happens to history then? Is he the same guy?"

We will never know that. We only know that history shows that with Rivera, Wetteland, Pettitte, Bob Wickman, and Sterling Hitchcock available to him, Showalter might have had one of the greatest bullpens ever. All but Wetteland were still kids, however, and Showalter had particularly lost faith in Wetteland. Now Rivera was out of the game. McDowell struck out Martinez and escaped the inning. In the top of 10th, Randy Johnson struck out the side, including Don Mattingly in what would be his final career at-bat. McDowell wiggled from more trouble in the bottom of the inning. Finally, in the 11th, the Yankees struck for a run against Johnson. But this was also a game of "what might have been" for the Yankees. In the sixth inning, Mattingly had slashed an opposite-field, bases-loaded double that, because it took a particularly long hop over the wall, scored two runs rather than three. Later in the inning, Mike Stanley, a judicious hitter who was 9-for-11 with the bases loaded during the regular season, swung at a high fastball from Andy Benes that would have been ball 4 with the bases loaded. Instead, he popped out to the catcher. Now here in the 11th, with Johnson pooped, the Yankees could not add to their lead.

In spring training, Mariner ownership had demanded a significant payroll cut, and with 3 years and better than $16 million remaining on his contract and his obvious attractiveness in the market, Johnson was the natural choice to go. Seattle GM Woody Woodward and Piniella, who both had served as executives under Steinbrenner, implored their ownership to give the 1995 Mariners a chance to win, and the ownership relented. Now, on the brink of the organization's most meaningful triumph ever, Johnson needed to find the reservoir of strength to keep the deficit at just one run in his third elimination game in a week. Johnson struck out Wade Boggs and intentionally walked Bernie Williams. That brought up Paul O'Neill, who was a Yankee only because he had failed in Cincinnati to become the power force desired by a demanding manager. A guy named Piniella had wanted the 6-foot, 5-inch lefty to post hulking numbers commensurate to his frame.

Now Piniella was in the other dugout. O'Neill had come to New York and grown into a big-time hitter, in part because Showalter protected him from tough lefties early in their time together and always kept him out against the elite such as Johnson. O'Neill, for example, had not started Game 3 when Johnson started. Neither did Boggs. And now with two runners on and two out, the last Yankee hitter of Showalter's tenure was Paul O'Neill versus Randy Johnson. O'Neill flailed at a 1–2 slider, his strikeout reenergizing the Kingdome as the Mariners came to bat.

Wetteland stayed glued to the bullpen bench. Showalter was going to decide this game with McDowell—6 foot, 5 inches and 180 pounds of thin arms, spindly legs, and unquestioned heart. His rock band was aptly called Stick Figure. Tim Belcher, who had served up the Game 2–winning homer to Leyritz, warmed to replace Johnson, in case there was a 12th inning. At that moment, Johnson stood to lose this game. In the key four-batter sequence against Wetteland the previous night in Game 4, Joey Cora had dragged a bunt toward first that went for a single when perhaps the greatest defensive first baseman ever, Mattingly, mentally flubbed by trying and failing to tag Cora rather than flip to second baseman Randy Velarde covering first. Feeling in his baseball bones that Cora, leading off the bottom of the 11th of Game 5, would try to drag a bunt again, Willie Randolph, the Yankee coach in charge of setting the infield, attempted to alert Mattingly to shorten up even more than normal against the speedster. But the crowd was just too loud, and Mattingly never heard or saw Randolph. Cora dragged a bunt toward first and once again evaded Mattingly's lunging attempts for an inning-opening single.

"I have beaten myself up ever since over that," Randolph says. "I was standing in the dugout, trying to get Mattingly's attention. I should have just gone out onto the field so he could see me or called time-out. I said, 'Oh, shit,' when I saw Cora drag that ball. That could have changed the complexion, if I had gotten Donnie's attention."

Instead, with Mattingly holding Cora, Ken Griffey grounded a single to right. It was first and third, and here again came Edgar Martinez, who had pounded the Yankees during the regular season by hitting .391 with 7 homers and 20 RBIs and was doing even more damage in October. The two mounds down the right-field line remained barren. Showalter was staying with McDowell. Mariner players raised their arms to further incite the crowd. Piniella blatantly smoked on the bench against league rules. Mounted police gathered beyond the left-field wall for postgame crowd control. The fifth clinching, extra-inning game in postseason history had come down to this.

With a 1-strike count, Leyritz, in the game now for Stanley, shifted toward the outside corner, but the splitter backed up over the inner half, belt high. Martinez smashed a ball to the left-field corner. McDowell darted his head over his left shoulder as left fielder Gerald Williams raced for the ball. Cora crossed easily for the tying run, and Griffey received a wave from Perlozzo not to stop. Williams's relay bounced once to Tony Fernandez, who whirled and threw homeward as Griffey passed the pitcher's mound down the third-base line.

It was 8:27 p.m. Pacific time and Mattingly, in his last act as a major league player, yelled from his cutoff position in the middle of the diamond to throw home. The crowd noise made the effort as futile as Randolph trying earlier in the inning to summon him. This was a young Ken Griffey, graceful and talented enough to draw comparisons to Willie Mays. His slide nudged Leyritz's foot out of the way before the ball even arrived. Griffey popped up and was bear-hugged by Alex Rodriguez, then knocked to the ground as Vince Coleman leapt on them, creating a pile quickly joined by euphoric teammates. Griffey's helmet bounded away, and frozen forever in memories is the smile on his face underneath a sea of bodies. The sound system pumped "Shout" through the Kingdome, fireworks exploded, and a banner reading "Yanks Are Sweepless in Seattle" waved frantically. Mariners 6, Yankees 5. But more than a season was done.

For an entire game, Showalter, as usual, had sat rather impassively, his left leg wrapped familiarly over his right. But inside the losing clubhouse, knowing he had probably lost the only job that ever mattered to him, Showalter cried at his desk, tears falling onto his midnight blue Yankee windbreaker. Cone and McDowell, also red-eyed after pitching their hearts and arms out, tried to explain how a game, a season, had gotten away from them. Mattingly, fidgeting with his bats, was feeling the ache in his chronic lower back after deciding to have a damn-the-pain, swing-all-out October. He also choked up, partly out of pride for hitting .417 and proving to himself that he could indeed excel in this forum.

Any other owner might have observed the scene and honored his team's fortitude for simply reaching this moment, while acknowledging the greatness of a series just ended that had helped baseball rebound with its fans after a canceled World Series in 1994. But George Steinbrenner had spent the past week out of control. He had been critical of his own fans for not showing up during the season, and he'd done nothing to stem the threats that he would move the Yankees to New Jersey if a new stadium were not built for him, preferably on the west side of Manhattan. He had lambasted the umpires, all but crying conspiracy against his team, and disparaged former University of Kansas chancellor and current AL president Gene Budig as "an educator" who might not have the faculties for the job. He blasted Mariner president John Ellis for lining up to take revenue-sharing money, yet expanding his payroll at the trading deadline to add, among others, Game 5 starter Andy Benes, rather than following through on the spring-training plan to subtract Randy Johnson. And, of course, the Boss ran down Showalter throughout this Division Series.

A victory over the Mariners would have advanced the Yankees to play the Indians, whom they had mastered over the past 2 years. It also would have given Showalter a near-ironclad case to be retained. The same was probably true for Stick Michael. If they had been kept in place, a group of players thought of as Showalter guys—Mike Stanley, Randy Velarde, Jack McDowell, Dion James, and, possibly, even Don Mattingly—also might have been kept. Before Game 5, Showalter had tried to inspire his club in a meeting by noting just how different the club would likely look in 1996 and that this was a chance to do something special together for the last time. But the Yankees did not win Game 5. They lost their poise on the road and with it a two-games-to-none lead. Steinbrenner was heard in the clubhouse telling his executives that this meant massive change was needed. But what if . . .

. . . There had never been The Baseball Network, and the Yankees had played Cleveland in the first round? What if Tony Fernandez had caught that line drive on August 24, 1995, to end a Yankee victory, rather than miss it and ignite one of the greatest runs in major league history by the Mariners to make the playoffs and turn their home field—a baseball mausoleum for 18 years—into a tremendous advantage in Year 19? What if Willie Randolph had gotten Don Mattingly's attention or Mattingly's Game 5 double had bounced and hit the wall, scoring three runs rather than two? What if Mariner ownership had ignored Woody Woodward and Lou Piniella and followed through on its spring 1995 plan to trade Johnson?

What if Mariano Rivera had not moved from shortstop to pitch that day in 1989, or had been picked in the 1992 expansion draft, or mysteriously and magically had not added 5 miles an hour to his fastball on the brink of being traded in 1995? All of that allowed him to be a Yankee on October 8, 1995, a weapon unidentified by his manager. Which leads to the biggest question of all:

What if Buck Showalter had known?

2 | THE PERFECT MANAGER

"When Edgar hit the ball down the line, I have no idea this is going to impact me. That is the bizarre part. If that [a Mariner victory] doesn't happen, I'm not here."
—*Joe Torre*

Joe Torre tuned in to the Division Series from the living room of a rented house in his pregnant wife's hometown of Cincinnati. He watched with dread, as he always did in the postseason. He knew that at some point the whole nation would be informed what a big loser he was. Inevitably the subject would come around to those who had played the most games without ever appearing in a World Series. Sometimes photos would be arrayed to accentuate the point. And there, along with others such as Luke Appling, Ernie Banks, and Buddy Bell, Joe Torre would see himself, part of a loser fraternity. For Torre, the misery was far more intense. He also had never managed a team to the World Series. All told, he had played 2,209 games and managed 1,897. That total was 4,106 games, and only Gene Mauch had ever spent more time in uniform between those two jobs without ever participating in even a single World Series game.

As a teenager, Torre had shuttled between Milwaukee and New York, when his older brother Frank was the starting first baseman for the Braves, who won the 1957 World Series and lost in 1958, both times against the Yankees. But that was as close as Joe Torre came to experiencing the Fall Classic. As a pro himself, he had become a baseball Javert; the World Series, a tantalizingly close yet out-of-reach Jean Valjean. In the 8 years before Torre joined the Braves as a regular in 1961, Milwaukee not only had those two pennants with brother Frank but also never finished below third place. Yet, while Torre developed into an All-Star in his eight seasons as a Brave, the team never finished above fourth.

Following the 1968 season, Torre became embroiled in a nasty and personal contract dispute with then Braves general manager Paul Richards, who was infuriated by Torre's considerable involvement with the burgeoning Players Association. Richards nearly traded the Brooklyn-born Torre home to the Mets in a deal that involved Nolan Ryan coming to the Braves, but instead swapped him to St. Louis for Orlando Cepeda. In 1969—the first year of division play— the Braves won the National League West and the Mets won the National League East, clinching on September 24, when Gary Gentry closed a four-hitter by getting Torre to hit into a 6-4-3 double play. After beating the Braves for the National League penant,the Mets won the title, with the first baseman they obtained instead of Torre, Donn Clendenon, earning the World Series Most Valuable Player award. "I could have been Clendenon," Torre says, looking back. He was a Cardinal instead. St. Louis had played in the World Series in each of the 2 years before Torre arrived. In 1969, the Cardinals finished fourth, 13 games out of first place. As a Cardinal, Torre won the NL MVP award in 1971 but never made the playoffs. In Torre's final two seasons in St. Louis, 1973 and 1974, the Cardinals finished $1\frac{1}{2}$ games out of first place both times. Torre was close enough to dream of the playoffs but not enter them.

Torre became a Met in the discouraging middle ground between the "Ya Gotta Believe" NL champions of 1973 and the rise with Davey Johnson, Dwight Gooden, and Darryl Strawberry of the mid-1980s. In August 1976, Mets GM Joe McDonald informed Torre he could be traded to the contending Yankees, but Torre preferred not to go if it would cost him a chance to manage the Mets. Torre remained a Met, and the Yankees reached their first World Series in 12 years. Torre did indeed become the Mets' player-manager during the 1977 season, and 2 weeks into his stint, the Mets traded their best player ever, Tom Seaver, to the Reds. With Torre as their full-time manager from 1978 to 1981, the Mets went 237–352, by far the NL's worst record. In 1982, Torre guided the Braves to an NL West title before the Whitey Herzog–managed Cardinals eliminated Atlanta in three straight playoff games. The Braves followed with consecutive second-place finishes, which were viewed as insufficient by impetuous team owner Ted Turner, who fired Torre.

From 1985 until August 1990, Torre was a well-regarded broadcaster of California Angels games before the Cardinals hired him to replace Herzog, who in his nine seasons in St. Louis had won three NL titles and one World Series. In his autobiography, *You're Missin' a Great Game*, Herzog insultingly wrote, "Joe Torre was the worst catcher I ever saw. The fans in the center-field bleachers knew his number better than the ones behind home plate did."

However, more vital to Torre's tenure than replacing the successful and popular Herzog was that August Busch Jr. had died the previous year. Gussie Busch loved his baseball team. His inheriting son, August Busch III, did not. Torre maneuvered a young core to above .500 from 1991 to 1993. But the ownership promises to Torre to expand payroll went unfulfilled; instead, Busch III ordered financial retreat that negatively impacted performance. Torre was sacrificed on June 16, 1995, and felt out of more than a job. He had managed the Mets, Braves, and Cardinals, the three teams for which he had played and had ties. For much of the past $3\frac{1}{2}$ decades, he had been in vexing proximity to championships. He was 55 now, too young not to care about the emptiness, too old to believe there were fresh chances out there for him. His wife, Ali, remembers it as "the low point. He just figured he would never realize his dream."

"Not winning drove him crazy," Frank Torre says. "It put a hole in his stomach. He had borderline ulcers that he never won a World Series."

Joe Torre knew he could land a good broadcasting job. But what resonated was something Super Bowl–winning coach turned TV analyst Hank Stram once said in an interview: "When you leave the broadcasting booth, you're not sure if you've won or lost." So while his agent pursued on-air possibilities for the 1996 season, Torre pined for the dugout and a chance at the World Series. But how? Torre could not see the combination of opening and connection necessary to get a fourth strike as a manager. What he did not know was that an ally from his past was participating in a palace coup in the Bronx. He did not know that the most bizarre off-season of the George Steinbrenner Era was already under way.

No manager in the Steinbrenner Era had served longer continuously than Buck Showalter's 4 years. Yet if his tenure was long, his enemies' list within the organization was longer. He had surrounded himself with loyalist coaches in Brian Butterfield, Rick Down, and Glenn Sherlock, all of whom—like Showalter—had never played in the majors. Many Yankee employees outside the tight circle theorized that Showalter had a stabbing insecurity when it came to former major leaguers milling around the team. Catfish Hunter stopped going to spring training, citing Showalter's coolness, and Reggie Jackson said he, at times, felt unwelcome. Coaches Clete Boyer and Frank Howard, both of whom enjoyed accomplished playing careers, did not survive long on Showalter's staff. But most damaging to Showalter was the 1995 dismissal of pitching coach Billy Connors, a fringe major leaguer in the 1960s who had been a longtime major league pitching coach. The two had bonded as Yankee coaches in 1990 under manager Stump Merrill, and Connors had actually championed Showalter as a replacement for Merrill.

But Showalter became convinced Connors was a Steinbrenner clubhouse spy and waged a behind-the-scenes smear campaign, in part leaking that Connors's obesity was jeopardizing his health and causing him to fall asleep on the bench during games. Showalter's plan worked. On July 13, 1995, Connors was summoned for a phone call from Steinbrenner in GM Gene Michael's office. Showalter knew the call was to fire Connors, yet he innocently asked Connors if he had angered a Yankee powerbroker such as Steinbrenner confidant Dick Williams. It was a particularly sly misdirection. Showalter knew Williams and Connors had warred when Connors was Williams's pitching coach for the Seattle Mariners. After Steinbrenner removed Connors as Yankee pitching coach, Showalter hugged Connors and told him the manager's office was open. But soon after, Connors found the office door locked, galvanizing his burgeoning suspicion of just who was most responsible for his dismissal.

The episode revealed Showalter's Machiavellian side, and it backfired. Connors was out of the clubhouse but in a far worse place for Showalter: near Steinbrenner's ear. Connors had built enough collateral with Steinbrenner as a gossip and self-promoter to avoid being ousted altogether. Instead, Steinbrenner brought him to his hometown and the franchise's minor league base of Tampa, where he was officially put in charge of running the organization's pitching program and unofficially put in charge of running down Showalter. Steinbrenner was always changing his flavor of the month as far as which executives he listened to, but Connors had staying power. Steinbrenner's natural tendency was to scare and repel people, and because of that, he had few true friends and rarely felt like one of the guys. Connors seized upon this, telling the Boss dirty jokes or accompanying him to the horse track or wrestling matches.

The other key person Showalter alienated was Arthur Richman. Officially, Richman was a "senior advisor" assigned to the Yankee media-relations department. But he more resembled a Las Vegas casino greeter, having formed a kinship with many prominent baseball people as the brother of United Press International Hall of Fame reporter Milton Richman, as well as from his own half century as either a newspaper reporter or working for the Mets and Yankees as a traveling secretary or publicity man. Access to the clubhouse in general and the manager's office in particular were lifeblood to Arthur Richman, satisfying his staggering sense of self-importance and his hunger to be around baseball people. Showalter imperiled that way of doing business. The Yankee manager disapproved of Richman tottering into the postgame clubhouse—win or lose—with vodka in a clear plastic cup. He considered Richman another spy with access to Steinbrenner. And he thought Richman was excessively negative, seeing the worst in everything. It was not uncommon for Richman to bitch about a Yankee player's salary, even following a victory, as if the money came out of his pocket rather than Steinbrenner's.

Believing Richman poisonous to the clubhouse culture, Showalter tried to curtail Richman's access, particularly to the manager's office. Showalter's most loyal coaches felt similarly about Richman. Hitting coach Rick Down recalls that while eating breakfast at the team hotel before the decisive Game 5 against the Mariners, Richman came across a group of the support staff and disparaged the 1995 Yankees, comparing their fortitude unfavorably to the Yankees of the late 1970s. Down, infuriated by Richman's incessant pessimism, unshackled years of restraint. He told Richman the 1995 Yankees had a game that night and if he were not confident of victory to "fuck off."

Richman began a front-office smear campaign against Down, designed mainly for Steinbrenner's ears. Richman did not stop there, deriding Showalter to Steinbrenner, other club officials, and to the media. But Showalter's biggest problem was not in New York.

In Tampa, Connors was skewering Showalter to Steinbrenner, harping on the theme that Showalter conned the New York media into favorable treatment by keeping certain reporters in his confidence. Showalter was roundly hailed as the hardest-working man in baseball. He had teamed with then GM Gene Michael to reverse the perception of the roster from unprofessional doormats to focused contenders. For all the talk about how badly Steinbrenner aches to win, he aches to win under his parameters: No one is to be bestowed more credit for success than he. So Michael and Showalter, both in the final year of contracts, were in Steinbrenner's crosshairs throughout 1995. They had committed a Yankee sin in the Age of Steinbrenner: They were getting far too much credit. "If we had just won against the Mariners, we all would have been fine," Michael says, looking back. But the Kingdome came crashing down on the Stick and Buck era.

"I assumed, based on George's indictment of Buck in the Kingdome, that he was a condemned man," David Sussman says. "I also felt throughout 1995 a lack of connection between George and Buck because Buck was not his guy [Showalter was hired by Michael as manager after the 1991 season, while

Steinbrenner was under suspension]. The manager of the New York Yankees is one of those key roles where George wants his person, someone he can relate to. Temperamentally, Buck was not George's kind of guy. He was quiet, cerebral, taciturn."

Showalter was, in fact, Stick's guy. And in a cost-cutting vengeance after the highest-payroll Yankees' playoff setback to the small-market Mariners, Steinbrenner zeroed in on Michael. For much of his 5-year tenure, Michael had exhibited a golden touch in player acquisition that infused the lineup with high on-base percentage hitters and the clubhouse with a sense of mature purpose. He said he deserved to have Steinbrenner honor his $600,000 option for 1996. The Boss balked, offering $400,000. Still, Steinbrenner recognized Michael's acumen and did not want to lose him, so for $150,000 he allowed Stick to devise his own job: director of major league scouting. The idea was to allow Michael to escape the paperwork he hated and instead concentrate on the scouting he loved and at which he excelled.

But instantly Steinbrenner blurred responsibilities and warped the chain of command by authorizing Michael to find his GM successor. Eighteen years in the organization had educated Showalter on the necessity of a unified front when dealing with Steinbrenner. The Boss loved to pit employees against one another, dividing and conquering uncomfortable workers. In response, Showalter and Michael had formed a counterbalance to Steinbrenner's irrationality. Now Michael was no longer GM and, at the least, Showalter wanted the replacement identified before committing to more time under Steinbrenner. Torre actually flew from a Las Vegas vacation to Tampa to be interviewed by Michael and Steinbrenner's son-in-law/general partner, Joe Molloy, for the GM position. He likely could have had the job, but when he heard the salary was only $350,000, he rebuffed the offer, citing the heavy workload and his pregnant wife. He did tell the Yankee executives, however, that he was more comfortable on the field and "if I can help in any other way, let me know." The clear implication: Torre still hankered to manage.

Torre was not alone in turning down the GM job. Besides Torre, Michael reached out to friends in the business such as Tom Grieve, Sandy Johnson, Bill Lajoie, Dal Maxvill, Mike Port, and Jerry Walker, only to have them snub advances, mainly because they did not want to work for Steinbrenner. Bob Watson, who was serving as the Houston Astros' GM, had been the first free-agent player Michael had ever signed in his initial stint as Yankee GM in 1979. But in this case, Michael was emptying his Rolodex and actually pondering the possibility of elevating his unpopular and untested assistant GM Tim McCleary before Watson's name eventually arose. Watson had a year left on his deal as Houston's GM but was worried the Astros might move, possibly to northern Virginia, so he was receptive to outside offers. Houston owner Drayton McLane permitted Watson to talk with the Yankees on October 23, and in three phone calls with Molloy during a 4-hour negotiation, Watson accepted a 2-year, $700,000 pact with two option years.

Looking back, Watson says he jumped because Steinbrenner, through Molloy, promised he was "stepping back," and Watson and Molloy would "run the baseball operation" with Steinbrenner participating only on "real big-ticket items." As was his wont, Watson waxed boldly in public, saying at his introductory press conference, "I will speak my mind. We [he and Steinbrenner] will probably not agree on all issues, and I don't think he expects us to. If you are asking if I'm going to be a yes-man, no. He didn't hire me to be that." In actuality, that is exactly why Steinbrenner hired him. From the outset, Watson's job consisted mainly of taking abuse from Steinbrenner. His influence on personal matters was far less than he had enjoyed in Houston.

By the time Watson was hired, Torre already was considered the internal front-runner should Showalter be jettisoned. Earlier in October, Richman had confided to Steinbrenner that he could hook him up with Torre, Davey Johnson (like Torre, another ex-Met manager with whom Richman had ties), or Tony La Russa, with whom Richman had formed a friendship. But Steinbrenner did not want to spend heavily on a manager, either. Richman reported to Steinbrenner that the Orioles were willing to pay Johnson $700,000 annually and the Cardinals were offering La Russa $1.5 million a year. Both men wound up taking those jobs. That left Torre. "It came through loud and clear in the organization that this was Arthur's guy," Sussman recalls.

Torre had already passed the Arthur Richman entrance exam. When he managed the Mets from 1977 to 1981, Torre welcomed Richman, then the Mets' traveling secretary, into his office and into his life. Richman responded by in effect becoming Torre's valet. On the road, he secured a two-bedroom suite for himself and Torre and took care of the manager's phone calls and ticket requests. But Richman was more than a nuts-and-bolts functionary. In the parlance of old-time baseball men, Richman was the type who could round up booze, broads, and bail in any city at any hour. Richman himself says his falling out with Mets GM Frank Cashen in the late 1980s was out of "jealousy because wherever we went, people knew me and not him. And there always was a beautiful dolly waiting for me." A Mets front-office employee at the time, though, calls Richman a "sycophant" and says, "Arthur was always in Joe's office and always went out socially with him in New York and on the road. He fawned all over Joe. Arthur treated Joe like a king."

Steinbrenner convened a meeting in Tampa of his top executives shortly after Watson's hiring to nail down the managing job. Then assistant GM Brian Cashman, speaking for a significant faction in New York, says he voted to "stay with Showalter. His style had worked here." However, Showalter had become a boxer without cornermen. Clete Boyer and Billy Connors were out of his coaches' room, but in Steinbrenner's good graces in Tampa. Richman was running the anti-Buck sect in New York. Stick Michael was no longer GM. And Showalter's most loyal players—Don Mattingly, Mike Stanley, Randy Velarde—were all free agents and tenuous to return.

Showalter had received a 3-year, $1 million extension after his rookie season managing in 1992 when the Yankees finished tied for fourth place. Now Steinbrenner proposed a 2-year contract with the Yankees having just gone to the playoffs for the first time in 14 years. More important, Steinbrenner told Showalter that coaches Brian Butterfield, Glenn Sherlock, and Rick Down could not return. "It fit George's time-honored tactic that if you didn't like a manager or chief executive, rather than go directly after him, he would cut the legs out by firing a secretary or coaches," Sussman says. Showalter believed fewer years on his contract and the removal of loyal coaches weakened his position in the organization and in the clubhouse. Showalter, at 35, had arrived as the youngest Yankee manager since 23-year-old Roger Peckinpaugh served for 14 games as a player/manager in 1914. But he was never naive. By age 39, he saw his allies within the organization diminishing and his enemies gaining more power. He believed his detail-oriented style had rid the roster of unmotivated players and made a team owned by Steinbrenner likable to fans and media and desirable to outside players. The Yankees mattered again, which was not true when he first sat in the manager's office.

His reward had come in Game 1 against the Mariners when, aside from Mattingly, he had received the largest ovation during introductions from the 57,178 people packed inside Yankee Stadium. The fans were there for the organization's first playoff game since Steve Howe induced Bob Watson to fly out to end Game 6 of the 1981 World Series, sealing a Los Angeles Dodgers title. The ovation turned Steinbrenner jealous, rather than prideful. As much as the Yankees meant to Showalter—he still had a separate bank account for the $13,000 check he received after signing as a fifth-round pick out of Mississippi State in 1977—he saw staying as untenable, friends of his say. Still, his departure remains rife with intrigue.

What is certain is that during a 10-minute conversation, Showalter, in Pensacola, rejected a 2-year, $1.05 million offer from Steinbrenner, in Tampa. What has remained in dispute, as Cashman remembers, is "whether Buck left or was fired." Showalter said he merely spurned that offer and was awaiting a counterproposal. Steinbrenner claimed Showalter resigned and cut off further negotiations, despite Steinbrenner's indication that he was malleable on every issue except Down's retention. Steinbrenner told reporters he would not publicize his reasons for rebuking Down. Showalter has maintained there was never an option to keep negotiating, citing his payments through the end of the month as proof he did not quit. Steinbrenner issued a press release, written by Richman, in Cleveland an hour before World Series Game 5 to announce Showalter's departure and his version of events. Showalter insisted it was not until reporters began calling his home that he realized what the Yankees were declaring. But, perhaps, Showalter was just being cagey.

Showalter was already considered a front-runner for managing jobs in Detroit and Oakland (and many people around those teams thought Showalter was the one leaking his front-running status). Showalter said he did not talk to another team until after his contract expired on October 31 at midnight. Arizona owner Jerry Colangelo said he contacted Showalter at 2 minutes after midnight October 31 to begin discussions on what would become a 7-year, $7 million deal for Showalter to manage the expansion Diamondbacks, who were not due to play until 1998. But Cashman, Down, and Mark Newman, who was then the Yankees' assistant director of player development and scouting, say they believe Showalter had received enough signs that he was the Diamondbacks' man to allow him to confidently say no to Steinbrenner. One member of the organization went as far as to say that Showalter knew as early as September that the Arizona job was his if he wanted it. Showalter denied this.

Neither Steinbrenner nor Showalter budged to phone the other between October 26 and 31 to see if they could remedy their differences. Meanwhile, Steinbrenner proxies Connors and Richman were publicly persecuting Showalter, spinning a cover story for their Boss on why such a popular manager was not retained.

Richman went so far as to contend he was in the room with Steinbrenner on October 26 and heard Showalter say, "I don't think I want to come back." The conversation was not on speakerphone. Richman, at the time 69 years old, declared this was possible because his hearing had improved as his eyesight weakened. Meanwhile, behind closed doors, the Yankees already had settled on a new manager before October 31, though Watson adamantly told reporters a search was ongoing.

Watson's behavior fit a pattern that off-season in which it was difficult to determine whether he was horrified to concede a truth while working for the oppressive Steinbrenner, or simply out of the loop on most decisions. For example, on the day Watson was hired as GM, word leaked of the deal, and a few reporters called Watson at his home. Watson, who had already agreed to his contract, told the reporters he had not even spoken with Yankee officials. Watson also informed reporters that no accord was reached with Tino Martinez a day after the Yankees completed the second-largest contract in team history with the first baseman. He also said the Yankees were finished chasing front-line pitchers after the signing of David Cone, only to have the team pursue David Wells, Chuck Finley, Ben McDonald, Livan Hernandez, and Kenny Rogers.

Watson kept up his facade about his managerial search at the November 2 press conference at Yankee Stadium, during which Torre was introduced as the skipper. In explaining his process, he told reporters he had considered four candidates for the job, but named six: Torre, Sparky Anderson, Chris Chambliss, Butch Hobson, Gene Lamont, and—amazingly—Buck Showalter. But besides Torre, he had spoken only to Hobson and Lamont, and they both had called Watson. Watson never could explain how he was contemplating Showalter with no plans ever to talk to a man he hardly knew. It is conceivable that when Watson asked for permission to speak to Milwaukee manager Phil Garner and Pittsburgh skipper Jim Leyland and was refused on both, he just did not know what was going on behind his back. Torre was already in.

Cashman says the coronation of Torre fit the strange-brew nature that percolates under Steinbrenner; that often Steinbrenner is soliciting advice from so many areas that no cohesive strategy is ever enacted. For example, Watson did not officially contact Torre until November 1, when Torre was on his way to play golf in Cincinnati. He was in Tampa later that day for what was more an hour-long chat with Watson, Steinbrenner, Molloy, Michael, and Cashman than an interview. And he was in New York the next day for an introductory

press conference to be named as the 14th different man among 20 managerial changes in the Steinbrenner Era. "We didn't do second or third interviews," Cashman recalls. "We didn't do any kind of psychological workup. Joe
was the man."

Watson's input was minimal, but he did endorse the hiring of Torre and
knew that the two would enjoy a fine working relationship. Watson had loved
playing for Torre as a Brave from 1982 to 1984. Torre had permitted Watson
to serve as an unofficial hitting coach, and, in what would be Torre's final game
as Atlanta's skipper and Watson's final game as a player—September 30, 1984—
Torre let Watson manage the game. More imperative to Torre's candidacy,
though, was that Gene Michael also blessed it. Michael told Steinbrenner, "Joe
won't panic, so that will be good for you and good for the team." Just 4 months
earlier, the Cardinals had fired Torre for the reason that Michael was now ex-
alting him to Steinbrenner. St. Louis president Mark Lamping said his office
had been inundated with letters complaining that "Torre doesn't do anything
in the dugout. He just stands there." Michael read that not as apathy but rather
as maturity and serenity, two ingredients he thought would play well working in
The Bronx Zoo. They were traits Torre needed on his first official day as
Yankee manager.

In November 1994, Showalter had been toasted as the American League
Manager of the Year in the Stadium Club at Yankee Stadium. A year later,
Torre was roasted in the same room. There were few of the niceties associ-
ated with the hiring of a new manager. Instead, Torre was carpet-bombed by
questions about his sanity in working for Steinbrenner, his unspectacular man-
agerial record, and whether he had the facility to replace the popular Showalter.
He was greeted by near-universal panning on sports talk radio, and in the New
York papers the next day he was fricasseed as overmatched, naive, and incapable, most famously in a *New York Daily News* back-page headline of "Clueless
Joe." In a *New York Post* fax poll asking readers who the next manager of the
Yankees should be, Showalter won as a write-in candidate at 45 percent. Of the
four possible alternatives provided by the newspaper, Willie Randolph received

17 percent; Sparky Anderson, 13 percent; Torre, 5 percent; and Dick Williams, 3 percent.

An unflinching Torre counterpunched each insult by simply acknowledging the realities: Steinbrenner was a tough boss, the lack of a World Series ring was more disturbing to him than anyone, and Showalter had been successful. The media had Torre on the run, and, interestingly, no one saw him sweat. "The first positive I attached to Joe was how deftly he handled the press," Sussman says. "I was not expecting much, but he seemed so easygoing, honest, and so smart in his ability to answer questions with a sense of humor and wry smile, disarming questions about George."

Steinbrenner did not even attend the introductory press conference, though he used the forum to again chide Showalter. In the first line of the press release, the Yankees included Torre's salary—$500,000 in 1996, $550,000 in 1997; in other words, the same deal Showalter rejected. Besides invoking Showalter on what was supposed to be Torre's day, Steinbrenner was insultingly paying Torre $50,000 less in his first year managing the affluent Yankees than he had made in his last season with the smaller-market Cardinals. Ominously, Ali Torre remembers, "George told us to rent in New York, not buy." Yet the indignities were about to grow. In its December 3 edition, the *New York Times* reported that less than a week after Torre's hiring, Steinbrenner had secretly flown to Pensacola, Florida, to meet with Showalter. According to sources in the story, Steinbrenner either requested that Showalter immediately return as manager with the ability to bring his *entire* coaching staff back, or he alerted Showalter he could be quickly rehired if Torre's Yankees stumbled early in 1996. In later interviews, both Showalter and Steinbrenner downplayed the meeting, indicating it was more about parting amicably. However, it was clear that the unkind fan and media backlash to the managerial change had given Steinbrenner instant buyer's remorse about Torre.

"George was lukewarm when Torre was first announced," Sussman says. "My sense was he had apprehension whether this would work or not. George was not 100 percent supportive. [In meeting with Showalter] George was trying to cover his bases and prepare a backup plan in case Torre did not work out. He wanted to mend fences with Buck so he could be someone he could turn to later on."

Steinbrenner had fired Bob Lemon after 14 games in 1982 and Yogi Berra after 16 games in 1985. But even for him this was a record, as he sought an escape hatch from Torre in the week after he had hired him. Privately, Torre was aggravated that November. But he focused on the big picture: next October. He kept a vow he had made to enjoy this journey and not be submarined by each inevitable affront and distraction. "It was good for my ego to be named the Yankee manager," Torre says, looking back at the Showalter-Steinbrenner meeting. "The other stuff I tried not to think about. I knew the other guy had won for him."

The ham-handed transition from Showalter to Torre was metaphorical for a Yankee off-season that was untidy, undisciplined, and—to a large degree—unprofessional. Even for Steinbrenner, this was more hands-on than he had ever been. In October, he prioritized signing a drug addict named Dwight Gooden before focusing on the expiring contracts of loyal aides Showalter and Michael. In one 4-day period in November, the Yankees had relationships end with perhaps their three most popular players, Don Mattingly, Mike Stanley, and Randy Velarde. In December, Steinbrenner nearly chased free agent David Cone away to the hated Orioles by mystifyingly lowering his offer at the 11th hour. And he fired his media-relations director for going home for Christmas. In January, Steinbrenner empowered deposed pitching coach Billy Connors to entertain Cuban defectors Livan Hernandez and Osvaldo Fernandez in Manhattan, and the night ended with Yankee officials and the free-agent pitchers ogling a girl-on-girl sex show at the Paradise Club on 33rd Street.

Tino Martinez was paid $9 million more than he was even seeking, Pat Kelly was retained because he made a favorable impression on Steinbrenner at a Wade Boggs barbecue, and Kenny Rogers was signed despite overwhelming evidence he was ill-equipped for New York. These mostly unpopular, disjointed, poorly devised, and—at times—classless maneuvers projected an impression throughout baseball of a team in rudderless disarray, especially because the *New York* Yankees more than ever were being run from Steinbrenner's home base of Tampa. The fans and media reacted to the series of unpopular moves by ceaselessly bashing the Yankees. Cashman says the sound he equates with that off-season is the endless whirring of fax machines in the New York office as angry missive after angry missive piled up on the executives' desks.

Daily News columnist Mike Lupica, the most powerful newspaper voice in the city, wrote that off-season: "An organization that actually seemed to be heading in the right direction as recently as the spring has once again become a laughingstock. Gene Michael is gone, Showalter is gone . . . good scouts are gone. Steinbrenner is more obsessed these days with sending out the likes of Billy Connors and Arthur Richman with their rambling, barely coherent attacks on Showalter than preparing a plan for next season. Because he has no plan."

Steinbrenner's mad maestro act looked even more destructive because the Yankees' main AL competitors appeared much more precise and effective in fortifying their clubs for the 1996 campaign. Sure, the nemesis Mariners had lost Tino Martinez, but they still had Ken Griffey, Randy Johnson, and Edgar Martinez, and they were ready to install 20-year-old shortstop Alex Rodriguez, hailed as the game's next great player. The Indians sold every home ticket for the 1996 season at 3-year-old Jacobs Field before Christmas—starting with the season opener against the Yankees—providing even greater resources to augment a club that had won 10 more games than any other in 1995. The Indians signed Jack McDowell away from the Yankees, adding the only piece seemingly absent from their championship designs—an ace. They also inked free agent Julio Franco; tied up Charles Nagy, Manny Ramirez, and Omar Vizquel to multiyear deals; and retained Orel Hershiser, Eddie Murray, Tony Pena, Jim Poole, and Alvaro Espinoza. All told, in one 10-day period, the Indians spent $53.425 million on 10 players, drawing complaints that a team from Cleveland was inflating the market.

The Red Sox, who had won the AL East by seven games over the Yankees in 1995, grabbed Mike Stanley, whose dismissal as the Yankees' everyday catcher and cruel off-season handling (no Yankee executive even called to tell Stanley he was no longer in the plans) heightened the hostility the Yankees were facing at home. Stanley and former National League Most Valuable Player Kevin

Mitchell joined a muscular lineup with reigning AL MVP Mo Vaughn, Jose Canseco, Mike Greenwell, Tim Naehring, and John Valentin that had actually produced a better slugging percentage in 1995 than the ferocious Mariners had. But the club that fixated Steinbrenner was the Orioles. While the Yankees brought in the tongue-twisted Bob Watson as GM, Baltimore hired Pat Gillick, the architect of the 1992 and 1993 Blue Jays, the first team to repeat as World Series champions since the Yankees of 1977 and 1978. In contrast to Torre, who began the 1996 season as the only manager in history to lose more than 1,000 games without winning more than 1,000 (894–1,003), the Orioles lured Davey Johnson, whose .576 winning percentage was the best among active managers.

And while Cone proved elusive, the Orioles added two lefties to their rotation: Kent Mercker and David Wells. Roger McDowell and Randy Myers joined another former member of Johnson's powerful Met bullpens of the 1980s, Jesse Orosco, in a Baltimore relief core that also had young fireballer Armando Benitez. The versatile B. J. Surhoff was obtained coming off a career-best .320 season. The coup of the Oriole off-season, though, was landing the best free agent available, Roberto Alomar, to team with Cal Ripken for perhaps the finest middle-infield setup in major league history. The Yankees countered with an untested rookie in Derek Jeter at short and a suspect hodgepodge of Mariano Duncan, Tony Fernandez, and Pat Kelly to select among at second.

"There definitely was a sense of, what are we doing?" Cashman says. "There was a building of the franchise, and all of a sudden Stick and Buck weren't there. It felt like we were blowing up the right direction. There was a sense what we were doing wasn't right. We were afraid we were taking a step backward."

But the fatalistic feeling about all that had transpired from the moment Ken Griffey slid into home plate to end the Yankees' 1995 season began to lift early in spring training in 1996. It did so because of one man. "I'm thinking World Series," Joe Torre said on the third day of spring training. "Other clubs I've managed, I've always said I want to be competitive. But I feel if we stay healthy, there's no reason why we can't win as many games as we need to win . . . I relish this opportunity."

That Torre ran toward the fire of expectation while employed by Steinbrenner slowly deflated much of the tension and apprehension that had hardened around the club during the winter, especially because it stood in such stark contrast to Showalter, who would have sooner dined daily with Billy Connors than provide such fireable ammunition to the Boss. Torre's assessment opened eyes and minds. Sure the off-season was messy and discordant. But look at the end result, Torre thought. This was like a Jackson Pollock painting, the finished product belying the frenetic, unconventional style with which it was strewn on the canvas. There was $55 million worth of established talent scattered around the room, way more skill than Torre had ever had at his disposal. Reporters stoked the Yankees' brewing spring-training controversy of having to concoct a five-man rotation from seven experienced candidates, and Torre laughed the laugh of a man who knew what it was like to try to win when Craig Swan and Pete Falcone were your best starting pitchers.

And every time the mean-spirited impulsiveness of Steinbrenner was thrown into his face, Torre puffed smoke from one of his ever-present Padron cigars and patiently told his inquisitors that he had worked for the rash Ted Turner in Atlanta and the parsimonious August Busch III in St. Louis and had been canned from three jobs in all. He was no managing virgin. "From the first day, you guys have predicted all the horror stories," Torre said to reporters in spring. "What's the worst thing that can happen? Get fired? Nobody's going to line me up and shoot me."

It was the kind of unflappable statement that spoke to Torre's endless comfort in his skin, a nature that made him so ideal to be managing this stormy team at this stressful time. It was as if Torre had been preparing through a career of baseball misery for this, the role of his dreams. Torre played the Yankees that spring like Mozart at a piano, instantly, intuitively, and incredibly. But he was no boy genius. As a pudgy child—he had a size 40 waist at age 16—Torre struggled with self-confidence growing up on Brooklyn's East 34th Street and Avenue T. He despised loud noises after watching his screaming father abuse his mother. Informed by his childhood, Torre imbued his managing style with building self-esteem and doing it in a low-decibel fashion—the mode that Lamping, the Cardinals' president, had disparaged. Torre admits he wondered about altering this method for the Yankees. But just before camp opened, while on a StairMaster at the team's new $30 million spring base, Legends Field, Torre read an item stressed by Bill Parcells in his autobiography *The Biggest Giant of Them All* about the need to be true to what you feel works as a leader. "That," Torre recalls, "really stuck with me."

Thus, Torre remained devoted to his tactics, despite being 109 games below .500 as a manager. The pudgy kid in Torre worried about his new roster's self-respect after an off-season in which the organization was so enwrapped in pessimism and disapproval. So on the first day of spring training for his full roster, according to Tino Martinez, Torre told the players: "I am really excited about this season. I have never had a collection of players this good." Torre pointed to a coaching staff that, unlike Showalter's, was populated only by accomplished former major leaguers—Willie Randolph, Mel Stottlemyre, Jose Cardenal, Chris Chambliss, Tony Cloninger, and Don Zimmer—and said, "They all have World Series experience. It is time for me to get my first." But he didn't stop there, telling his new team, "I don't want to win two World Series rings. I want to win three."

It was heady stuff from a man with no World Series rings. But Torre was hungry for the players to share his vision. He wanted them to ignore the off-season chaos and behold the beauty formed from that chaos: a roster that could win. In that way, Torre benefited from the end of the Showalter era. This was not like Showalter taking over the carnage from the inept Stump Merrill. Through his organizational skills, work ethic, and weighty baseball IQ, Showalter had transformed the culture around the Yankees. He restored pride in the uniform and seriousness to the clubhouse and field. Torre inherited a roster primed to win, in large part due to Showalter's heavy lifting.

"Joe would not have been the manager for us in 1992 in my mind," Cashman says of Showalter's first year. "He was the perfect manager for us in 1996, though I didn't know it at the time. But 1996 going forward doesn't happen without what Buck did beforehand. Everything is connected."

Torre even profited from how Showalter was removed. It was so unpopular that Steinbrenner grasped the importance of winning in the immediate aftermath, since it did not take a special *CSI* crew to find the Boss's fingerprints all over every off-season transaction. Since he would be blamed most for failure, Steinbrenner retreated from his original call for a $38 million payroll, approving an outlay beyond $50 million. And it was in comparison to Showalter that Torre gained so much that spring. As Yankee manager, for example, Showalter would not release his lineup card until the other manager had sent his over, had once waited until Opening Day to name Pat Kelly the starting second baseman over Mike Gallego (and never did get around to telling Kelly), and was a contrarian by nature who would never publicly concede a player who was hitless in 20 at-bats was in a slump. It all exemplified a nitpicking, untrusting, controlling nature that slowly wore out an organization. Meanwhile, Torre named David Cone his Opening Day starter before hitters had even reported to camp. He took stock of the potential talent in his rotation and stated, "I have no excuses now. I can't tell someone we don't have the players."

Unlike Showalter, Torre had no overriding passion to have his hand in every decision or a conceit that he knew how to do everybody's job best. Early that spring training, pitching coach Mel Stottlemyre, as he had done for each of his previous managers, supplied a detailed daily report on what the pitchers had done. Stottlemyre was stunned, especially since Torre had not hired him, when Torre told him, "Hey, that's your department. You take care of it. You don't need my okay. I'm behind whatever you do."

"[Showalter] wanted to be involved in everything around here, and you have to let some things go," remembers Willie Randolph, who coached for both Showalter and Torre. "Buck was prepared. At times, he was overly prepared."

He was also tight. It was quickly evident to media and Yankee personnel that Torre was looser, more honest. He was a stickler for one thing in particular, and that was promptness. Showalter seemed to have rules about his rules. He had his coaches playing private eye into players' personal lives; one member of the Yankee staff said Showalter and his coaches would find out which players had been drinking the night before and determine lineups based on that information. Torre treated players like adults until they dishonored his faith. He slowly built alliances through the power of his fraternal nature and the goodwill engendered by his calming, fatherly demeanor. He then empowered those players to police their own clubhouse. He removed air from an overinflated balloon, a skill he had been crafting since his pudgy childhood.

But that pudgy childhood also included watching his brother, Frank, play in the World Series. That was a part of him as much as his soothing nature. He was consumed by an image: himself in October. To feed that obsession, Torre had swallowed the insults that had dominated his introductory press conference. He had accepted only marginal control of picking that accomplished coaching staff. He had even braved the affront of Steinbrenner meeting with his predecessor to discuss the manager's job. Torre recognized how treacherous it was to be guiding a team in New York in this era. Earlier in March, the venerable Don Nelson stepped down as Knicks coach not even three-quarters of the way through his first season and was replaced by Jeff Van Gundy. Torre knew it would be even more treacherous working in New York for arguably the rashest owner in sports. However, Torre was willing to sleep on Steinbrenner's bed-of-nails ways in exchange for this last best chance.

"I knew the history here," Torre says, looking back. "But on all the teams I was with, we were either a player short or a dollar short. That was the over-riding factor for me. I knew George was committed to win at any cost. I always felt I could manage, but you are judged on your accomplishments. I wanted to see my capabilities on a team that had a chance to win."

This team had a chance to win, and Torre knew it. This was Torre's October opportunity, an opportunity that was enough to make him overlook a disre-specting Boss and the crude choreography that formed the 1996 Yankees. Edgar Martinez hit the ball down the line. The Mariners won a Division Series. Joe Torre was here. He did not care how. He only cared about all the wonderful possibilities in front of his team.

3 | THE PERFECT SHORTSTOP

"We can't win this year with Derek Jeter playing shortstop every day. He's not ready."
— *Clyde King*

The Yankees were renowned for having the most fractious management in base-ball. George Steinbrenner lived in Tampa, the home of the organization's minor league complex. So minor league officials had access nearly every day to the Boss, and that proximity—and Steinbrenner's refusal to adhere to a chain of command—gave these executives influence in major league decision making. That fostered paranoia and anger with the major league executives in New York. Yet, for the most part in 1996, the coalition-forming skills of assistant general manager Brian Cashman and Mark Newman, who was now running the minor league program in Tampa, brought a level of discipline to the dysfunctional process.

But a third power base had long existed within the Yankees organization that was more nebulous and, thus, more uncontrollable and much more unpredictable. Steinbrenner had for years empowered a group that operated as a shadow cabinet, a society that included sportswriters, agents, and a few Yankee employees stashed on the payroll by Steinbrenner. This bloc fed the Boss's lust for second-guessing and assigning blame on a near-daily basis. Billy Connors and Arthur Richman, for example, were members who played roles in designing the 1996 Yankees. But no one in the shadow cabinet had exhibited quite the survival gene of Clyde King. In the 1980s, Steinbrenner had changed his manager, general manager, or pitching coach more than 40 times, and King was the only man to have operated in every capacity. In perhaps his most well-known act, King, as general manager in 1985, served as Steinbrenner's henchman by telling

Yogi Berra he was fired as manager after just 16 games. Berra vowed never to set foot inside Yankee Stadium again while Steinbrenner owned the team, a promise he was still keeping in 1996. King, however, had lingered on the company dole without interruption, a baseball dinosaur yet still with a conduit to the ultimate Yankee authority. He was officially a member of the Yankees' "special advisory group." But like another member of that body, Dick Williams, King advised only Steinbrenner.

At age 71, watching through soda-pop glasses, King felt he had seen enough in spring training to advise Steinbrenner that 21-year-old Derek Jeter was incapable of handling the offense or defense necessary to be the everyday shortstop for a championship Yankee team. It was always easier to feed Steinbrenner a negative forecast; he was a pessimist by nature. But the Boss had actually been upbeat as camp began, mostly because, on the back of Tampa taxpayers, the Yankees had unveiled Legends Field that spring training. The opening made Steinbrenner even more money and an even bigger man in his hometown. The stadium also was of great tactical use to the organization because the dimensions were the same as Yankee Stadium. More important, it brought major league spring training across the street from the minor league complex. The Yankees had trained in Fort Lauderdale from 1962 to 1995. The new setup meant the organization could send prospects over to play in major league spring-training games or that a major league pitcher rehabilitating an injury could face minor leaguers in a more controlled atmosphere. Of course, it also meant Steinbrenner was always around. He kibitzed and cajoled regularly with the media early in the spring training of 1996, good-naturedly predicting 15 wins for Dwight Gooden and that the New York Rangers and Detroit Red Wings would play for the Stanley Cup.

But as spring training rolled along, Steinbrenner turned more familiarly abusive. That pitching bounty Joe Torre had crowed about in February was melting away in March. With each outing, Gooden looked more washed up than a 15-game winner; Scott Kamieniecki failed to impress Torre; and Kenny Rogers stoked the worst fears about lacking the temerity to play for a New York team.

What most unnerved Steinbrenner and elevated anxiety in Yankee camp, however, was the state of the middle infield. Pat Kelly, initially tabbed as the starting second baseman, never had a healthy right shoulder in camp. Tony Fernandez had lost his starting shortstop job to Jeter before Legends Field even opened, and he requested a trade upon his arrival. However, with Kelly ailing, Torre flipped Fernandez to second base, and the veteran switch-hitter reluctantly acquiesced and actually adapted well to the position while hitting superbly in spring. As the final week of exhibition games approached, Fernandez was Torre's starting second baseman. But on March 24 at Legends Field, in the fourth inning against Houston, Fernandez hurled his body to backhand a well-struck grounder by James Mouton. He landed with full force on his right elbow, the ball popping out of his glove on impact. Fernandez attempted to barehand the ball to toss to Jeter covering second. But he could not even close his hand around the ball. He had fractured the tip of his ulna. Fernandez would be sidelined at least 3 months.

Mariano Duncan had been signed to replace Randy Velarde as the Yankees' jack-of-all-trades. But with Kelly and Fernandez unavailable, the defensively suspect Duncan was now the regular second baseman, although he had not played even 100 games at any single position in the past 5 years. Besides losing their second baseman so close to the season, the Yankees also had their shortstop safety net removed. Fernandez was dour and finicky, but he was a four-time Gold Glove winner at shortstop. Jeter, meanwhile, was a defensive work in progress. Fernandez was only in position to be hurt because the previous batter in that March 24 game, Brian Hunter, had hit what should have been an inning-ending double-play ball at Jeter. But Jeter threw wide of Fernandez. That permitted Mouton to bat. It was yet another worrisome snapshot concerning Jeter's readiness for such a vital role on the most expensive, pressurized team in the majors. Clyde King and his more than half a century of professional baseball experience told him Jeter was not prepared.

Steinbrenner ached to be taken seriously as a baseball man, and one of the services rendered by his shadow cabinet was to furnish the Boss with concepts about the team and game that Steinbrenner then parroted as if they were his own. On Tuesday night, March 26—a day after *Braveheart* won the Academy Award for Best Picture of 1995 and less than a week before the season opener—Steinbrenner summoned more than a dozen of the club's most powerful executives to Joe Torre's Legends Field office. Steinbrenner broached "his" frets about the Yankees going with a rookie shortstop on Opening Day for the first time in 34 years—and Tom Tresh had started in 1962 only because Tony Kubek was in the military. Gene Michael saw a subject too important to stay quiet about and challenged Steinbrenner on how he formulated such a negative impression about Jeter's preparedness. Though he was no longer the Yankees' general manager, Michael engendered unrivaled respect in the front office because he had never backed down from Steinbrenner on vital issues just to protect his job or to make the yelling stop. The Boss buckled, giving up King and summoning him to speak in front of the assembled group and repeat his assertions that Jeter was not ready for the Yankees.

A Yankee season was in crisis before it had even begun. The double-play combination of Jeter and Duncan was unsettling, and the backups now were rookies Robert Eenhoorn and Andy Fox. Bob Watson was hunting middle infield possibilities. Steinbrenner had a jones for Minnesota standout second baseman Chuck Knoblauch, but Twins general manager Terry Ryan was not interested, no matter how often Watson called at Steinbrenner's behest. Philadelphia second baseman Mickey Morandini was discussed, as was Milwaukee's Pat Listach. Because Seattle was going with Alex Rodriguez at shortstop, Felix Fermin and Luis Sojo were expendable. Since both played shortstop as well as second base, the Yankees honed in on them. In fact, Yankee officials went into this meeting mulling a Seattle offer of Fermin for either Bob Wickman or the pitcher that had so impressed the Mariners in the Division Series the previous October: Mariano Rivera. So on March 26, 1996, this possibility existed: Rivera traded to Seattle and Jeter demoted to Columbus. A dynasty was teetering, and no one knew it. Rick Down, who had recently been deposed as Yankee hitting coach but continued to monitor the team, says, looking back, "If George had a Plan B, there would have been no Derek Jeter."

Michael did not want there to be a Plan B, so, at that tense meeting, he reminded Steinbrenner of Plan A. The previous October, the Tampa and New York officials had rare simpatico in resolving that Jeter should be the full-time shortstop in 1996. Stick had counseled Steinbrenner when that evaluation was made to not even watch the first month of the season to avoid an impulsive decision after an inevitable rookie mistake. Now Michael, recognizing the need to inject humor, directed Steinbrenner to abstain until after the All-Star break. Steinbrenner laughed, and after a few others weighed in (infield coach Willie Randolph, for example, lauded Jeter's work ethic and, thus, likelihood to improve), the Yankee executives departed Torre's office once more in agreement. Jeter would start. Neither Wickman nor Rivera would be sacrificed for Fermin, who would be waived a few weeks later by the Mariners, play briefly for the Yankees' Triple-A team, appear in 11 games for the Cubs in 1996, then never play major league baseball again.

Still, regardless of the renewed commitment to Jeter in late March, this was George Steinbrenner. He was never going to wait until the All-Star break or even the first month to judge Jeter. In 1984 Steinbrenner had busted 23-year-old shortstop Bobby Meacham down to Double-A for making a two-out, eighth-inning error against Texas that cost the Yankees the fourth game of the season. Then manager Yogi Berra protested. Steinbrenner told reporters, "Meacham isn't ready for New York."

Was Jeter?

This was not the first time Jeter's abilities were questioned within the organization.

He would go on to be the most popular Yankee of his generation, a Mickey Mantle of his time. However, in his early years in the organization, before his 1996 breakthrough, Jeter was universally adored by the Yankee hierarchy only during the dating process. That was when Bill Livesey's scouting department fixed its collective heart on a skinny shortstop from Kalamazoo Central High, who scuttlebutt also indicated was the fancy of the Cincinnati Reds. The Yankees drafted sixth overall on June 1, 1992. The Reds selected fifth.

The Yankees had set up their draft headquarters in the Harbor View Room, a conference room about the size of half a basketball court, just off the kitchen on the first floor of George Steinbrenner's Radisson Bay Harbor Hotel in Tampa. The Yankees had three boards set up in the front of the room on which the draft-eligible players were sorted by position in order of desirability. To the left of each youngster's name was a grade known as the OFP (Overall Future Potential), designed to project a player's future status—from merely an organizational player with no chance of making the majors all the way up to a franchise cornerstone. On the right was a number that showed how many of the five standard tools—hitting, hitting for power, throwing, fielding, and running—the player was likely to be at least average at in the majors. If a player had a plus next to the skills, it meant a projection that he would be above average at that facet of the game.

Jeter had an OFP score of 60, commensurate to a high-end projection of a regular All-Star and a low-end projection as a franchise player. He was listed to have all five tools, with a plus next to each but power, though Livesey had a hunch power would eventually come to the skinny kid. Jeter topped the shortstop list, but he topped more than that. Livesey had been a Yankee employee from 1978 to 1995 and was the organization's director of scouting from 1992 to 1995. In Jeter, Livesey saw all he loved in a player, a marriage of already burgeoning skills and mouth-watering possibilities still untapped. Livesey had crafted his department to revere all the qualities in prospects he admired, and so Jeter was an easy sell within those walls, although the Yankees already had used their top draft picks the previous two years on high school players: Carl Everett in 1990 and Brien Taylor in 1991.

"Our reports were so high on (Jeter) compared to other reports," Livesey says. "This kid had a feel for the game you just don't get from other northern high school players. This kid was the diamond in the rough."

When word came across the speakerphone that the Reds had taken Chad Mottola with the fifth pick, a roar surged in the Yankee draft room. There was an identification number assigned to each draft-eligible player. Kevin Elfering, the Yankees' director of minor league operations, was on the phone to the Commissioner's Office and gave the number 19921292; with that, Derek Jeter was part of the Yankee organization. "It was almost too good to be true," Livesey says.

The Yankees had drafted Taylor a year earlier with the first pick overall, and acrimonious negotiations followed that ended in Taylor receiving a record $1.55 million bonus and then GM Gene Michael being humiliated by the process. Because of that series of events, Yankee officials did not avail themselves to the media to discuss Jeter. They were afraid to rave too much and stack ammunition for Jeter in negotiations. The Yankees limited their public comment to this Livesey canned statement: "Jeter was the best athlete available when it was our opportunity to select. We feel in due time he will become a frontline shortstop in the major leagues." That is all they had to say at the time they drafted the player who would soon become the greatest shortstop in their history.

Jeter had a scholarship waiting at the University of Michigan and was a serious enough student to be contemplating premed courses. But he had been a fan of the Yankees since his youth, dreaming from his childhood of playing shortstop for them. So, 2 days after his 18th birthday, on June 28, Jeter agreed to a contract for $700,000 that would include money to attend Michigan. In truth, the education of Derek Jeter was just beginning.

Jeter was gangly and not yet fully developed, just 162 pounds at his first Yankee weigh-in. Brian Butterfield, then the Yankees' minor league infield instructor, said Jeter looked "like a baby Doberman pinscher, all arms and legs going in every direction." This Doberman started with Tampa in the Gulf Coast League in July 1992 still carrying his equipment in a bag supplied by his Summer League team, the Kalamazoo Maroons, and wearing high-tops to protect an ankle badly sprained in his senior high school season. The Yankee minor league heads were sticklers for uniform uniformity, and among the items banned were high-top shoes. "People were ragging him, like, 'Who is this guy?'" Jeter's GCL teammate Ricky Ledee recalls.

It got worse. After striking out once as a high school senior, Jeter whiffed in his first two at-bats and five times overall, going 0-for-8 in a doubleheader to begin his pro career. He made an error that cost the Tampa Yankees the opener. Jeter did not have a hit in his first 14 pro at-bats. Jeter's game was miserable and so was he. He had never spent extended time away from home, except to be with his grandparents in New Jersey. He had excelled only as a baseball player. Now he was 1,200 miles from home. He was the youngest player on a team consisting mostly of players ages 19 to 21, more than half of whom had already played at least a year of pro ball. The limited experience afforded a high school player from a cold-weather state could not be hidden. A month earlier at the Radisson Bay Harbor, Yankee executives exalted at being able to select Jeter. Now Jeter returned daily to his room at George Steinbrenner's hotel to eat his meals, cry, and run his phone bill home as high as $400 a month. Jeter hit .202 and struck out 36 times in 173 at-bats for Tampa.

He finished that first pro season with an 11-game jump from the Rookie League to the Single-A Sally League. In his first game playing shortstop when Andy Pettitte started, Jeter went 0-for-5 with four strikeouts and committed two errors. Pettitte remembers, "I kept thinking, 'This is our first-round pick? This is our best prospect?' I didn't think he was worth flip." Jeter made nine errors in just 48 chances at Greensboro. He was aching to return home, to begin his first semester at Michigan in the off-season. However, his GCL manager Gary Denbo recalls, "What stood out for me was how he handled his failure. Him and Ricky Ledee were always at the cages waiting as the first guys out to hit when we came out of our staff meetings. Honestly, I had no idea about the crying and how much he was calling his parents. You would have never known by his actions at the complex that he was insecure. You would have thought he was the most confident guy in the world."

What Denbo did fret about was Jeter's atypical hitting approach. Most batters move their hands back to initiate a swing and the barrel of the bat goes straight up. With Jeter, the barrel tilted toward the catcher. It is usually a tip-off for a long swing. Denbo and Triple-A Columbus manager Rick Down, who at the time was the most trusted organizational voice on hitting, conferred and were unable to come up with a single example of a major league hitter who successfully used this approach. Nevertheless, Denbo became Jeter's hitting sherpa, beginning an annual process of countering the unorthodox bat dip by lowering what at the time was an exaggerated leg kick. Jeter moved to Tampa and worked daily in the off-season with Denbo, reinforcing within the organization how serious-minded he was. By 1993 the worries about Jeter's hitting became secondary. Playing for Greensboro of the low Class-A South Atlantic League, Jeter hit .295 with 11 triples (second in the league) and 152 hits (third in the league). But he committed 56 errors in 128 games.

"Talk about the ugly duckling becoming the swan," Livesey says, looking back. "For the first 2 years, Derek was the ugly duckling."

It was so unsightly that some sentiment grew within the organization to shift Jeter to center field. According to Mark Newman, as early as spring training 1993, when Jeter spent a few weeks in big league camp, a feeling emerged that he did not move smoothly enough to handle shortstop. Clete Boyer, then a Yankee coach who would later become part of the anti–Buck Showalter faction and leave the organization angrily, says, "I don't care what they say now, I am telling you the goddamn truth, every person who had some power said Jeter should be moved to center field." But many coaches and executives who were then part of the organization claim he is covering up — that it was Boyer who saw Jeter in big league camp in 1993 and thought his footwork was so choppy that he would never play shortstop in the majors. Livesey remembers then GM Gene Michael becoming "so sick of answering questions about when [Jeter] would be moved to the outfield that we had a conference call to talk about it.

Our reply was, nobody in Tampa feels he can't play shortstop. We felt the 56 errors were part of a normal progression."

Michael could believe that. In an amazing coincidence, he had botched his way to a Northern League–leading 56 errors in 124 games in his pro debut of 1959 and committed more than 50 errors in each of his first three pro seasons. So Michael was sensitive to the shortcomings; besides, he had actually visited Jeter at Greensboro midway through the 1993 campaign and left impressed by Jeter's athleticism, intelligence, and earnestness. Noticing Jeter's main problem was altering his mechanics from groundball to groundball, Michael recommended that the 19-year-old watch Cal Ripken. Michael thought Ripken was like a conveyor belt, fielding each grounder and completing each throw in an identical fashion: same footwork, same arm slot, same follow-through. Jeter said that advice impacted him, but not as much as the 5 weeks he spent in Brian Butterfield's boot camp did. Jeter had been hit on his left hand late in the 1993 season; "a blessing in disguise" he calls it now. That meant in the postseason Instructional League he could only field, not hit. For 35 straight days he worked exclusively with Butterfield.

The two interacted in drills all morning, then watched film of the session and returned to address the mistakes in the afternoon. Jeter's skills were so raw that student and teacher literally began with playing catch because Butterfield observed Jeter giving with the ball each time, subtly moving his glove back to cradle the ball rather than aggressively moving his glove and feet forward. Jeter loved to hit, so this was mentally exhausting. Yet there he was, day after day, absorbing the lectures. "He's as good a pupil as you could hope for," Butterfield says. "He wanted to be great, and he had great aptitude."

Jeter melded all the tutorials into a 1994 in which he was widely hailed as the minor league player of the year. The Yankees of that era were conservative in promoting prospects. But Jeter could not be constrained. He was the Single-A Florida State League Most Valuable Player despite playing just 69 games, was named the third best prospect in the Double-A Eastern League by Baseball America—though he played just 34 games for Albany—and performed so well in a 35-game cameo for Triple-A Columbus in the International League that Yankee executives visiting during the major league players' strike actually toyed with beginning the 1995 season with a 20-year-old shortstop in the Bronx, since both Mike Gallego and Randy Velarde were free agents.

"I saw Jeter in Albany in 1994," says Carlos Tosca, then the manager of Florida's Double-A affiliate. "This guy did everything you can ask a guy to do to win a baseball game. He bunted against us for a sacrifice, and he bunted against us for a hit. He hit the ball to the right side to advance runners, and he pulled inside pitches for hits. He stole bases—and not just at any time; he'd steal a base when everyone knew in a late-game situation that he needed to steal a base. His only problem was footwork on defense. He played to beat you. I don't think you can teach that. With Jeter, unless you know what you are watching for, you very well might not see it. But if you are really watching you will see stuff every night that helps his team win a game."

Jeter hit .344 over the three levels in 1994 and reduced his error total to 25 in 138 games. But the Yankees, who had the American League's best record in 1994 when the season-ending strike hit, were a team built to win now. So they signed Tony Fernandez to a 2-year, $3 million contract. When Fernandez was hurt in late May 1995, Jeter was summoned for his first 2 weeks in the majors. He was promoted again after September 1 and mainly watched from the bench as the Yankees surged to the wild card and suffered postseason heartache against the Mariners. In between, Jeter had another superb year, though not as electric as the previous season. Playing at Triple-A, he hit .317 and had 29 errors in 123 games.

Jeter slipped from fourth to sixth on Baseball America's major league–wide prospect list. Ruben Rivera of the Yankees was fourth. Paul Wilson of the Mets was second. The Mets, with their Generation K starters of Wilson, Jason Isringhausen, and Bill Pulsipher—all projected to make the big-league rotation to open the 1996 season—had begun to appear a stable organization on the rise, as opposed to the chaotic Yankees, who were trying to revive the career of a fallen Mets ace from a decade earlier, Doc Gooden. Steinbrenner hated that the

Mets might prevail in any New York battles, so before Bob Watson was even hired as general manager, it was decided the Yankees would counter on the youth front with Jeter as their shortstop in 1996. On December 12, 1995, Joe Torre announced publicly that a player he had never even met was going to replace Fernandez. Torre reiterated for years afterward how wise the then rookie was to respond to Torre's unintentional disrespecting of Fernandez by saying that what he had was an "opportunity" to start at shortstop, not a firm job.

Jeter did not help himself early that spring training. As he had at Tampa and Greensboro in 1992, and again in Greensboro in 1993, Jeter started unimpressively. In the opening intrasquad game, he threw high on the first grounder he handled to produce an unearned run. In the first inning of the first spring training game against Cleveland, Jeter's pivot on a double-play grounder skidded errantly in the dirt. Jeter struck out looking against Orel Hershiser in his first at-bat and began the exhibition season hitless in 11 at-bats with four strikeouts. There was youth in Jeter's face, hairstyle (shaved on the sides and bushy up top), and game. Steinbrenner said to the media after the spring opener, "I would not have gone with a Jeter in the past. I think I've changed. I was too demanding. Too hasty." He had changed so much that he convened a secret meeting not long after to scream behind closed doors about the wisdom of going with Jeter. Bobby Meacham was in the air. This was not the time for a bad first impression.

Jeter did not need to leave this camp to see how ephemeral being acclaimed as the next big Yankee could be. In the worst Yankee season in more than half a century, 1990, Kevin Maas had arrived with jutting chin and dynamic power. He set major league records for fewest at-bats to reach 10 and 15 homers. Maas had matinee looks and a lefty stroke seemingly ideal for Yankee Stadium. Yet he was back in the minors by 1993, released in 1994, and after failed stints in the Padres, Reds, and Twins organizations, Maas returned to Columbus in 1995 to be teammates with a kid named Jeter.

"Everyone teased him because he did not have power," Maas recalls. "He could only really get the ball to the warning track at that big ballpark in Columbus. But we teased him about that because that was all we could really tease him about. He was solid at everything else. And, more than that, he was so young [just 20], yet he was the guy everyone looked up to on that club to be the leader. He was a go-to guy, and he had professionalism, though he was the youngest guy on the team."

Kevin Maas, 31 in the spring of 1996, made one final major league bid in that Yankee camp. But he was reassigned to minor league camp after just the third exhibition game and released for good on March 22. He never played in the majors again.

Besides Maas, the only other positive of the 1990 season had been that the Yankees were so terrible they earned the first pick in the June 1991 draft. If Maas's lefty stroke was ideal for Yankee Stadium, the organization could just as easily imagine the lefty power arm of Brien Taylor in the same way. Taylor's 181-strikeout/$161\frac{1}{3}$-inning debut in Single-A in 1992 was so overwhelming that Baseball America made him the top prospect in the minors (Pedro Martinez was 10th). Despite a bout with wildness at Double-A in 1993, Taylor slipped behind only Atlanta's Chipper Jones in the prospect rankings. On December 18, 1993, Taylor unwisely picked a fight in defense of his brother and during the altercation fell on his left arm, tearing up his shoulder. Lost forever was the thunder in his pitches. He missed all of the 1994 season and pitched horrendously back at the rookie level in 1995. In January 1996, Taylor was part of the regular workout group at the Yankees' minor league complex readying for big-league camp. So was Jeter. When it was mentioned to Jeter that it would be frigid in New York in April, Jeter sagely said, "You know what my father told me? He said it's colder in Columbus than New York."

Taylor, clearly not getting the true meaning, responded, "Really? I guess that is because the wind blows in off the water." It became apparent that spring that without a pitching intellect to adapt to his lesser arm, Taylor was never going to make it. He was gone from major league camp on March 7 and never appeared in a single major league game. Taylor, instead, became the subject of the longest-running debate at the Yankee minor complex: What would he have been had he not foolishly gotten into that fight?

Even at 21, Jeter was smart enough to know how things worked in the Yankee world. On those annual summer retreats to his grandparents in New Jersey, Jeter had become a Yankee fan in part because of Dave Winfield. Winfield retired on February 8, 1996, on the brink of this pivotal spring for Jeter. Steinbrenner conceded at about the same time that this was the most he had been involved in the day-to-day decision making of the team since he had returned from his suspension for trying to destroy Winfield. Therefore, with Steinbrenner so fully exposed to criticism if these Yankees underachieved, Jeter recognized he could not have another slow start.

And that was before the Yankee season began in turmoil.

Prior to injuring himself, Fernandez had injured Kenny Rogers. On February 25, Rogers decided to throw batting practice without the protective screen in front of him and was drilled on his left shoulder by a Fernandez line drive. Rogers was so determined, though, to scuttle all the worries that he was not New York tough that he misled Yankee officials, telling them he was fine. But, by mid-March, it was obvious the lefty was not fine, and Joe Torre was furious at being misled. An uneasiness emerged in the Torre-Rogers relationship that would never fully dissipate.

Rogers was signed for 4 years at $20 million to be the No. 2 starter behind David Cone, who had helped recruit Rogers with a few phone calls. It was the most money ever guaranteed a Yankee pitcher. But his poor spring caused, at least partially, by trying to pitch with shoulder pain led Torre to announce before the penultimate exhibition game that Rogers had not made the rotation. Rogers reacted by saying he would tear up his contract if the Yankees let him hook on elsewhere. Rogers had been banished to the bullpen so that Melido Perez, coming off a 1995 season wrecked by shoulder problems, could make the rotation. Then in the final spring game in Tampa, Perez's radar-gun readings fell to the low 80s in miles per hour. So Torre did a U-turn, returning Rogers to the rotation and asking Perez to fly to New York to have his arm examined. Perez hurled duffel bags and drink containers around the Legends Field home club-house. Rogers, disgusted by the original decision, was hardly appeased. Torre looked foolish for announcing the choice without full information about Perez.

Meanwhile, Scott Kamieniecki was so openly disturbed by what he felt was no real chance to make the rotation that he told reporters he was being parked on the disabled list although he really was not hurt. Tom Reich, a longtime member in good stead of Steinbrenner's shadow cabinet, had persuaded the Boss to acquire Tim Raines to be the speedy leadoff hitter Steinbrenner was so convinced the team needed. But Raines had fractured his left thumb in spring training, and so the slow Wade Boggs was reinstalled atop the lineup. With all of this going on, it seemed fitting that the regular-season opener in Cleveland was scheduled for April Fools' Day. But, by 9:30 a.m., the game was postponed due to snow. To lighten the mood, Torre joked, "Kenny Rogers is still in our starting rotation."

But what was happening back in New York hardly had Steinbrenner laughing. The Mets opened on April 1 at Shea Stadium in icy rain and rallied from 6–0 down to beat St. Louis 7–6. And the first rookie shortstop to make the highlights did not play for the Yankees. In the seventh inning, Rey Ordoñez, a Cuban defector in his major league debut, dropped to his knees like a child in a rush to pray, scooped a relay peg from left fielder Bernard Gilkey, and— without rising—spun and threw a 150-foot dart to nail the fleet Royce Clayton at the plate. Ozzie Smith, in the visitor's dugout, remarked that he had just seen a younger version of himself. The Mets had Generation K and now they had a young Ozzie Smith, as well. Suddenly there was even more pressure on Derek Jeter.

Torre had tried to lower the stress, saying his shortstop needed to hit just .240 to .250 and make all the plays. Jeter swatted away such notions. He was no braggart. In fact, he hated when peopled crowed about themselves. He did not play or talk or dress flashy. He had a maturity about him, and in a veteran clubhouse that was noticed immediately. "He was like a 10-year veteran when

you first met him," says Mike Borzello, the Yankees' longtime bullpen catcher.
He may not have strutted, but Jeter did not lack self-confidence. The kid who
cried daily in George Steinbrenner's hotel was long gone. Jeter believed he belonged, and .240 to .250 was not good enough for someone who belonged. It certainly was not going to be good enough for Steinbrenner.

The Yankees reached Opening Day with the majors' highest payroll, $52.9
million, and Steinbrenner was not of the mind to let his youngest player, making
just more than the minimum wage, undermine the investment. Steinbrenner
did not travel to his native Cleveland to watch the season opener because he was
on the *Seinfeld* set, but his presence was everywhere. David Cone, the Opening
Day starter and tacit team spokesman, grasped how the anxiety level could
quickly spiral beyond control if the Yankees did not placate the Boss—and fast.
"Obviously here it is important to get off to a good start," Cone said, refer-
encing how the ghosts of Don Mattingly, Buck Showalter, and Mike Stanley
could overwhelm the team by comparison should the Yankees break out poorly.

If Rey Ordoñez's Opening Day acrobatics had cast a pall over the Yankees,
the University of Kentucky's NCAA basketball title under Rick Pitino that
night provided encouragement. On the four previous occasions that the
Wildcats had secured the championship—1978, 1958, 1951, and 1949—the
Yankees also captured the World Series. But while Kentucky finished strongly,
Jeter again opened unpromisingly on April 2, a sunny but chilly afternoon at
Jacobs Field. Batting ninth, he struck out looking on a 2–2 fastball on the outside corner when crafty 40-year-old righty Dennis Martinez dropped down
side-arm with two on to close the second inning. But Jeter did not take the
strikeout or Rey Ordoñez onto the field. In the bottom of the second, Jeter
turned a flawless pivot on a double play initiated by Tino Martinez and ended
the inning by sliding on his knees to backhand a Sandy Alomar smashed
grounder before rising to throw out the Cleveland catcher. So he was feeling
good about himself when his second at-bat came to open the fifth inning, the
Yankees leading the Indians 1–0.

Jeter had made his mark as a minor leaguer with mounting hit totals, mostly using his inside-out approach to serve balls toward right field. Over the years, with the tutelage of Gary Denbo, Jeter had incrementally lowered his leg kick and gradually incorporated trying to pull in certain counts. Still, he had managed just two homers in 534 at-bats between Triple-A and the Yankees the previous season. Dennis Martinez fell behind 2–0 and fired a fastball that backed up tantalizingly over the inner half. Even though his bat barrel still tilted toward the catcher at a point in his swing, Jeter had the hand speed to whip the bat through the strike zone and send a crushing drive about 15 rows beyond the 19-foot fence in left field—the first Opening Day homer by a Yankee rookie in 27 years. Denbo, watching on a satellite in the Yankee complex, felt goose bumps rise on his arms.

Cone carried a one-hitter and the 2–0 lead provided by Jeter into the seventh. But something was wrong. His right hand was unnaturally cold and clammy, even considering the nippy weather. He was having trouble feeling the ball and had walked six Indians. Nevertheless, the bulldog in Cone pushed him on. He blocked out the strange condition, knowing there was no other choice. This Indian lineup was just too good; so good that two of the best young hitters in the league, third baseman Jim Thome and right fielder Manny Ramirez, were batting sixth and seventh. Cone retired that duo to begin the seventh before Sandy Alomar doubled to the right-field corner. That brought up Omar Vizquel, the ninth-place hitter and the only player in the Indian lineup who had not hit at least .300 the previous year (Julio Franco did it in Japan). On the first pitch, Vizquel looped a ball toward the Bermuda Triangle of the Yankee defense, a near central point from Jeter, left fielder Gerald Williams, and center fielder Bernie Williams. If the ball dropped, the Indians would have their first run, Vizquel on base as the tying run, and the majors' most dangerous lineup would turn over to the top again. The 42,289 fans bracing against 38-degree temperatures roared, sensing the key moment in this game. There was not much air under the ball, and it was heading toward a place where perhaps only Vizquel, the AL's best shortstop, could reach.

But Jeter's strength as a defender was the ball in the air. While managing

Triple-A Tidewater, Bobby Valentine had marveled from the opposing dugout at how the young shortstop innately understood baseball geometry, deciphering the parabola of a ball to anticipate the landing spot and, thus, run without having to watch the ball the whole way. On this occasion, Jeter sped toward the outfield like a wide receiver on a fly pattern, the No. 2 on his back visible at home plate. Cone was sure the ball was going to fall safely, sure he was about to be pulled for a warming Bob Wickman. Joe Torre, wearing No. 6, the only other single digit besides Jeter's not retired by the Yankees, was sure he was about to pull Cone. Jeter was sure of the opposite. Brian Butterfield, watching at a friend's house in Tampa, smiled as his student extended his left arm above his head and snared the ball.

Jeter had begun this game as the least likely of the 18 starting position players to homer and a distant second to be the defensive star at shortstop, since Vizquel had won the last three AL Gold Gloves at the position. But the Yankees were about to learn their shortstop had timing—a flair for the poignant moment. Willie Randolph was good-natured but old-school. He did not bestow compliments easily and hardly ever on a young player. But even he conceded that Jeter's retreating catch was "the biggest play of the game." Cone remembers the play as establishing from Day One that Jeter belonged. The Yankees scored three times in the top of the eighth and won 7–1. The next day the FBI raided a cabin in Montana and arrested Unabomber suspect Theodore Kaczynski, and Jeter had three hits in three at-bats with three runs to help Andy Pettitte beat Jack McDowell in a 2–0 Yankee victory.

"Jeter wouldn't have made the team if Fernandez had not gone down," Tim Raines recalls. "In spring training he couldn't even turn a double play. I wasn't real sure about him. But he took off right from the first game of the season."

For the first time since Tony Kubek became the full-time shortstop in 1958, the Yankees had a homegrown shortstop with star qualities. Clyde King had been wrong.

"Someone in the organization said we can't win with Jeter at shortstop," Gene Michael says. "It turned out we couldn't win without him."

4 | THE PERFECT FORMULA

"This Rivera guy, we don't want to face him anymore. He needs to go to a higher league. I don't know where that league is. He should be banned from baseball. He should be illegal."

—Tom Kelly, Twins manager

The ball flew in April of 1996. Conspiracy theorists suspected baseballs were wound tighter than ever to promote run scoring in general and home runs in particular. In the aftermath of the labor war that led to the cancellation of the 1994 World Series and a shortened 1995 season, the conjecture went that the Office of the Commissioner was looking to reinvigorate apathetic fans. And nothing quite captivates like the long ball. In 1996, the 40-year-old record for homers per game in April was smashed and the 10.58 runs averaged per game were the fourth highest for the month in history. Three players—Brady Anderson, Barry Bonds, and Gary Sheffield—hit 11 homers in April after just three players had ever done so before.

If it was not simply a livelier ball, then there was a collaboration of factors that helped explain the phenomenon, including smaller ballparks and tiny strike zones. The players were bigger, and more substantive discussions were ongoing about the use of illegal performance enhancers such as steroids. It all created a run-scoring orgy that made it open season on pitchers, which influenced how the games were being played. Starting pitchers were more averse to throwing strikes and having muscular hitters have their way. So they nibbled around the plate, swelled their pitch counts, and were relieved earlier than usual. That exposed the soft underbelly of every team, as pitchers not good enough for either the rotation or to close were being called upon sooner and more frequently with pinball-like results. Middle relievers on every club were feeling the remorseless onslaught of offense. Every team, that is, except Joe Torre's Yankees.

In April of 1996, Torre trusted his eyes in a way that Buck Showalter had not just half a year earlier. As the month went on, Mariano Rivera corroborated that his performance the previous October against the Mariners was no fluke. And Torre kept defining a more and more vital function for Rivera, from mop-up man when the season began to a hybrid role that united middle and setup relief. Rivera was asked to get as many as nine outs to bail out a rotation that was proving far more unreliable than Torre had forecast.

"It was like a gift to us," Joe Girardi remembers. "Mo was our righty setup man, lefty setup man, long man, middle man, and setup man all in one. And no one could hit him."

Rivera's metamorphosis from nonentity to cornerstone under Torre was not all that different from his introduction to the organization. In 1990, Rivera's first pro season, he played on a Tampa squad in the Gulf Coast League that featured Carl Everett, Ricky Ledee, and Shane Spencer, fresh from a June draft in which the Yankees also selected Andy Pettitte and Jorge Posada. The minor league policy, implemented by then vice president of player development and scouting Brian Sabean, was to let the prospects play the most. So a top hitter was never pinch-hit for regardless of the matchup, and the most well-regarded pitchers were used as starters or closers. Mariano Rivera was buried in middle relief, a sign that the organizational leaders did not think much of the right-hander, even if he had added enough velocity to reach 90 miles per hour—just as Herb Raybourn had predicted when signing Rivera the previous February.

Rivera accepted his fate, then Tampa Yankee manager Glenn Sherlock remembers, with the stoicism and excellence that came to embody his Yankee tenure. No matter what the role given him, Rivera flourished. In 21 appearances, all in relief, Rivera had only one save, but he pitched 45 innings, produced a 5–1 record, and permitted just one earned run. Noticing Rivera needed just five innings to qualify to win the GCL ERA title, Sherlock successfully appealed to the director of minor league operations, Mitch Lukevics, to let him start

Rivera in the first game of a season-ending doubleheader. On August 31, 1990, Rivera registered a seven-inning no-hitter of the Bradenton Pirates to finish the season with a 0.17 ERA. After the game, Rivera had a secretary in the minor league department track down minor league executive Mark Newman, who was watching the Yankees' Single-A Carolina League team. "You owe me $500," Rivera told Newman. Rivera wanted to remind the minor league coordinator that organizational policy was that players who produce a special achievement get a monetary bonus. But Rivera earned way more than that. "That no-hitter put him on the map with the organization," Sherlock says.

Still, Rivera experienced plenty of detours. Even in spring training 1996, Torre did not discern the assets in a player who was going to most change his professional life. What he did see was a straight fastball that made Rivera's role murky. Torre actually told Watson he should take all the trade offers for Rivera seriously. It was another dangerous moment for an organization unsure of what it had in its midst. In early April, the Yankee middle-infield situation, specifically second base, remained so unsettled that Watson had to listen as rival GMs honed in on Rivera and top pitching prospect Matt Drews. Yet as Watson warded off suitors, Rivera was still mainly roster filler when the season began. Just like in the GCL in 1990, he was in the netherworld of middle relief.

John Wetteland had returned for his second year as the Yankee closer, and his primary setup man from 1995, Bob Wickman, was still in place. Jeff Nelson, a side-winding whiz devastating against right-handed hitters, had been obtained as part of the deal that brought Tino Martinez from Seattle to New York. Unable to acquire a lefty specialist all off-season, the Yankees brought back the troubled Steve Howe just as spring training began. That quartet formed Torre's late-game arsenal as the Yankees followed the stress-releasing euphoria of winning two games in Cleveland to open 1996 by dropping three straight in Texas. The Yankees won their home opener against Kansas City in a driving snow behind Andy Pettitte. Newcomers replacing popular players—Tino Martinez and Joe Girardi—received a crowd-wide cold shoulder when they were booed during lineup introductions. The Panamanian Rivera was completely out of his element, shivering despite "12 layers of clothes on, a parka and mittens, and he was still probably the coldest guy in the ballpark," Howe said. Those in attendance were briefly warmed by a new edition to Yankees home games. While raking the field after the top of the fifth inning, the five-member grounds crew broke out in dance to the Village People song "YMCA." The 2 minutes of gyrations would become a staple at every Yankee Stadium game thereafter.

Through 12 games, the Yankees were 6–6 and had yet to develop a character or a consistent phase of the game. David Cone and Andy Pettitte were the lone dependable performers out of the rotation, but Girardi kept noticing how often between pitches Cone would rub his thumb against the other fingers on his pitching hand, as if he were trying to remove crumbs. What he was trying to do was get feeling back into a hand that continued to tingle, turn cold, and worry a whole organization. Jimmy Key managed just 13²/₃ innings in three starts as even he began to fret about whether a fourth operation to his pitching arm had left him without enough strength to weave his art. Kenny Rogers, due to rainouts, off days, and growing organizational doubts about his stuff, had yet to make a start, a slap of disrespect for a pitcher signed to be the No. 2 starter. On April 19, Dwight Gooden started the 13th game of the season, already having tanked his first two outings. He desperately hungered for some indication that a piece of his past could be recaptured. Instead, he had his worst performance yet, permitting 10 of the 17 batters he encountered to reach base as the Minnesota Twins swarmed for six runs in three innings. The next day's newspapers were filled with stories about Gooden facing the bullpen, a demotion to the minors, or perhaps outright release. He was 0–3 with an 11.48 ERA, and, after this 7–1 loss, the Yankees were a below .500 team and already four games behind the Orioles in the American League East.

So hardly anyone noticed that the same Twins lineup that had bulldozed Gooden for three innings was tranquilized for the next three. But Torre was noticing as Rivera struck out five batters and did it rather effortlessly. Just as important, Torre was already registering that Wickman had limited control of his pitches; that Nelson minimized the impact of his stuff by constantly falling behind hitters; and that wear, tear, and cocaine abuse had diminished Howe's 38-year-old left arm. Three nights later in Kansas City—2 days after the New York Jets had used the first overall pick in the NFL draft to select Keyshawn Johnson—Cone willed his way through five innings of two-run ball, though he was losing feeling regularly in his right middle finger and was unable to command the ball.

The Yankees led 5–2. Nelson, Howe, and Wickman all had relieved the previous day in Rogers's first start of 1996, and Torre was staring at nine outs before he could summon closer John Wetteland. A concept was born—what Torre would come to refer to as the Formula. Rivera was asked to not only protect a lead but protect it for an extended period, to become a long bridge between starter and closer.

Rivera entered against the Royals on April 22 and sliced through the lineup one complete turn without a glitch. Nine up, nine down. No hits. No walks. Perfect. The Yankees won 6–2 and drew within one game of the slumping Orioles. After the game, Cone said blisters on his pitching hand had undermined his control. But before their game of April 26, the Yankees announced that Cone would not make his start the next day, the first time in 9 years he would fail to fill his turn in a rotation. The blisters were a cover story. The Yankees acknowledged not only the disturbing cold sensation in Cone's right middle finger but also discomfort in his pitching forearm. Cone was sent to Columbia-Presbyterian Medical Center to undergo an angiogram.

Torre weighed starting Gooden or Rivera in place of Cone. Rivera had been working on a changeup to deepen his repertoire because he thought the bullpen was a pit stop on the way to his desired job in the rotation. The theory was that he needed something soft to go through a lineup successfully several times. Torre, though, liked what he saw from Rivera as a reliever and didn't want to disrupt that, so he tabbed Gooden.

Cone's potential loss to injury only turned a greater focus on Rogers, and the lefty simply could not handle the scrutiny or redirect the coaching staff's concerns about his makeup. On April 26, Rogers allowed 10 hits and 4 walks in five innings against the Twins. He exited with the Yankees behind 4–0 in the top of the sixth, runners at first and second, and no one out. It was obvious that if Cone were lost for an extended period, Rogers could not fill the void, regardless of how much the Yankees were paying him.

Rivera relieved Rogers and walked Chuck Knoblauch. The bases were loaded. The Twins were on the verge of breaking open a game that would again reduce the Yankees to a .500 team, this time 20 games into the season and with Cone possibly facing a serious arm injury. At that moment, Minnesota had scored 47 runs in its previous 31 innings, and the Twins' second, third, and cleanup hitters were due to bat. But Rivera hurled 95 mph fastballs at the dilemma. One pitch, one result: success. Jeff Reboulet grounded to third baseman Wade Boggs, who threw home for a force out. Paul Molitor popped out to second baseman Mariano Duncan, and Marty Cordova popped out to the catcher, Jim Leyritz. A crowd of just 14,450 rose to salute Rivera. The momentum of the game, perhaps of a season, had changed.

Brad Radke had a three-hit shutout going to the bottom of the sixth before the Yankees erupted for five runs capped by a Bernie Williams grand slam. Rivera authored two more innings of perfect relief, giving him three hitless innings for this game and six over his last two games. Wetteland pitched the ninth to save Rivera's win. The Yankees prospered, 5–4.

Gooden pitched well in place of Cone that Saturday, but the Yankees lost 8–6 when Wickman was crushed for four runs in the 10th inning. The churlish Wickman sensed his job slipping away and, in the bullpen during games, complained about how his new manager was using him. He also railed against the expanding role of Rivera, slamming the notion that any hurler with just one pitch could thrive for an extended period. It was just a matter of time, Wickman told the veterans in the pen, before the league deduced the parlor trick and began walloping one-pitch Mariano Rivera. Plus, if the one-pitch inventory did not eventually nullify Rivera, then he was certain to be undone by his size — or lack of it. Rivera had an athletic body that more resembled a no-hit, all-field shortstop than a pitcher, especially compared to the 6-foot, 8-inch Nelson and burly, barrel-chested Wickman and Wetteland. Rivera did not have thick legs or a big butt, so how was he going to keep generating that fastball over the long season? And where would Rivera find the endurance for this expanding role that Torre was creating for him?

Gene Michael heard scouts rumbling over the same notions, yet he was becoming a true believer. Nicknamed "Stick" for his thin frame, Michael was an avid golfer who carried his scout's eye onto the links. He was mesmerized, in particular, when a skinny person walloped a ball off the tee. He determined that it was about form, moving all the parts in ideal synchronicity as to maximize power. Michael concluded Rivera was like that as a pitcher, with each phase of his delivery so fluid that the end result was effortless, elite arm speed. Rivera's greatest asset, though, was in the deception of his delivery. He unfurled toward the plate without the manic gyrations of obvious power relievers such as Goose Gossage or even Wetteland, large men who announced their fastball intentions with the violence of their deliveries. Rivera was easy-listening smooth, no clues betraying the lightning to come. Sure, he had only one pitch. But boy, was that one pitch hard to pick up.

Derek Jeter, who had the best seat in the house at shortstop and had climbed the minors with Rivera, says, looking back, "He had one pitch in A-Ball and no one hit it, no one hit it at Double-A. No one hit it at Triple-A. Now it is the majors. There is no place else for him to go. They just aren't going to hit it."

As a onetime top-tier hitter, Torre appreciated the difficulties presented by Rivera. Hitters needed a clear read of a release point and a rhythm within their swing, and Rivera messed up both. Torre also loved that Rivera was belying his body type. As pitching coach Mel Stottlemyre recalls, "We learned early that Mo is a lot stronger than he looks." In that 8-day period from April 19 through April 26, Rivera threw the equivalent of a complete game shutout—a trio of three-inning stints—firing 154 pitches in all without any deviation in his stuff. Torre and Stottlemyre recognized a weapon, a pitcher who could influence two or three games in 1 week amid this year when more games were being decided in the sixth, seventh, and eighth innings.

The need for a reliever who could be used often and for many outs kept getting more vital for the Yankees. Before the series finale, April 28, against Minnesota, the Yankees announced Cone had a "mild circulatory problem" in his right hand that was causing tingling, discoloration in the ring finger, and an inability to grasp the ball comfortably. The organization spoke more bravely in public than its members truly believed internally about the situation. Their worries about Jimmy Key were only expanding as well. Between every inning against the Twins, Key had to apply heat to ease tightness in his surgically repaired shoulder. He lasted just five innings, leaving with a 3–2 deficit. Torre turned once again to the antidote to short starts and pitching worries: the one-man, one-pitch, momentum-turning machine.

Rivera relieved to start the sixth. He was operating on just 1 day's rest following a 56-pitch effort. Yet his fastball hopped as always. His style did not change. Joe Girardi put down signs only for location, since there was only one pitch selection. Girardi started at the upper realms of the strike zone with his requests, moving Rivera up a few inches with each strike. The pitch tempted hitters. There it was—a fastball up in the zone. And, boom, it was by them. Rivera struck out Dave Hollins, Roberto Kelly, and Ron Coomer, demoralizing the Twins yet again and infusing the Yankees by whiffing the side. In the bottom of the inning, the tone of the game having changed, the Yankees tied the score on an RBI single by Girardi. Rivera opened the seventh with his fourth straight strikeout, fanning Pat Meares. Greg Myers popped out, Knoblauch walked, and Reboulet popped out.

The top of the inning was over. The Yankees had a chance, if they completed this rally, to move into a first-place tie with Baltimore, which was not an inconsequential matter. Eleven days earlier the Orioles had led the Yankees by 4½ games, and life around the Yankees was not good, not good at all. The Orioles were George Steinbrenner's obsession, his measuring stick for Yankee success. The Yankees could not let Baltimore get away. The Formula helped, but the Yankees had been a good team for several seasons now, in part because of yet another pleasant surprise.

That Paul O'Neill was a heck of a player.

Time diminishes what a risky trade Gene Michael made on November 3, 1992, the same day Bill Clinton defeated incumbent George Bush and Ross Perot to win the presidency. He obainted O'Neill and a minor league first baseman, Joe DeBerry, from Cincinnati for Roberto Kelly. Kelly had just reached his 28th birthday. He was a center fielder with speed and hints of burgeoning power. The Yankees had believed enough in Kelly's gifts that he had displaced Don Mattingly as the primary third-place hitter to start the 1992 season, emerging as the team's lone All-Star representative. O'Neill, meanwhile, was 20 months older than Kelly, played a less premium position of right field rather than center, and was a .259 lifetime hitter coming off a career-worst .246 campaign. O'Neill was in jeopardy of not even being a full-time player, since he had just a .215 career mark against lefties. Five days before the trade, the Yankees had dumped corner outfielder Mel Hall, who had 161 RBIs over the previous two seasons. O'Neill had 157. "You know this is a gamble because Kelly could still be a star," Michael said at the time.

But as he finished up his second full year as Yankee GM, Michael was shaping a roster to fit a set of beliefs established over nearly 4 decades in professional baseball, a majority of those years as a Yankee player, coach, manager, or executive. Some of these beliefs were tangible. More than a decade before *Moneyball* detailed how Oakland GM Billy Beane used statistical analysis to defy expectations and win with the underfinanced A's, Michael was employing many of the same tactics to rebuild a Yankee team. Michael became Yankee GM on August 20, 1990, with the team en route to the worst record in the AL. Atlanta was on the way to the National League's worst record. That the Yankees and Braves would go on to be the teams of the '90s owed much to the genius of their construction, and no person was more responsible for the Yankee rise than Michael.

Tim McCleary, who served as an assistant GM under Michael, remembers his supervisor circling several statistical categories to emphasize areas that the Yankees needed to upgrade, as well as players on other teams whom he thought the Yankees should pursue. Michael, for example, felt that innings per start by pitchers and the ability to produce extra-base hits for batters were vital pieces of data when conceptualizing the assembly of a roster. But, just like in *Moneyball*, Michael championed on-base percentage as the most important statistic. So he was mortified that his 1990 team was at .300 — 20 points worse than any other team, the worst in the AL in 9 years, and the worst by a Yankee team since 1968, a club that had a scrawny shortstop with a .218 on-base percentage named Gene Michael. Among players with at least 200 plate appearances, the Yankees had 5 of the majors' 17 worst on-base percentages in 1990. Mel Hall was in that group, and so were Oscar Azocar, Alvaro Espinoza, Bob Geren, and Randy Velarde. Michael emphasized plate patience as he began his roster renovations, which is how, for example, he found Mike Stanley. The Rangers had released Stanley after both the 1990 and 1991 seasons because he hit just .249 each year, but his on-base percentages were .350 and .372, and that motivated Michael to sign the catcher, whose true value he thought was being missed by others.

Kelly might have begun the 1992 season as the third-place-batting center fielder. But by August, Mattingly was back in the third spot, and, with the Yankees out of the playoff race again, Bernie Williams was called up to play the final 2 months as the center fielder. Michael loved that such a young player worked at-bats from both sides of the plate with a keen-eyed savvy. He was not seeing that from Kelly, which was a big reason he had summoned Williams and moved Kelly over to play left field. What Michael did see from Kelly fell into the intangible set of principles he had honed during his professional life and which he relied upon even more than the stat sheet. Michael formed an idea that began in his baseball gut and ended up as a steadfast opinion. Kelly was not what Michael called a grinder, a player who treated each pitch, each at-bat, and each game with focus and seriousness. Michael thought Kelly gave away games, some-times weeks-long stretches, of at-bats. He believed that Kelly had an overin-flated opinion of his own abilities, thinking himself a star simply because he was possibly the best player on a poor team. That mind-set, Michael reasoned, led Kelly to mentally quit on the 1992 season when he was moved over to left to ac-commodate Williams.

Together, Michael and Buck Showalter had unanimity about what kind of makeup they wanted in their clubhouse. That's why Michael cleansed the roster of players such as Espinoza, Hall, and Steve Sax because of their lack of day-to-day sincerity about the importance of the games. He carefully refurbished with players such as Stanley, Steve Farr, and Mike Gallego, who may not have been elite talents but were allergic to excuse making and burned daily to win. Kelly was neither a grinder nor a player who burned to win. But O'Neill was, and Michael saw him, too, as an undervalued stock. Yes, he had hit just .256 and .246 the past two seasons, but his on-base percentage both years was .346, which was better in that time frame than supposed stars Cecil Fielder and Ruben Sierra. O'Neill's walk totals had risen each year from 18 to 38 to 46 to 53 to 73 to 77. Michael loved that trend line. And no major league outfielder had more assists than O'Neill's 37 from 1990 to 1992.

Michael wanted to reconstitute his outfield to be strong on defense and pa-tient on offense, and he wanted to sprinkle his lineup with more lefty bats to capitalize upon the configuration of Yankee Stadium. He envisioned O'Neill in right and the switch-hitting Williams in center. He hoped that Danny Tartabull would be taken in the expansion draft, freeing the money to go after a free agent named Barry Bonds to play left. But that did not happen. He was going to have to live with O'Neill as his big outfield catch of the off-season, having completed this trade on the advice of an unlikely source. Lou Piniella and Michael were pals, dating back to their Yankee years together. After the 1991 season, when O'Neill had hit 28 homers, Piniella had told Michael that he was going to turn the strapping lefty swinger into a 40-homer monster.

But what ensued was an emotional war between two fiery personalities.

Piniella kept pushing his pupil to get closer to the plate and drive the ball, and as the failures mounted, so did the abuse. O'Neill was sometimes called Big Country, and when he would, for example, pop out, Piniella, according to a person affiliated with the Reds at the time, might mutter "Big Fucking O'Neill"—or worse. Looking back, Piniella says, "Probably when I managed him, he reminded me of me a lot in a red-ass sort of way. I knew myself it was a little unproductive for me. I tried to see if we could take some of that away." All that was removed was O'Neill's confidence. In a love-hate relationship, he tried to appease a manager he knew was running him down and asking him to be what he was not. His homer total did not climb to 40; instead, it was cut in half to 14 as he found that trying for long balls was against his natural tendencies.

Now, after the 1992 season, Michael decided to seek counsel from Piniella, who had recently left the Reds to become Seattle's manager. "Stick told me by phone he could trade Roberto Kelly for Paul O'Neill: 'What do you think?'" Piniella remembers. "I said, 'Stick, what the hell are you waiting for? Paul is a good outfielder, good hitter, and solid fielder. Plus in New York, you need good, solid lefty hitting with the short porch.' Kelly was a good player, too. But when you can get a premium lefty hitter in New York, plus a good-throwing right fielder, that is a good ingredient."

Jim Bowden, in his first trade as Reds' GM, was looking to make his team more athletic with Kelly. The feeling had been that the Yankees would use either Kelly or Williams to get pitching. Instead, they had received another outfielder. But, as O'Neill says, "timing was everything, and I came at the perfect time." It was an ideal union of a player to a new city, a new hitting coach, and a new team.

O'Neill was born in Columbus, Ohio, as a Reds fan, and he figured it would be heaven to play so close to home. It was the opposite. Friends and family besieged him for tickets and for insights into slumps, both his own and the team's. For a player who treated each at-bat as a mandate on his ability, the pressure was too great. O'Neill's wife, Nevalee, cried when she heard the Yankees had obtained her husband, so distraught was she that they could no longer live year-round in one home. But the move was a blessing. O'Neill was loath to talk about himself, and in a big city like New York, he could actually hide. Don Mattingly was in the clubhouse to do the talking and provide guidance, and O'Neill gravitated to the team captain. They were both midwesterners with a devotion to hitting, family, and basketball.

O'Neill developed such respect for the man he affectionately called Cap that it was difficult for him to replace Mattingly as the primary third-place hitter on July 20, 1994. Mattingly, however, made it easy. On his first day as Yankee manager in August 1989, Bucky Dent had made Kelly the third-place hitter and moved Mattingly into the second slot. Mattingly protested by bunting and derisively saying afterward that is what second-place hitters do. Over the first 4 months of the 1992 season, Kelly again was the main third-place hitter, with Mattingly bouncing between second and cleanup, not wholly pleased with that situation, either. But nobody endorsed O'Neill's move to be the third hitter more than Mattingly did. He said, "If I were managing, I would have done it a long time ago, the way Paulie's hitting."

O'Neill was hitting great. He had batted .311 in his first year as a Yankee and was leading the majors in hitting at the time he was installed as the third-place hitter en route to an AL batting title of .359 in 1994. Being away from Cincinnati, around Mattingly, and part of such a professional clubhouse had helped O'Neill gain comfort. But perhaps nothing had helped more than Rick Down.

Down had been one of the minor league hires in the late 1980s and early 1990s, when Yankee executive George Bradley repopulated the system with industrious coaches. Down graduated from managing Columbus to become Buck Showalter's hitting coach in 1993, and during his first spring on the job and O'Neill's first as a Yankee, the two bonded. Down noticed that O'Neill's opening move as a batter was forward. Together they devised a pattern that made O'Neill's initial move back so that he could see the ball longer and drive through it. O'Neill turned his right foot inward, pigeon-toed, and tapped it to create a timing device before lifting his right leg as the pitch was coming. "I told him to think of how you throw a ball, you go back to go forward, and this is the same thing," Down says. "He got it right away. It was about rhythm. Piniella thought he was afraid of the ball and was not competitive. It had nothing to do with that." O'Neill recalls, "I was searching for something. I was always lunging at pitches. The leg kick kept my weight back. More important, Rick Down ingrained in my head that your next swing is going to be your best one."

It was the kind of confident talk that O'Neill needed to cleanse Piniella from his brain. And, unlike Piniella, Down did not force theories on any hitter, especially O'Neill. He agreed that O'Neill's natural style was to drive the ball to all fields, not to pull for home runs. The reward was the blossoming of O'Neill. Because the Yankees had four established outfielders in 1994—O'Neill, Luis Polonia, Danny Tartabull, and Bernie Williams—the quartet drew straws to decide who would not be on the All-Star ballot. O'Neill lost, yet he made the All-Star team, finished fifth in the AL Most Valuable Player voting, and amassed a .460 on-base percentage, the best ever by any Yankee not named Babe Ruth, Lou Gehrig, or Mickey Mantle. Nevalee O'Neill was not crying any more. Paul O'Neill and his high school sweetheart loved living in Westchester, and the marriage between player and team had gone so swimmingly that he signed a 4-year, $19 million contract to stay rather than test free agency.

Meanwhile, in 1994, the Reds gave up on Roberto Kelly, who began a nomadic journey to the end of his career that had stops with the Braves, Expos, Dodgers, Twins, Mariners, and Rangers before finishing with 10 games as a Yankee in 2000. Gene Michael had been right about Kelly. He did not have the discipline or grinder mentality to capitalize on his wonderful skills. And Michael had been right about O'Neill, whose on-base percentage from 1993 to 1996 was a team-best .404 to help the Yankees produce the best on-base percentage in the majors in that time frame. Michael had churned the roster from impatient hackers to a deliberate group that performed batter's box Chinese water torture on pitchers; drip by drip, pitch by pitch, they wore down the opposing staffs by refusing to swing at anything but strikes, and that mentally and physically broke pitchers. O'Neill exemplified that style. But Michael's influence on the roster went beyond that.

There were many contributors to the Yankee dynasty, but Michael's fingerprints were everywhere. At 6-foot-2 and 180 pounds, Michael was a basketball star at Kent State. He was not built all that different from Derek Jeter, and with more modern concepts about weight training and nutrition, he might have grown to be more than a Stick. But in a second-rate, 10-year major league career, Michael managed just 15 homers and a .229 batting average. Michael was a Yankee from 1968 to 1974, amassing a .296 on-base percentage, the second worst in franchise history for players with at least 2,500 plate appearances.

But Michael was a baseball savant. He understood instinctively the most important facets of the game, even if he could not execute them. He was not couth or worldly, and certainly not as funny as he thought. But Michael could look at players and divine their strengths and weaknesses. He was astute at projecting in his mind what they could and could not be. From 1990 to 1995, Michael held the title of GM, but a desk and paperwork for Stick Michael were like a cage for a lion. He was a scout at heart, a man who wanted to dissect players, not figure out budgets or decipher the rule book. He delegated those chores as often as possible, so he could concentrate on what he loved and excelled at: player evaluation and deal making.

There were times, in fact, when he seemed a magician. In 2½ seasons as a Yankee, Tim Leary produced the worst winning percentage (.340) and second-worst ERA (5.12) ever by a Yankee pitcher with at least 400 innings pitched, and he was also caught on television in June 1992 discarding a piece of sandpaper that he had used to cheat on the mound. Buck Showalter told Michael he would perform oral sex on the GM if he were able to trade the righty. On August 22, 1992, Michael went into the manager's office and jokingly dropped his pants, having successfully moved Leary to Seattle. That off-season he shocked Showalter again by turning the expensive, defensively inept Steve Sax into three viable arms, Melido Perez, Bob Wickman, and Domingo Jean.

Michael was treasured within the New York office for being both inclusive with and protective of his staff. But he was constantly in conflict with the Tampa-based minor league head, Bill Livesey, because, as Tim McCleary recalls, "Bill was always saying, 'Let's keep the foundation for the future,' and Stick was always saying to Livesey, 'We have to give some players to get some players.'"

It was not as if Michael was profligate anyway. In 1993, George Steinbrenner's first season back from his suspension, the pressure was intense for the Yankees to win to satisfy the Boss. But Michael simply did not believe that his team was ready yet to overtake the Blue Jays. So, late in the season, he augmented by trading nonprospects for pitchers Lee Smith and Frank Tanana to upgrade what he perceived as a slim chance to make the playoffs. As Brian Cashman says, "He didn't give up good prospects. He refused to trade our best guys when in his heart he knew we weren't good enough. You have no idea how tough that is—when you have our fans, our media, and our owner—not to just try to appease everyone instead of doing the right thing. Gene Michael kept perspective."

But when he felt the team was ready to win in 1995, Michael fixated on acquiring elite players. In that quest, he traded six homegrown talents (Keith Heberling, Lyle Mouton, Fernando Seguignol, Marty Janzen, Jason Jarvis, and Mike Gordon) to obtain Jack McDowell, John Wetteland, and David Cone. This was his genius. Michael had a sixth sense of which prospects to protect, such as Derek Jeter, Andy Pettitte, Mariano Rivera, Bernie Williams, and Jorge Posada, and which ones to move. After an era in which the Yankees notoriously traded eventual stars Jay Buhner, Doug Drabek, Willie McGee, and Fred McGriff for veteran waste, Michael was never burned by any of the young- sters he dealt. Some turned into good players, such as J. T. Snow, but most did not, and none became star performers elsewhere.

All in all, his ability to shield the right players and consummate a series of vic- torious trades positioned the Yankees to be the dominant team of the late 1990s. But no acquisition within this period was more important than that of O'Neill. For in O'Neill, Michael found a player about to run off the six best seasons of his career, a player capable of replacing Mattingly without rancor and with great production. He was a cornerstone to build around. The Yankees had finished below .500 in each of the four seasons before O'Neill arrived, and they never finished fewer than 13 games over while O'Neill was a regular. But more than that, this team fit O'Neill, and O'Neill fit the team. The Yankees of Michael and Showalter were a serious outfit, and no one took each at-bat more seriously than O'Neill. They were holy wars for him. If he singled, he beat himself up for not doubling. If he doubled, he beat himself up for not homering. If he made out, he became a threat to batting helmets and water coolers everywhere.

"O'Neill was the ultimate grinder," Joe Girardi says. "He was the person who was never satisfied. He always thought he could get more out of himself. O'Neill would say he was happy with his career, but he was never happy with any individual game within it. He always thought he could get more. I felt bad sometimes, how he tormented himself."

What was hard for the outside world to fully appreciate was that frustration was Paul O'Neill's fuel. He needed the self-criticism to drive himself to perform. Because of that, O'Neill was an acquired taste, and not just for opponents and umpires who derided his constant whining about balls and strikes, and his destruction of equipment, as selfish and infantile behavior. Even within his own clubhouse, it took time for Yankee personnel to fully comprehend O'Neill's motives and motor. It was not uncommon for him to become so distracted in misery by a bad at-bat that he would loaf to first or not be fully focused in the field. On April 23, a ball fell between O'Neill and Bernie Williams for the go-ahead hit as the Royals beat Jimmy Key 5–2; afterward, Joe Torre made it clear to the media that he thought O'Neill should have made the catch. O'Neill was annoyed to be called out, and even more so the next day, when Torre removed him for defensive purposes in the ninth inning, inserting Gerald Williams. There had already been a couple of instances on the bases and in the field in April in which O'Neill did not appear to be giving his all.

Torre insisted he was not trying to send a message, at least not to O'Neill. Following the April 24 game, Michael Kay, in his role as the clubhouse reporter for the Yankee broadcast company, Madison Square Garden Network, asked Torre if O'Neill was either hurt or being punished. Torre said that neither was the case; he liked Paul O'Neill and wished he had a team full of him. What he did not like was being put on the spot like that. So the next day, in the middle of the clubhouse and in full view of many players, Torre irately told Kay, "Don't fuck with me." He accused the broadcaster of trying to create unease between the manager and his players. The setting was deliberate. Torre wanted his players to see that he had a temper and would not allow the media to create rifts between the manager and his players. That Kay was probably the media member who had the best relationship with Buck Showalter did not escape Torre, either.

Later that day, O'Neill saw his manager in the exercise room and clarified that he was not mad at Torre, and Torre said he had no problems with the right fielder. Torre was in the midst of educating himself about his team. He was coming to understand that O'Neill's implosions did not mark him as selfish. Torre had noticed that there was not a single player on his roster who had a greater ratio of wanting to talk about the team and never wanting to discuss himself than O'Neill. O'Neill had developed a pleasant repartee with the regular reporters who covered the Yankees, even becoming more willing to expand on club issues now that Mattingly was gone. But no one was going to confuse O'Neill with his distant relative Mark Twain. By the end of the first month of the regular season, Torre had learned to tolerate O'Neill's eruptions and that it was important occasionally to steer his hot-tempered right fielder's attention to matters beyond the batter's box. And Torre had certainly learned that one-pitch Mariano Rivera was one of a kind.

There was no doubt about O'Neill's concentration and hustle against the Twins on April 28. In the fourth inning, he had made a leaping catch as he crashed into the right-field wall to rob Paul Molitor of a home run against Jimmy Key. In the following inning, O'Neill went sprawling when a purpose pitch from Twins starter Frankie Rodriguez was delivered toward his chin. Now in the seventh, O'Neill came up as the AL's leading hitter, a consistent bat in what had been a relatively inconsistent Yankee attack to date. There were two out and none on, and Rodriguez threw a first-pitch fastball, this time toward the middle of the plate. O'Neill tapped, tapped, tapped his right foot, raised his leg like a pitcher, and crushed a line drive toward the 408 sign in center. The ball never climbed much above 15 feet, so it looked as if the Twin center fielder had a chance at the ball. The center fielder was Roberto Kelly. But the drive cleared the fence. The Yankees led 4–3 on O'Neill's homer.

In the top of the eighth, Torre sent Gerald Williams in to play defense again, but this time for Tim Raines in left field. Facing the 3-4-5 hitters, Rivera sandwiched two groundouts around a strikeout, and the Yankees scored twice in the bottom half to gain a 6–3 lead. With the heavy lifting completed, Rivera stepped aside to have Wetteland save his win, a Yankee victory that did indeed move them into a tie with the Orioles atop the division, with a trip to Camden Yards next on the schedule. In the course of the week, Rivera had a trio of hitless three-inning stints or the equivalent of a complete-game no-hitter. But rather than one victory, Rivera had influenced three outcomes: one against Kansas City and two against Minnesota. The Yankees had enjoyed a 4–3 week, and Rivera was the determining factor in three of the four triumphs. He had both of the Yankees' wins in the just-completed weekend series against the Twins and a 12-inning scoreless streak, and he had retired 29 straight batters without allowing a hit. His April ERA was 1.38 at a time when the entire AL's mark was 5.31, and the rest of the Yankee bullpen was at 5.19. There were 439 homers hit by AL batters in April, one every seven innings. Rivera pitched $21^{2}/_{3}$ innings and yielded no long balls.

"He was just blowing people away with one pitch," Tino Martinez says. "Batters did not have a chance. We didn't have a high-powered offense, so he was vital. It was like Little League baseball, six-inning games. We just had to be ahead after six innings, and we won. After the sixth inning, it was the Mo Show."

The Yankees had a one-pitch dynamo no other team could counter early in 1996, a force so overwhelming that two-time World Series–winning manager Tom Kelly made it clear he hoped never to see Rivera in a game against his team again. The Yankees were 12–10, and Rivera was emerging as the biggest reason the team did not bury itself early in the campaign. The ball was flying, and now suddenly so were the Yankees. They had the only middle-inning pitcher in the majors who was defying the offensive ambush. Suddenly the Yankees had developed a Formula to win.

Get the ball to Mariano Rivera.

5 | THE PERFECT 2 DAYS

"I take you back to Baltimore. I take you back to two games that I think set the tone for the whole '96 season. I take you back to two games that gave us confidence and took the wind out of the Baltimore Orioles' sails."
—*Bob Watson*

The retro clock above the center-field scoreboard at Camden Yards showed 7:36 p.m. when Arthur Rhodes threw the opening pitch on April 30 to Derek Jeter. The first meeting of AL East powers began with the Orioles in first place by a half-game over the Yankees. Jim Mecir was on the Columbus Clipper roster, and Tino Martinez was still dragging the ghost of Don Mattingly around with him from at-bat to at-bat. All that changed over the next two nights—and part of one morning—was the major league record book, the AL East standings, and the tenor of the 1996 season. Oh, yeah—and Tino Martinez's Yankee career. Over 9 hours and 55 minutes of play—as April turned to May—the Yankees and Orioles defined their baseball souls.

Baltimore began the season as if to confirm all of George Steinbrenner's worst visions about which organization had won the off-season. The Orioles opened 9–1, their best start since 1966, when they sprinted to a 12–1 record en route to sweeping the Dodgers to win the World Series. Davey Johnson played second base on that championship squad and on four Oriole pennant winners. When Buck Showalter's chances of returning to the Yankees were in limbo in October, Johnson had been viewed initially as the front-runner to be their next manager. Steinbrenner had a longtime infatuation with all things Mets, especially mid-1980s championship Mets. So who better to manage Dwight Gooden, David Cone, and Darryl Strawberry in the Bronx than the man who had brought such greatness out of them in Queens? And Steinbrenner had a ready-made conduit to Johnson, dating back to his days managing the Mets, in Arthur Richman.

But Johnson revered his Oriole roots. He had been crushed to be bypassed for their managing job the previous year for Phil Regan. Baltimore, with great expectations, had finished 71–73 in 1995, leading to the ouster of Regan and general manager Roland Hemond. Johnson was hired to manage, and to his great joy, the GM job went to Pat Gillick. The two had been teammates together in 1963 for Baltimore's Single-A team, the Elmira Pioneers, who were managed by Earl Weaver. Johnson and Gillick had five World Series titles combined as players or executives—five more than Joe Torre and Bob Watson. Johnson was a disciple of Weaver, who disdained the sacrifice and managed to build big innings. In New York, Johnson had played bulky Kevin Mitchell occasionally at shortstop during the 1986 season, just to get another impact bat into the lineup. As a player, Johnson had been at the vanguard of using computers in baseball, employing his expertise to write an analysis entitled *How to Optimize the Orioles' Offense*. Interestingly, it always had Johnson as the cleanup hitter and always wound up in the garbage after he presented it to the crotchety Weaver, who used his own well-kept data to make decisions.

These 1996 Orioles were a reflection of Johnson, which explained both their April ascension and their decline. Brady Anderson epitomized the team. He had transformed from a player noted for speed to set a major league record by hitting a homer to lead off the first inning in four straight games during the third week of the season. Baltimore, however, lost all four of those games. Anderson tied the major league record with 11 April homers, yet after an 11–2 start, the Orioles had fallen apart.

Weaver's great Oriole teams had not only home-run might but elite pitching as well. These Orioles had only half of the equation. Baltimore lost 9 of 12 games after the hot start because its pitching, particularly after the top three starters, was odious and its defense was insufficient, even with the Cooperstown-coated double-play tandem of Roberto Alomar and Cal Ripken. Johnson had made only one real concession toward better defense, and, in many ways, that was hurting the team most. Under Regan, Bobby Bonilla was moved between third base and right field, neither of which he was particularly adept at. The Orioles signed free agent B. J. Surhoff to play third and added Mike Devereaux and Tony Tarasco to form a more defensively sound righty-lefty platoon in right. But Bonilla was now in the last season of a 5-year contract, and with free agency looming, he knew his value would be compromised if he were a full-time designated hitter and could not market himself as a two-way player. Bonilla's persistent carping to the media about his deployment began before the season even commenced. Johnson was inflexible at first, not wanting to be seen as capitulating to a player. However, Bonilla's offense was so rancid that Johnson bent by shifting him between right and third again midway through April. That angered Manny Alexander.

Alexander was Baltimore's top prospect, but he played shortstop, the same position as the Iron Man, Ripken. Alomar had been signed for second base and Surhoff for third. Alexander saw all the places he was blocked, but he was offended that now even Bonilla was playing ahead of him at third. He also took his complaints to the media. The shabby defense motivated No. 3 starter Scott Erickson to air his grievances, proclaiming he would have been undefeated rather than 1–2 with better fielding support.

April 29 was an off-day for the Yankees, and *Rent* opened on Broadway. Meanwhile, Orioles No. 4 starter Kent Mercker reacted to what he thought was a premature hook in the third inning by berating Johnson on the mound before the two got into heated exchanges in both the dugout and the clubhouse. But the Orioles illustrated why they were a dangerous team, rallying from a 5–0 deficit to beat Texas 8–7 and gain that half-game lead on the idle Yankees. Baltimore had an offense capable of cleansing bad pitching, bad defense, and even bad actors.

As if to accentuate the point, the Orioles wiped away Yankee leads of 2–0 and 4–3 before the series opener was even two innings old. Andy Pettitte, to that point the only Yankee starter not to worry Joe Torre due to injury or

ineffectiveness, lasted just one inning plus six batters, none of whom he retired in the second inning. He was charged with nine runs. In the period
between taking the ball from Pettitte and waiting for Scott Kamieniecki to
reach the mound, Torre told his assembled infielders that this was the AL in
1996, so no game was ever over. He likened it to choosing up sides in the
streets, playing until dark, and scoring so much that no one could keep count.

The message was for all the infielders gathered on the mound but for
Martinez most of all. In their short time together, manager and first baseman
had developed an affinity for each other. Torre admired how much Martinez
cared about each at-bat, each game, and each teammate. Martinez burned to
succeed as much as Paul O'Neill did. But, unlike O'Neill, he internalized his
fury. He did not throw bats, helmets, or tantrums. The anguish was nevertheless evident on his face. He simmered, and his response in bad times was to grip
his bat tighter and always—always—take more batting practice. If anything,
Torre worried Martinez cared too much; that his new first baseman might be
overdoing extra batting practice in hopes that somehow he could ward away
Mattingly's ghost through sheer pluck.

"I got off slow," Martinez says. "Through all that time of me not playing
well, Joe Torre never made me feel the pressure that I could lose my job. He
never seemed to feel the pressure of working for George Steinbrenner. He was
always just positive and relaxed. He didn't forget what it was like to be in a hitting slump or a team slump."

As a Mariner, Martinez had worn No. 23 in tribute to Mattingly. But
Martinez was now finding out just how big Mattingly's uniform was to fill.
Martinez had switched to No. 24 as a Yankee, but he was still playing first base,
still following Mattingly. Martinez totaled just three hits in his first 34 at-bats
as a Yankee and was hitless in his initial 17 at-bats with runners in scoring position. Particularly at home, Martinez followed one overanxious swing with another to go hitless in his first 16 at-bats at Yankee Stadium, unleashing torrents
of "Donnie Baseball" chants. He admonished himself to stay back, stay back,
and then an off-speed pitch seduced him into shooting for the short right-field

porch, and he would top another ball to the right side of the infield. He did not get his first hit at home until Torre moved him from fifth in the lineup to second, and even that hit was an unimpressive grounder that simply found its way through the middle of the diamond. It took Martinez 66 at-bats to homer, connecting off Cleveland lefty Jim Poole, to turn the chants temporarily to "Tino, Tino." But that homer merely made a 7–2 Yankee lead 10–2. Even with a bit of a hot streak, Martinez was batting just .226 with two homers and no meaningful hits heading into the series at Camden Yards.

In the second inning against the Orioles, with the Yankees ahead 4–3, the bases loaded and two out, Martinez had detected a statement moment: the chance to blow open the first game of the year against Baltimore. But Rhodes, wild all inning, jumped ahead 1–2 and pumped a fastball knee-high on the inside corner. Martinez froze, reading ball 2. Home-plate ump Terry Craft, however, emphatically signaled strike 3. Martinez grimaced, challenged Craft's call without theatrics, and placed his hitting gloves in his helmet to retreat to first base, distressed that another statement moment had disappeared.

Leading off the fifth inning, Torre's encouraging words still with him, Martinez crushed Rhodes's first pitch toward the top of the 25-foot scoreboard in right. A fan reached for the ball. Martinez thought he had a homer. First-base coach Jose Cardenal pleaded with first-base umpire Rich Garcia that he had missed the call. Torre came out to argue to make the same point. The umpires correctly ruled that the ball had hit the ledge projecting atop the scoreboard and caromed back to the field, perhaps the brim of Martinez's helmet from a home run. Martinez had hit the ball as far as possible at Camden Yards without achieving a home run. He had only a single. On Madison Square Garden Network, announcer Jim Kaat said, "You talk about tough luck for Tino Martinez."

Yet that hit ignited the Yankees. Gerald Williams doubled in one run, and attrition finally won out over Rhodes, who was removed following the dissatisfying exchange of 113 pitches to obtain just 13 outs. The Yankees were into the Orioles' terrible middle relief. The game was more than 2 hours old and not yet half over, and here came a 27-year-old rookie named Jimmy Myers to make his ninth career appearance.

Joe Girardi had been enduring a month much like that of Martinez: lousy hitting attracting boos at home. He had managed just three RBIs heading into Camden Yards, but—like Martinez—Torre was sticking with him. The manager said defense was first when it came to his catchers, and he praised the subtle excellence of Girardi's work behind the plate. Now, for the first time in 1996, Torre could praise the offense, too, as Girardi's single snaked under Myers's glove, drove in two runs, gave him three RBIs for the game, and moved the Yankees within 9–7. Heading into the season, Jim Leyritz had not played third base since September 2, 1992. But, unlike Davey Johnson with Bobby Bonilla, Torre willingly decided in spring training to find places in the field for Leyritz, figuring whatever he gave away defensively he gained at bat. In the first inning of his third game of the season at third base, Leyritz had undermined Pettitte with a throwing miscue. Reparation came in the fifth, when he launched a mammoth two-run homer off Myers. The score was tied. The Orioles, who had erased a five-run lead the previous night against the Rangers, had just blown a five-run lead.

The score was still 9–9 when the seventh inning began. Derek Jeter had been hitless in 15 at-bats before this game. Pitchers had uncovered a weakness by working inside on the shortstop's hands. But Torre had made a determination that his new administration was intrinsically tied to the new players. That is why he had invested such faith in Martinez and Girardi during their struggles. And that is why he remained steadfast behind his rookie shortstop. While Johnson bickered in April with Orioles, Torre quickly constructed a bond with players he sensed cared passionately about winning, playing hard, and fostering clubhouse goodwill. Those types of players came to find a resolute public defender in Torre. He always found a way to accentuate positives about this core group in down times: Girardi's game calling, Jeter's precocious nature, or the determination of Martinez. Because of that style, by the end of April, Torre was already gaining a loyal flock.

Perhaps no one was a more devout member of this society than Jeter. He loved the positive air Torre had exacted around him. Here Torre was batting him leadoff for the second time in 1996 despite the slump, and Jeter rewarded the confidence by laying down a bunt single, his second hit of the game. In the first inning, O'Neill had homered against the type of lefty, Arthur Rhodes, whom Showalter probably would not have started him against. The shot was so impressive, over Boog Powell's barbecue joint in right and onto Eutaw Street, that it left an impression. With one out, Davey Johnson had another of his weak righty relievers, Keith Shepherd, intentionally walk O'Neill. Ruben Sierra flied out. Two down. And Martinez was up again, another shot at vanquishing the myth of Don Mattingly.

For the final six seasons of his career, Mattingly was among the major leagues' worst offensive first basemen. He was the proverbial pinstriped elephant in the lineup. It was hardly spoken about because Mattingly had what Martinez did not: collateral. From 1984 to 1989, Mattingly just might have been the best player in the game. He hit and fielded majestically, further burnishing his reputation by handling all that came with his success with midwestern humility. He was New York's Larry Bird, just without the championships. If anything, his fruitless quest for a title only endeared him further to Yankee fans. They exonerated him and blamed George Steinbrenner and a Yankee management that could not assemble a team worthy of his abilities.

In reality, the Yankees were getting better and better as Mattingly's career wound down, reaping the benefits of Gene Michael's vision and Buck Showalter's stewardship. His loyalists wrapped Mattingly in pity, forgiving him because he was trying to soldier on with a chronic back problem that had left him unable to create the torque necessary in his swing to damage even the most delectable of hanging breaking balls. This was the decade of runaway offense, and Mattingly just could not keep up anymore. From 1990 to 1995, only seven players who batted as often as Mattingly hit fewer than his 58 homers. Since one was Wade Boggs, the Yankee front office did not gaze quite as sentimentally upon Mattingly as the smitten fans did. Team executives knew the Yankees were being diminished by lack of power at the infield corners. That is why, one official from that era remembers, "we needed Mattingly out. We all hoped Mattingly would retire. We were afraid he would say he wanted to be back, and then we would have to make either the right decision or the fan-friendly decision."

Mattingly had obliged. He had excelled against the Mariners in the playoffs, but he did so by swinging with full might, with no regard for his back. The result was such anguish that Mattingly had to stand up during nearly the entire flight from Seattle back to New York. Shortly after that series, Mattingly informed the front office he was going to retire because, he says, looking back, "I couldn't live with the exchange anymore" of being away too much from his wife and three children in Evansville, Indiana, to play baseball in pain.

The Yankee officials should have been free of Mattingly. But they worked for Steinbrenner, which meant nothing was that simple. On June 27, 1995, as Mattingly's tepid bat factored significantly in the Yankees' surprising struggles, Bill Madden of the *New York Daily News* wrote that Mattingly was hurting the team and should retire after the season. Because Steinbrenner was quoted in the piece, disparaging the power production of his corner infielders, and was known to have a chummy relationship with the writer, Mattingly was convinced the Boss had motivated the column.

The Yankee owner was right, of course. But Mattingly was cherished while Steinbrenner was reviled. Stung by outraged fan and media reaction, Steinbrenner heeded the counsel of Tom Reich, player agent and member in good standing of the Boss's shadow cabinet. Though he did not represent Mattingly or any of his potential replacements, Reich advised Steinbrenner that the only way to prevent falling further into disdain was to be perceived as wanting Mattingly back and—absolutely—not to look in any way as if he was hurrying a decision. So, to the paralysis and horror of the front office, Mattingly agreed to Steinbrenner's request to take more time before a final announcement. Now only in the most below-the-radar way could the executives strategize on filling such a vital position, while uncertain if Mattingly would change his mind, scuttle the plans, and damage first base for yet another season with lifeless offense.

New GM Bob Watson devalued his already skimpy hold on organizational influence when, at a November 16, 1995, press conference to announce Torre's coaching staff, he told reporters that Mattingly had agreed to call the next day to reveal his decision. Mattingly's representatives, annoyed at having a deadline imposed, responded that Mattingly had made no such promise. After all of his tightrope walking to avoid even the scent of disrespect, Steinbrenner was irate that Watson depicted a ticking clock over Mattingly's head. The Boss berated his general manager, threatening to remove his right to even speak to the media. On November 21, Ray Schulte, Mattingly's business manager, finally released a joint six-paragraph statement with the Yankees in which Mattingly never used the word *retire*. He simply blessed the Yankees to move on without him. And Schulte conceded that if Showalter had not been forced out, Mattingly might have kept on playing.

It made sense. The two had become good friends as minor league teammates at Double-A Nashville in 1981, when Showalter was becoming the first client for an agent named Jim Krivacs. Slowly, over four agonizing seasons mostly at Double-A, Showalter recognized the futility of his major league aspirations. "I could out-stat you in the minor leagues, but I could not make it here," Showalter says, looking back. He could hit, but not for power. He was neither fast nor a particularly adept defender. His greatest asset was his baseball mind, which allowed him to stay employed in the game. Showalter had already developed the eye of a scout. He recommended the fruit of the Southern League and Yankee system to Krivacs, who signed as clients Alvin Davis, Howard Johnson, Jim Presley, Dave Valle, Fred McGriff, Otis Nixon, and, yes, Don Mattingly. Each off-season, back at their alma mater, Jefferson High School in Tampa, McGriff and Tino Martinez worked out together in preparation for spring training. That friendship led to Martinez choosing as his agent Jim Krivacs.

Now, in the gulf between the 1995 and 1996 seasons, Krivacs was in a unique insider position. Mattingly had vacated first base for the Yankees, who prioritized two of Krivacs's other clients, McGriff, a free agent, and Martinez. The Yankees briefly pondered trades for Oakland's Mark McGwire and Detroit's Cecil Fielder, as well as free agent Mark Grace. The Yankees even toyed briefly with putting Boggs at first base and breaking in well-regarded prospect Russ Davis at third. But Martinez was the first choice. He hit left-handed, had an underappreciated glove that Gene Michael likened to that of the lumbering but defensively expert Kent Hrbek, and was in his prime, having made the All-Star team for the first time in 1995 at age 27, a late substitution to replace the injured McGwire. McGwire had been plunked on the head by a pitcher by the name of David Cone, who 3 weeks later was traded to the Yankees. Martinez was picked to be an All-Star over Fielder by the AL manager, Buck Showalter.

Martinez had finished 1995 with 31 homers and 111 RBIs, yet he learned shortly after the Mariners' magical playoff run ended in the AL Championship Series against Cleveland that he almost certainly would not be back. Seattle needed to cut $5 million in payroll, and manager Lou Piniella leveled with Martinez that his removal would probably be part of the solution. Piniella liked Martinez. Both were Tampa natives. Piniella had grown up across the street from Tony Gonzalez and remained best friends with him. Gonzalez's sister, Sylvia, married Rene Martinez, and their middle son, Tino, grew up to play first base in Seattle for Lou Piniella. Now Piniella thought a trade might be worked out sending Martinez to the Padres, but he asked Gonzalez his nephew's preference. To Martinez, there was only one place to relocate.

The Yankees were opening Legends Field in Tampa, which would mean spring training at home. But it was more than that for Martinez. The sound of Yankee Stadium during the opening two Division Series games lingered in his ears. He knew it was no nouveau love affair between fans and team, like he suspected Seattle was with the Mariners. Martinez had grown up a Yankee fan. Of course he had. Piniella was a Yankee. Martinez understood the team's history. Now he was imagining making history as a Yankee, hearing that sound as a home player. Piniella promised Gonzalez to try to steer Martinez to New York. The Yankees and Seattle GM Woody Woodward haggled throughout November about Martinez, working as covertly as possible before Mattingly's press release. Seattle wanted Andy Pettitte; the Yankees countered with Sterling Hitchcock. To further cut payroll, the Mariners had to trade third baseman Mike Blowers. Once the Yankees decided to retain Boggs as a free agent, they knew they could deal a young third baseman, either Russ Davis or Andy Fox, to help the Mariners replace Blowers.

But the key moment came on December 2, when Steinbrenner summoned an old friend of both the Yankee family and the Martinez family. Circumventing his baseball people yet again, Steinbrenner wanted to hear in a face-to-face with Piniella whether Martinez had the character to replace Mattingly. Piniella provided a glowing report, just as he had about Paul O'Neill to Gene Michael. Martinez's lefty swing was made for Yankee Stadium; his seriousness and perfectionism were made for Steinbrenner. Piniella had been a player, coach, GM, and manager for the Boss. He knew what that look in Steinbrenner's eye meant. Piniella had sold Steinbrenner on Martinez, so now Steinbrenner would do just about anything to have him—move heaven, earth, or Jorge Posada. "I knew Mr. Steinbrenner was salivating," Piniella says.

Piniella advised Woodward to take advantage of Steinbrenner's desire. He had heard wonderful things about the switch-hitting Posada, who actually had been on the 25-man roster in the Division Series as Showalter's third catcher. Just wait Steinbrenner out, Piniella counseled, and he will break down and throw in Posada. For a few moments the next day, the Yankees included Posada but annoyed Woodward by removing Russ Davis from the offer for Martinez. In fury, Woodward bluffed that he was done with the Yankees and was now in serious talks with the Cubs and Padres. Seeing Fred McGriff re-sign with the Braves, the Yankees returned Davis to the proposal on December 5, along with Hitchcock. Posada was no longer in the deal. But Davis was the player

Woodward craved. That package was deemed good enough, despite Piniella's protests, to deal Martinez and two relievers. The Yankees made the trade conditional on signing Martinez to a multiyear contract. A meeting was scheduled at Carmine's, an Italian restaurant in the Ybor City district of Tampa. Steinbrenner had sent his son-in-law, Joe Molloy, to handle negotiations. Molloy had once coached the St. Lawrence elementary basketball team against a St. Joseph's team with Tino Martinez. Tampa was proving a wondrous enclave for the Yankees.

On the way to the negotiation from his Tampa offices, Krivacs quizzed his client on what would make him happy. Two or 3 years, Martinez said; do not ask for too much. Martinez did not want to spoil his chance of being a New York Yankee. The two agreed that 3 years at $11 million was ideal. What they could not know was that Steinbrenner—against his baseball officials' wishes—had prioritized making an immediate statement of long-term belief in Mattingly's replacement. Lunch had hardly begun when Molloy spread out a yellow legal pad with a 5-year offer. "Where do I sign?" Martinez thought. Krivacs told his client to leave the room. When he returned, the Yankees had added an option year. The package was $20.25 million. The next day, December 7, the contract was finalized, Martinez celebrated his 28th birthday, and his wife, Marie, gave birth to their third child, Victoria. "I was blown away," he says.

Yet, with all he had joyously received, Martinez noticed something missing—a no-trade clause. He was fine with it, thinking to himself, "These are the Yankees, and I will never last the length of this contract." Now, as his first month ended as a Yankee, Martinez was feeling the heat of supplanting an idol, in New York, with Steinbrenner as the owner. The noise from the crowd was not the stuff of his October memories but, rather, mocking chants. Mixed in were the relentless questions from a media group bigger on a Saturday afternoon in April than anything he had ever experienced in Seattle. Martinez talked quickly by nature, but in these near-daily, postgame dissections, his words raced. He agreed with the boos, flogged himself for not performing well, and admitted how much he had devoted to a strong start "to show the hometown fans what I am about."

Now here was a new chance to make a strong impression. Two on. Two out. Tied score. Keith Shepherd worked Martinez with hard stuff and, at 2–1, made a mistake with a fastball right over the plate. But Martinez could not get his bat head out quickly enough, fouling a ball on top of the Oriole dugout, a few feet away from the third out. With the count now 2–2, Shepherd missed just outside with his fifth straight fastball. The count was now full. Another fastball was coming. Martinez was sure. But as he took a practice swing away from the plate and readjusted his batting gloves, Martinez lectured himself for the final time in April 1996 not to be too quick, stay back, let the ball travel to him. He did. Gregg Zaun had set up again on the outside corner. But Shepherd missed badly, the ball boring toward the inner half about thigh high. Zaun reached to backhand the ball, but it never reached his glove. Martinez made contact on the barrel, feeling the love in his hands that meant no scoreboard was going to knock down this drive to right-center. Martinez had his first big hit as a Yankee, a tie-breaking, three-run homer. The score was now 12–9.

Martinez was surprised by his thoughts as he rounded the bases — that the reporters would be coming to his locker, and "finally they were going to write some nice stuff about me." But there was still work to do. Torre had hoped not to use the overextended Mariano Rivera again. However, Mariano Duncan botched a double-play ball in the bottom of the seventh, and Jeff Nelson infuriated his manager by losing the plate. Torre had sent messages of support for Martinez, Girardi, and Jeter by sticking with them through difficulties. But he thought Nelson was guilty of negating elite stuff by nibbling around the strike zone rather than attacking, especially early in a confrontation with a hitter. So when the count went to 2–0, Torre sent another message, this one of impatience. He removed Nelson. There had been too much work done to lose this game now, Torre thought, especially because his lineup had outplayed the supposedly superior Baltimore offense. Rivera, bringing fastball artistry to the messy affair, threw six straight strikes to begin what would be two more hit-less, shutout innings. He was now up to 11²/₃ straight hitless innings—35 straight at-bats without a hit—and 14 innings without permitting an earned run.

By the time John Wetteland threw the last of the 400 pitches in this game, and Mike Devereaux hit it deep to center for the final out of a 13–10 Yankee triumph, it was 11:57 p.m., establishing this as the longest nine-inning game in major league history. But for the Yankees it was worth a 4-hour, 21-minute investment, as they won when trailing by five runs for the first time since August 1993. Martinez and Girardi had broken out. The relief quartet of Kamieniecki, Nelson, Rivera, and Wetteland had delivered eight innings of three-hit, one-unearned-run pitching, underscoring an area of advantage against the Orioles. With 3 minutes left in April, the Yankees were in first place alone for the first time in 1996. An encore would be difficult. And yet . . .

The game of May 1, 1996, began with Cal Ripken as the Orioles' shortstop for the 2,180th straight game. Andy Pettitte was sitting in a warmup jacket next to Jimmy Key in the Yankee dugout, and Jim Mecir was now in the Yankee bullpen for the first time, having been summoned from Columbus to supplement the overworked relief corps. David Wells versus Kenny Rogers represented not only the pitching matchup for the series finale but the last major move and countermove of the off-season between Orioles owner Peter Angelos and Steinbrenner. After signing David Cone, Steinbrenner had told his baseball people that the financial faucet was closed. Then the Orioles traded prospects to Cincinnati for Wells. Wells had been traded from Detroit to Cincinnati the previous July, shortly after Mariano Rivera's radar-gun readings soared and Gene Michael pulled him out of consideration to be included in a trade for Wells. When Steinbrenner's late attempts to inject himself into talks with the Reds failed, the bank was suddenly back open, and Rogers had an unexpected suitor, underscoring Steinbrenner's fear of the Orioles.

The hope in this series finale was that with two strike-throwing lefties starting, the pace of the game would quicken considerably. But offense ruled early again. Brady Anderson led off the bottom of the first with his 12th homer, which was tied for the most in the majors. The Yankees answered with three runs in the second and gave Rogers leads of 5–1 and 6–3. But Rogers proved unequipped yet again for the stress of the Yankees, leaving with two runners on in the sixth and none out. And this time Mariano Rivera was absolutely, positively not available to save the Yankees—at least not in regulation. Instead, Bob Wickman allowed a two-run single to Ripken.

It was 6–5 in the eighth when Ripken singled to right to send Bobby Bonilla to third with none out. The tying run was 90 feet away. But Davey Johnson was thinking about the win; his bullpen was simply too taxed and too awful to entrust with a tie score. Nelson was the pitcher. At 6 feet, 8 inches he was built like a basketball player—in fact, he played in the renowned games at Ripken's home court—but his size and side-arm sling deprived him of the fluidity to deliver a pitch quickly. Johnson saw opportunity. Sure, Ripken was a heady base runner almost certain never to blunder. But it was almost 2 years since he had last stolen a base. Manny Alexander had started only one game all year, but speed was his asset, and Johnson sent him in to pinch-run, unaware that for the last 14 seasons—since May 30, 1982, when his consecutive game streak began—Ripken had been removed 68 times from a game, but never with the outcome in doubt, as it was now. Ripken trotted off, accepted handshakes, and sat on the bench, his facial expression screaming, "What am I doing here?"

Alexander had a green light but no order to steal. He danced off the base, aiming to distract Nelson. The Yankees played the infield back, conceding the tying run at third. From the bench, with the count 0–1 on B. J. Surhoff, pitching coach Mel Stottlemyre relayed a signal to Joe Girardi to have Nelson fake to third and wheel to first. It had been one of Showalter's favorite plays, and it almost never worked. The design mainly was to shorten the lead of the runner at first. For a portion of a second, Nelson was stunned when he completed his ruse, and Alexander had actually broken to second base. Nelson flipped to Jeter, who tagged Alexander while Bonilla held third. It was a staggering gaffe, made all the worse because it came at the expense of such a high-profile maneuver, removing Ripken from a game in doubt. Alexander returned to the bench to sit next to Ripken, whose arms remained crossed over his chest and his icy stare fixed on the field. Now Torre pulled his infield in, which kept Bonilla at third when Surhoff grounded out. Tony Tarasco flied out. The lead had survived. Temporarily.

In the ninth, Yankee second baseman Mariano Duncan made his fifth error in this two-game series, and Baltimore scored an unearned run against John Wetteland to tie. But with the winning run on second base, Bonilla struck out to end the inning. After the longest nine-inning game in history, the Yankees and Orioles were going to extra innings. It was just after 11 p.m., and thick clouds were moving in. Torre had gone as far with his familiar relievers as he could go. Earlier in the day, to supplement the bullpen, the Yankees had waived Dion James and summoned Mecir, who arrived shortly before game time to the good-natured clubhouse chants of "fresh meat, fresh meat." As part of the trade for Tino Martinez, the Yankees had the choice of either Nelson or Bobby Ayala, and either Mecir or Tim Davis. The Yankees hated Ayala's makeup but loved how Nelson devoured righty hitters with a side-winding slider that swept like a Frisbee across the plate. The Yankee scouting reports on Mecir were marginal. But the Yankees took him as the throw-in because the scouting eyes they always trusted the most saw something in him.

On September 4, 1995, the Yankees had built a 9–2 lead against Seattle by devastating Salomon Torres and Ayala through two-plus innings. The Mariners sent in Mecir to make his major league debut. Mecir had a clubbed right foot that forced him to walk with a limp and wear a cleat two sizes smaller than the 12½ on his left foot. Yet that is not what struck Gene Michael. It was the rarity of a righty pitcher deploying a screwball. Lefties such as Eddie Lopat and Luis Arroyo had helped the Yankees win titles with the baffling pitch. From the opposite side, however, Mecir suppressed the Yankees' lefty-saturated lineup, yielding one unearned run in 3⅔ innings. Michael indexed that Mecir might be a good throw-in to a trade someday. Michael was no longer GM when the Martinez deal was consummated, Watson was. But Michael had a long-standing relationship with Mariners GM Woody Woodward, so he did a lot of the leg-work and negotiations, to the point that Brian Cashman, when asked to re-member the swap, says, "Stick did that trade."

So here was part of another Stick Michael acquisition in Jim Mecir, fresh meat to the Oriole lineup. The Orioles loaded the bases with one out against Mecir, who induced Jeffrey Hammonds to pop out. No big deal. It was just vic-tory delayed. For Brady Anderson, who'd already established that this would be the season of his life, took three straight balls. A rookie reliever making his first appearance of 1996 had fallen behind 3–0 against the hottest power hitter in the game with the bases loaded, two outs, and the Camden Yards crowd growing louder with each pitch. It was about the worst situation imaginable. Joe Torre leaned against the bullpen phone in the dugout, helpless and out of moves. Mecir decided to throw the next pitch with no artifice straight down the middle, determining that ball 4 or a grand slam meant the same thing—a Yankee loss. Anderson took it for a strike. Mecir sank the next pitch, and Anderson uncoiled with another homer on his mind, but he fouled the ball back and, in frustration, swung his bat again in anger. He had not capitalized on a pitch to hit.

Despite his handicap, Mecir moved deceptively quickly off the mound, Gerald Williams recalls. But because he had so little growth in his right calf and no movement in his right foot, Mecir did not push off the rubber to gain power like most pitchers. The strength of his pitches came almost exclusively from his torso, which at times created a funky movement on the ball. He could not risk his screwball here, even though Anderson was a lefty swinger. "Give yourself a chance, forget who the batter is, throw a strike," Mecir told himself. His full-count fastball had the funky movement, arcing from the middle of the plate to-ward the outside corner. Anderson swung just beneath the pitch. Strike 3. Anderson flipped his bat down the third-base line and tossed his helmet toward the first-base dugout. Mecir jogged into the warmth of a jubilant, high-fiving Yankee reception line. This was even more stunning than Alexander getting picked off, and the Yankees celebrated the unexpected result. Meanwhile, Ripken was still on the Oriole bench, still cross-armed, staring at the field with a chilliness that would lead Thom Loverro of *The Washington Times* to write, "He made Anthony Hopkins [in *Silence of the Lambs*] look like Mister Rogers." The most important Oriole of all was not doing anything to hide just how irritated he was.

Strangely, Mecir's strikeout of Anderson had been met by a lot of cheering in the crowd. A large contingent of Yankee fans had made the trip and stuck out this game even as it started to rain. Mecir, a Long Islander who had grown up a Yankee fan himself, put runners on second and third with one out in the 11th inning. But the batter was Manny Alexander, not Cal Ripken, and Alexander struck out. Mecir put two more runners on in the 12th inning, but survived as well. Three innings, seven base runners, and no runs against Mecir, who was now done. But who could pitch?

Andy Pettitte had arrived at Camden Yards feeling miserable about his effort the previous night but doing fine physically; he had thrown just 45 pitches. He bumped into Torre late in the afternoon of May 1 and told the manager, "Gee, I would love to pitch today to make up for that lousy effort yesterday." Torre filed it away, but only because he admired the gesture. More and more, he liked the makeup of so many on this talented team. But now it was early in the morning of May 2, and Torre had flushed anything resembling a game plan. He wanted so badly to win that he had determined if the Yankees had taken a lead in the top of the 13th, he was going to use Mariano Rivera, despite promising himself that under no circumstances would Rivera be put into this game. The Yankees, though, did not take the lead in the top of the 13th because, with the bases loaded and one out after Davey Johnson ordered an intentional walk of Ruben Sierra, Tino Martinez had grounded Kent Mercker's first pitch into an inning-ending double play. Martinez had already struck out twice in extra innings. As he futilely dove headfirst into first base as the double play concluded, Martinez was back in a funk and back in the doghouse with Yankee fans as quickly as he had seemed out of it.

So, rather than Rivera, Torre called upon Pettitte a day after the lefty's worst major league effort. It was obvious immediately that Pettitte's stuff and sense of purpose were both terrific this time. He used a double-play ball to escape the 13th inning. Before the bottom of the 14th, "Thank God I'm a Country Boy" played over the public address system, signifying a second seventh-inning stretch, and with the good humor came a downpour. Pettitte finished off this half inning with a strike-'em-out, throw-'em-out double play when Girardi nailed Tory Tarasco trying to steal. That meant a 15th and, what seemed certain, final inning. The game was moving toward $5\frac{1}{2}$ hours, and if the rain did not end these proceedings, then the 1 a.m. AL curfew would. If the game were suspended due to curfew, it would be picked up again in July, top of the 16th inning, when the Yankees were next back at Camden Yards. So this long night had a chance to get much, much longer. The umpires, despite the deluge, were determined not to stop now. A rainout with the score tied was far worse than a suspended game; it would mean starting from scratch again, 0–0, first inning.

With men on second and third and one out in the 15th, Davey Johnson ordered Jimmy Myers to intentionally walk Ruben Sierra once more. It was the same scenario as the 13th inning, with Johnson forcing Martinez to try to be the hero with the bases loaded and one out. But for the first time in his eight plate appearances in this game, Martinez was facing a righty pitcher. From the previous night, Martinez remembered that the righties had worked him consistently away, and, sure enough, catcher Gregg Zaun set a target on the outside corner.

But just like the previous night, the ball did not reach Zaun's mitt. Myers delivered a pitch away but thigh high. Unlike most lefty hitters, whose power came on pitches low and in, Martinez favored pitches up and out over the plate, just like this one. Martinez did not open up his hips fully to pull the ball; rather, he drove it to the opposite field. Left fielder Jeffrey Hammonds, playing shallow, sprinted toward the wall. Wade Boggs retreated to third base to tag up. Hammonds, his back to the infield at the lip of the warning track, awaited a carom off the 7-foot-high fence. But Martinez, who had missed a mid-game homer by inches in the series opener, watched the ball carry into the first row of seats, just to the left of the 364-foot sign. Torre, normally the personification of calm, leaped with his arms in the air in celebration of the second latest grand-slam hit in major league history. Before the inning was complete, Gerald Williams became the first Yankee in 62 years, since Myril Hoag in 1934, to produce six hits in a game, his RBI single making it 11-6. Rafael Palmeiro grounded out against Andy Pettitte at 1:09 a.m., and this 5-hour, 34-minute odyssey was done. But the Yankees had much more than an 11-6 victory, and the Orioles had much more than an 11th loss in 14 games.

It was one thing for Davey Johnson to squander the clubhouse support of Bonilla, Alexander, Erickson, and Mercker, as he had during the season's first month. It was completely different to lose Ripken, who the previous September had passed Lou Gehrig's iron-man record. He was so popular with the local fans, Mike Mussina says, "Cal Ripken could have run for governor of Maryland and won." Within the clubhouse, Ripken controlled a bloc of influential veterans, including Brady Anderson, Chris Hoiles, Mussina, and B. J. Surhoff. After sitting inactive in a warmup jacket for more than 2 hours—an island in the middle of the dugout—Ripken sent word through the Oriole media-relations department that he would not talk to reporters, issuing a damning two-sentence statement: "I don't wish to make a comment one way or another. I'll just let that stand as my response." It was a passive-aggressive denunciation of the new manager, and Johnson was forced to spend the postgame walking the fine line between not ratcheting up an unwinnable war and not backing down from a decision he believed was in the best interest of winning a game. He was realizing that his dream job, managing his beloved Orioles, had minefields, and the biggest one of all played shortstop every day, every inning or else.

The Yankee clubhouse, on the other hand, was experiencing feelings even stronger than joy. This team had been shadowed from the off-season into spring training and through the first month of the schedule by unfavorable comparisons to its most recent iteration. The callous, shoddy way in which this group was assembled seemed as much a part of the day-to-day existence up to this point as the interlocking N-Y on the Yankees' caps. But because these wins were against the Orioles, in Baltimore, and conceived with such sturdy resolve, they unified the clubhouse and extinguished much of the grumbling about what had happened to the Yankees of Gene Michael and Buck Showalter. It was finally okay to be a 1996 Yankee.

"Everybody in spring training asked about our character," Torre said at the time. "I don't think after these two games that anybody can question the character, class, and ruggedness of this team. Not after these two nights. This should go a long way to what the rest of the season should be."

He was right. Those two games established the character of the 1996 Yankees. They would play into the night, into the parking lot, and into the back of its roster to win a game. This was the moment when the Yankees of Joe Torre showed that no game, no series, no season was ever over. Joe Girardi caught all 477 Yankee pitches and 24 innings of this two-game series. Jim Mecir had arrived with a 1–2 record and a 4.76 ERA at Columbus, yet unleashed a pitch—that full-count fastball to Brady Anderson—that would resonate all season. Andy Pettitte, who had faced 13 batters and recorded just three outs against nine runs in the opener, doggedly returned to throw three innings of scoreless relief to earn the win the next day. Derek Jeter had shaken his first rookie slump, and Mariano Rivera persisted in dominance. And Tino Martinez, who arrived at Baltimore with a month of boos in his ears and just 2 homers and 10 RBIs overall, had 2 homers and 8 RBIs in the most important series to date. He had put the Yankees ahead with homers in the seventh inning or later on consecutive nights, something Mattingly had done just twice in his final two seasons. No diehard Yankee loyalist was going to forget Mattingly, but this was like a get-out-of-Mattingly-jail card for Martinez. Never again would he hear wide choruses of "Donnie Baseball" at Yankee Stadium.

The Yankees had hopped over the Orioles and were in first place, on top by $1\frac{1}{2}$ games. Through 895 pitches and two games that covered parts of 3 days, the Yankees and Orioles had demonstrated a near evenness in every way, except that the Yankees were more together and mentally tougher. April began with the notion of the Orioles running away with the division, but by early in the morning of the second day of May, the tone for the season was set. The Yankees would always find a way to beat Baltimore. The Orioles were supposed to be the more dominant offensive team by far. But the Yankees had out-Orioled the Orioles in winning these games by a combined 24–16.

"That Oriole series is where that mentality was established for the year," Martinez recalls. "Grind it out. Grind it out."

This was the identity of the 1996 Yankees, and that identity was about to be needed more than ever. These Yankees were about to follow their greatest victory of this regular season with their greatest loss.

6 | ALMOST PERFECT

"That team had the ability that when someone was down, someone else came up. It was amazing."

—Joe Girardi

After the marathons at Camden Yards, the Yankees returned to New York at 5 a.m. on May 2, 14 hours shy of a home game against the White Sox. The players individually needed sleep, but as a team the Yankees craved innings from a starter. Unfortunately, nobody involved with the Yankees was sure what to expect from the starter. David Cone was on blood thinners for the circulatory problem in his right hand. He had to forgo the coffee he loved before and during games, as well as the cigarettes and beer afterward. He was willing to accept prohibitions on caffeine, nicotine, and alcohol to feed his greatest addiction: competition.

The strongest dependence of all, however, was how badly hooked the Yankee organization was on Cone. In that May 2 game, the reliance only grew more substantive as Cone provided the innings and excellence for which the weary Yankees yearned. Ten days after his last start and 6 days after being hospitalized overnight for a battery of painful diagnostic tests, Cone held the White Sox to five singles and one unearned run. In a 5–1 Yankee triumph, he threw 127 pitches and the Yankees' first complete game of 1996, despite needing the team physician's approval 2 hours before the first pitch to even take the mound and having to be monitored by a group of doctors between innings. The performance spoke to Cone's timeliness and toughness, as well as his status. George Steinbrenner had dubbed Cone "Mr. Yankee" upon signing him to a

3-year, $19.5 million contract in the off-season. Within the clubhouse, a few Yankees called Cone "Senator" for his polish in all arenas.

Cone's value transcended his elite pitching. Geographically, he was born and raised in Kansas City. But Cone was a New Yorker in every way. He kept his Manhattan apartment even while playing for the Royals and Blue Jays. He embodied the carousing Mets of the late 1980s and early 1990s. He had endured legal charges of rape and sexual harassment that included an allegation of masturbating in the bullpen. In fact, he more than endured it; he emerged with good humor and a great relationship with reporters intact. He thrived in this atmosphere, wrapping his arms around the idea of being the spokesman for a team in the biggest media market in the world.

Starting pitchers are not often accepted team leaders, owing to their once-every-5-days work pattern. Yet Cone was the Yankees' leader, in part for his expertise in dealing with the New York media. Normally, a cozy relationship with reporters is viewed suspiciously by teammates, and Cone was the rare player who knew the name, job description, and employer of seemingly every radio, TV, and newspaper reporter. Yet Cone did not inspire jealousy or distrust from his teammates. He was a chameleon, becoming whatever a distressed teammate required, from understanding big brother to raunchy sidekick. However, no one questioned his sincerity when it came to his passion for the city and for winning. As Tino Martinez says, "He was a great New York player. He knew how to handle everything here."

This club needed all Cone offered. In a rotation beset with uncertainty, Cone projected durable excellence. On a roster crowded with newcomers, Cone had the knack to lure reporters to his locker at times of trouble, keeping the media from overwhelming a teammate not as well equipped to cope with the swarm. Many pitchers refused to talk the day before their start, and almost none talked the day of a start. But Cone talked every day and on every subject. He arrived to the Yankees 2 hours before his first start on July 30, 1995, at the Minnesota Metrodome, carrying his bags from Toronto following his acquisition from the Blue Jays. Cone spoke to the media in a locker room adjacent to the main clubhouse until about an hour before the game, as his new manager, Buck Showalter, paced outside and occasionally peeked in to gauge when his just-obtained ace might actually get into uniform and game face. But there should never have been any doubt about Cone's deadly seriousness when it came to his craft. Cone threw eight winning innings in his Yankee debut.

So just about everyone in the Yankee family exhaled after Cone tamed the White Sox. He had improved to 9–0 at Yankee Stadium since his acquisition, exemplifying his New York heartiness, and was 4–1 with a 2.03 ERA in 1996, despite the hand problems. But the medical issues were not subsiding. The blood thinners were not working. The outstanding record and complete-game victory over Chicago were tributes to Cone's grittiness, just as those 147 pitches in the Kingdome the previous October had been. Now he kept looking at his hand and wondering about those 147 pitches, wondering if he had given away his career that night. Three days after the complete game, the anxiety about Cone intensified simply because he said nothing. He had always seemed more likely to author a no-hitter than a no comment. Yet on May 6, before a pitch had been thrown in a game against the Tigers, Cone left Yankee Stadium for his East Side apartment without talking to reporters. The numbness and cold sensation had extended beyond his ring finger; now it was in the three middle fingers of his right hand and his palm, as well. The nail on his ring finger was blue, the finger itself drained of all color.

When Cone had undergone his first angiogram on April 26, the symptoms suggested the possibility of an aneurysm, but none could be found. Nevertheless, due to the mysterious illness, he was monitored by a team of doctors for his May 2 start. Later stories appeared in which doctors questioned whether Cone should have even been on the mound that night, suggesting he had risked the loss of his arm or maybe even his life, had a lethal blood clot broken free from the aneurysm.

Cone had actually fought that angiogram. There were risks involved with the painful, intrusive procedure, in which a catheter is inserted in the groin and feathered to the chest so that dye can be injected to provide a clear x-ray of the aorta and arteries. Besides, he was David Cone. He had the American League's best ERA, even with the troubles. He would figure out how to cope, how to prosper. He wanted to believe all the problems were caused by a faulty grip on his splitter and were localized in his hand. He was David Cone, and George Steinbrenner had made him the highest-paid pitcher in baseball, and he was going to bull through this. He was David Cone, and he understood his place of leadership on a fragile club. And he was David Cone, which meant he was still saying he would stay in rotation and maybe — maybe — take the tests afterward.

Steinbrenner loved it. Team physician Stuart Hershon, MD, did not. He sensed the pitcher was at risk, and not just for his arm. A blood clot, for example, could break off and travel to the heart. He told Cone that if the pitcher started, he would resign. Cone and Steinbrenner relented.

The need for a second angiogram frazzled the entire organization. A pall invaded Yankee Stadium on the night of May 6. Faces were grim, voices somber. Suddenly, it was obvious to reporters that not just Cone's season or career was the greatest concern. The tests were not just for his hand anymore. Wade Boggs described the situation as "deadly serious," and John Wetteland told reporters he would pray for Cone, but it was general manager Bob Watson who promoted the most concern. He likened the tests to the early detection of his prostate cancer in 1994, saying, "This could be life threatening. The well-being of David Cone as a human being comes before the well-being of David Cone the pitcher. The number one thing is: Let's find out what the problem is. Early detection is the reason I'm standing here." Alerted by a club media-relations official about the gravity of his tone, Watson returned to the Yankee Stadium pressroom to temper his evaluation. "It is not life threatening," he said. It was too late. His initial words had sparked an avalanche of concern for a 33-year-old athlete who had an ailment that doctors had so far been unable to diagnose.

The answer came the next day. Cone had an aneurysm at the junction of the posterior circumflex humeral artery and the axillary artery, essentially a ballooning in the walls of the two arteries near his right armpit. Blood clots had been produced from this disturbance, broken off, and lodged in the smaller arteries in his pitching hand, blocking bloodflow and causing his symptoms. It was a rare spot for an aneurysm, and doctors surmised the repetitive violence of Cone's pitching motion had caused the problem. He needed surgery. His career was indeed in jeopardy.

Cone was distraught. Dr. Hershon was unable to convey the information to Torre and Watson until about an hour before the first pitch of May 7, so a decision was made to keep the news from the players until after the game. The Yankees rallied from a four-run deficit to beat the Tigers 12–5. Torre went into the players' lounge after the game and told those inside to go to their lockers for a meeting. Joe Girardi said what all the players understood tacitly, "This is about David." Torre, Watson, and Dr. Hershon stood before the club and revealed the disheartening results. Heads sagged; a few players fought tears. "You figure stiff shoulder, bursitis, something familiar to a pitcher," Paul O'Neill says, looking back. "There are a couple of words in the English language that send out alarms, and *aneurysm* is one of them." Former Yankee executive vice president and general counsel David Sussman adds, "No one expected this; there was a state of shock. It was not just a baseball-type issue. This was in the life-threatening category. It transcended the usual; it became more compelling and frightening. People were frightened David Cone might lose his life."

That fear was allayed as the information became clearer. The aneurysm was small and located in an area in which it was not life threatening. But the immediate feeling was that Cone had pitched his last game of 1996, and, Girardi remembers, "we just hoped he might pitch again." When the clubhouse door opened for reporters, there was none of the happy ambience associated with a victory. The Yankees had won for the eighth time in nine games but lost their leading man. Cone was in an intensive care unit, having taken the alias of the old-time umpire Nestor Chylak.

Cone was gone. The Yankee season could have gone with him. That it did not owes much to the intellect and sensitivity of the Yankees' new manager.

Nobody appreciated Cone's importance on and off the field more than Torre. He was loath to cite any one player as indispensable, yet Torre understood he was losing more than just 200 elite innings. Nevertheless, he was determined not to let anything derail his Yankees. He was, as Sussman remembers, "almost priestly, like a father confessor. Joe had strength and character, and this was a moment when everyone realized that."

"I was concerned about morale, and so was Joe [Torre]," says Gene Monahan, the Yankees' head trainer since 1973. "But Joe set the tone. Joe was our human conscious. He would put an arm around a neck, look you eye to eye. He would talk to you like a father. I have seen a great litany of managers, but this was like divine caring. This was like a father looking out for sons. How he dealt with the Cone issue set the stage for Joe's success. It was the first time I really noticed the human side of Joe. We became a real family because of how honest he was in dealing with this loss."

Torre used tenderness. He employed the pregame the way a boxer might treat the early rounds of a fight—feeling out players, sensing which ones might need an ear, a kind word, a pep talk. He also showed concern for the players' health. He stressed that no one play hero and try to persist through injuries to compensate for another player being sidelined. The big picture was most important. Sure, he wanted David Cone back at some point in 1996, Torre said, but he would let Cone dictate a return by his recovery and rehab, and if that were not until the following spring training, so be it. However, Torre mixed the warmth with a stern resolve. The bar would not be lowered for the team, despite the absence of its most vital person. Torre preached that there was still plenty of pitching and more talent than he had ever had at his disposal. No one was going to feel sorry for Steinbrenner's Yankees, he warned, so the Yankees could not indulge self-pity. "Joe always had this amazing ability to accentuate the positive to find the solution for something negative," Sussman says.

Still, there was a once-every-5-days void that all the calmness in the world could not alleviate. Cone's stature as an ace had actually expanded, now that every Yankee knew he had been the best pitcher in the AL with a condition that would have sent just about anybody else to the disabled list in panic. With that in the air, who could possibly rise up to be the Yankees' No. 1 starter?

Dwight Gooden had pondered putting Cone's No. 36 on his cap for his May 8 start against Detroit out of respect to a friend and inspiration for himself. He decided against it, worried about messing up and spoiling the tribute. The 36 he produced was 36 first-inning pitches, during which he allowed three runs and was booed by the home fans. Dwight Gooden was out on the ledge again. And then, astonishingly, he retired the final 22 batters he faced. The Yankees won 10–3, and Gooden won for the first time since June 19, 1994, which was 9 days before he was suspended for violating his drug after-care program, effectively terminating his Met career and leading to his absence from the 1995 season. He left his sixth start of 1996 after eight innings to a standing ovation from 18,729 at Yankee Stadium, a noise from his past that made Gooden call this his sweetest victory and a "miracle," considering his recent visit to rock bottom.

"He's got that look in his eye again," Torre said at the time.

On May 11, a day after a sudden storm engulfed Mount Everest, leaving eight climbers dead and inspiring Jon Krakauer's bestseller *Into Thin Air*, Cone underwent a 3-hour surgery to remove the aneurysm and graft a 1-inch segment of vein from his left thigh to reconnect the arteries and reestablish normal bloodflow. The previous day, the *New York Daily News* had loudly reported — based on information from a person familiar with the situation — that Cone would not pitch again in 1996. However, Cone's surgeons were more optimistic. Yes, this was uncharted terrain for a pitcher of Cone's status, but no muscles, nerves, or veins in the shoulder had been disturbed. The surgeons expected Cone to fully recover, and privately they even thought it could be as soon as 4 months. But to what? On the day of the surgery, the Yankees lost their third straight game since Gooden's victory, and on May 12 at Comiskey Park, they fell behind 8–0 after three innings against White Sox ace Alex Fernandez. Perhaps the Cone loss was just too much, physically and psychologically, for these Yankees.

And then Andy Fox hit a routine groundball to first baseman Frank Thomas. Fox was playing only because Mariano Duncan had joined fellow second basemen Pat Kelly and Tony Fernandez on the disabled list. The Yankees had scored twice in the fourth and twice in the fifth, but when their fourth-string second baseman hit his grounder to first, they still trailed 8–4. Thomas waved off Alex Fernandez; he was going to take this ball to the bag himself—except Fox met Thomas's insouciance with inspiration, firing out of the batter's box. Thomas recognized his quandary too late, panicking and missing the bag totally as Fox reached safely. By the time the inning was over, the Yankees had scored five times to take the lead, Girardi producing the go-ahead, three-run double, his biggest hit so far with his new team. The Yankees won 9–8.

"This reinforces what I think about this team," Torre said. "*Quit* is not in its vocabulary."

It also reinforced a sense of destiny within the clubhouse, a feeling that players would step up to a challenge. They needed that resolve because the marauding club that had eliminated the Yankees from the 1995 playoffs—the Mariners of Ken Griffey Jr., Edgar Martinez, Jay Buhner, and a new force named Alex Rodriguez—was coming to town.

Even with the power of Tino Martinez and Mike Blowers dispatched, Seattle still had tied a major league record for most homers after 37 games with 65. Paul Sorrento, Tino Martinez's replacement, joined Griffey and Buhner with double-digit homers already, and Edgar Martinez led the AL in doubles. This was not the worst-in-baseball Tigers anymore. Gooden needed to neutralize a team with a mighty lineup and a mightier hold on the Yankee psyche. The Mariners of Lou Piniella were so embedded in George Steinbrenner's head that the Boss had reacted to October's playoff loss by changing his manager,

GM, five position players, and three main components of the pitching staff, which was how Gooden gained employment. Bernie Williams, a key Yankee holdover, also would not play against the Mariners, having already been sidelined two games with an injured left calf. Williams had started 237 of the previous 240 games before suffering the injury and had reversed his penchant for slow starts by leading the Yankees in homers (7) and RBIs (27). That his bat was lost against the potent Mariners should have been devastating. But these were the 1996 Yankees.

Gooden began the game ominously by walking Darren Bragg after opening with two strikes. Alex Rodriguez then smashed a ball to deep center and thought he had an RBI triple. Why shouldn't he? "I knew the ball was over his head, and I was 20 years old," he remembers. The only man who could catch such a drive was likely on deck in Ken Griffey, who had won Gold Gloves the past 6 years. Bernie Williams's strength as an outfielder dated to his past as a high school track star. He did not read flies well, but if the ball had air under it, he was fleet enough to go get it. But liners that demanded quicker decisions— such as this one—were diabolical to Bernie Williams.

But Bernie Williams was not playing center field. Gerald Williams was. He broke instantly back in full stride. He turned left, turned right, and a step before the warning track threw his glove in the air, and, incredibly, the ball stuck into the top of his mitt, forming a snow cone. Bragg, assuming what everyone at Yankee Stadium assumed, was well on his way to third as Gerald Williams rifled the ball back to Derek Jeter, who threw to Tino Martinez for a double play that made Yankee radio broadcaster John Sterling proclaim, "Gerald Williams made a fabulous catch. Who knows if he didn't just turn this game around?" Instead of one run in, runner on third, no one out, and the Mariner offense off and rampaging again, Gooden had two out and none on. "Gerald was as good a player as we had defensively," O'Neill says, looking back, "so you do ask, 'What if?'"

The whole Yankee season was starting to feel this way. What if Mariano Duncan had not gotten hurt? What if Andy Fox did not hustle in Duncan's place? What if the Yankees had followed through on their initial instincts in April when it came to Dwight Gooden?

Gooden had followed up a dispiriting spring training in which he was 0–3 with an 8.88 ERA by beginning his season in even worse fashion. In his first three starts, Gooden looked as if all the cocaine, late nights, and youthful fastballs had left him a sad vestige of the kid who once evoked comparisons to Walter Johnson and Bob Feller. Just 31, Gooden opened 0–3 with an 11.48 ERA, managing just 13⅓ innings against 17 runs and 20 hits. Gooden hardly seemed worth George Steinbrenner's obsession; he seemed more publicity stunt gone horribly wrong. Steinbrenner had negotiated a deal for Gooden with Ray Negron, who was many things to Gooden—counselor, gofer, friend—but not certified agent. Players Association associate general counsel Gene Orza had initially forbidden a contract agreement because Negron was not certified. The infighting and insults were nasty, but in the end a certified agent, Steinbrenner's pal Tom Reich, was brought in to finalize the language on an $850,000 guarantee. Now that all appeared a waste of time, bile, and money. Three starts into his comeback, Gooden was banished to the bullpen. There was talk of demoting him to the minors, even releasing him outright. But—again—these were the 1996 Yankees. There was magic in the air.

Gooden's closest friend on the Yankees was Cone, going back to their days as part of the Mets' traveling circus. When Hershon demanded that Cone get his initial angiogram, the righty missed his first start since he had fractured his right pinky on May 27, 1987, while trying to bunt against San Francisco's Atlee Hammaker. Cone actually stayed in as a base runner and warmed up in the following half inning before having to be removed. His surgeon said he would not return before September, but Cone was back 11 weeks later, in mid-August. Cone actually had been acquired by the Mets from the Royals 2 months to the day before fracturing his finger and was designated the long man in the bullpen.

But he had begun the year in the rotation because, on April 1, the defending champion Mets announced their ace had tested positive for cocaine and was admitted to the Smithers Center for Alcohol and Drug Rehabilitation in Manhattan. Cone was in a major league rotation for the first time because Gooden was out of it. Now, with Cone out of the rotation, Gooden was being given one last shot.

It also just so happened that the pitching advisor Gooden trusted most was Mel Stottlemyre, from their decade together with the Mets as student and teacher. Stottlemyre's appearance in a Yankee uniform was as much about the stars aligning as anything else. He had resigned as Astro pitching coach after the 1995 season because his wife had an allergic reaction to the Houston climate. His intention was to sit out a year to sample life without baseball. He certainly had no intentions of ever being a Yankee again. In the late 1960s and early 1970s, Stottlemyre was the ace of the postdynastic Yankees. He tore his rotator cuff during the 1974 season and shunned surgery under advice that his best chance to pitch again was to rest his arm, then slowly build back strength and stamina. Then GM Gabe Paul told Stottlemyre to take his time and aim for May 1, 1975. But the Yankees waived Stottlemyre on March 29 because, he said, they wanted to pay him $80,000 rather than the $95,000 guaranteed if he were on the team after May 1. Though Steinbrenner was serving a suspension at the time due to his illegal campaign contributions to Richard Nixon, Stottlemyre sensed the Boss's offstage deviousness and held him responsible, vowing never to return to the Yankees. So when an old friend from his years as Mets pitching coach called to ask if he would be interested in joining Torre's staff and told him that Steinbrenner personally wanted to discuss the matter, Stottlemyre asked Arthur Richman, "Have you been drinking?"

But, in another fortuitous coincidence, the man who had hired him as Astros pitching coach, Bob Watson, was now the Yankees' GM. Stottlemyre liked and respected Watson. So, after contemplation, Stottlemyre agreed to talk with Steinbrenner, who blamed the whole 1975 matter on Paul. Stottlemyre rescinded his divorce from the Yankees. He had no previous relationship with

Torre and was hired by the front office, not the new manager. Torre recognized the ugly possibilities. In 1984, as Braves manager, Torre believed he was undermined by hitting coach Eddie Haas and pitching coach Johnny Sain, who were planted in the clubhouse by owner Ted Turner. Torre was fired at the end of that season. However, Torre and his new pitching coach built an instant rapport. Torre liked how honest, positive, and hardworking Stottlemyre was. So when Stottlemyre recommended in April something that had been on his mind ever since Gooden was his protégé with the Mets—altering Gooden's mechanics—Torre concurred.

Stottlemyre had been after Gooden almost from his teenage years to add a changeup and hold runners better. As a Mets coach, Stottlemyre had endured some criticism that he had reduced Gooden's natural effectiveness by getting him to overthink what came so naturally. But now, with his career in the balance, Gooden was a more willing student. Stottlemyre instructed Gooden to separate his pitching hand from his glove quicker, compact his delivery, and stop thinking of himself as Doctor K—a fireballer who could live at the top of the strike zone with his fastball. Eliminating his dramatic arm swing in exchange for more precise location with his breaking stuff, Gooden yielded just four runs over 20 innings in his next three starts.

But Gooden nearly did not make his fourth start since the alterations, on May 14 against the Mariners. His 64-year-old father, Dan, was scheduled for open-heart surgery the next morning in Tampa. Dan Gooden's body had been ravaged in recent years by kidney failure, diabetes, and circulatory problems. The operation had been delayed 5 weeks so he could regain some strength, but now it was decided that there was no more time to wait. Dwight Gooden's sister, Betty, told her brother by phone to brace for the worst and not hesitate in returning home.

Torre was serious about nobody playing hero and feeling all the weight to replace Cone, so he recommended Gooden prioritize family and leave. Touched by the gesture, Gooden nevertheless told Torre his father had raised him to be tough and would want him on the mound. Gooden decided to pitch at night and fly home first thing in the morning. In between innings, however, he cocooned himself in the tunnel that connected the dugout and clubhouse and cried, thinking about the man who had taught him to pitch in the family backyard. Kenny Rogers, whose spot in the rotation was forfeited early in the year so that Gooden could begin his climb back, spent a few of those awful half innings offering comforting words to his teammate. Then Gooden would regain his focus, go back out to the mound, and act young again. "His father was on my mind, so I know it was on his mind," Joe Girardi recalls. "To concentrate that night was remarkable."

Gooden walked 4 of the first 11 batters he faced; 3 others smoked line drives for outs. But to finish the third inning, Gooden provoked Griffey to swing through high heat, and it was as if he had found 1985, when Doctor K roamed the major leagues. For the rest of the game, his fastball tiptoed to 95 miles per hour, and his curve sliced through the strike zone in a physics-defying north-to-south, east-to-west path. But there was more. Gooden was now complementing his familiar repertoire with changeups and, especially, sliders so good, Luis Sojo says, that "every time somebody came back to the [Mariner] dugout, they said, 'What happened to this guy? He's dealing.' Man, when you have Edgar Martinez come back to the dugout with a concerned look on his face, you have great stuff."

As outstanding as Gooden was, he was being matched in zeroes by Seattle's Sterling Hitchcock in his first start against the Yankees since being traded for Tino Martinez. It was still a scoreless game in the sixth when Bragg led off with a ferocious two-hopper that slammed off Martinez's left biceps with such force it reached the stands. For a few seconds, the crowd of 31,025 was quiet. And then, in the press box, official scorer Bill Shannon ruled, "Error first baseman, E-Three," and on the big scoreboard in center field, a 1 lit up in the Yankee error column rather than in the Mariner hit column. The stadium occupants bellowed their pleasure at the ruling.

Bragg reached third base with one out, and up next were Griffey and Edgar Martinez, the duo that had done so much the previous October to exact regime change in the Bronx. The infield crept in, and Gooden went to a full count on Griffey before winning the confrontation with a dart to the outside corner that Griffey swung on and missed. Edgar Martinez followed with a sinking liner to center. If it fell, the no-hitter was over, and Seattle would lead 1–0. Once again, though, Gerald Williams had the right geometry, racing over toward right and in to snare the ball at his knees. In the bottom of the inning, the Yankees scored twice off Hitchcock, with Tino Martinez fittingly delivering the first run with a sacrifice fly. It was 2–0, still too tight to overlook that the game was in the balance but impossible to ignore what was going on with Gooden.

The ovation he received going to the mound in the seventh inning made Gooden realize for the first time just what was happening, stirring him out of the between-inning daze in which he ricocheted between the ailing health of his father and just how close he was to never having a night like this again. At this time a year earlier, the nearest to a baseball field the 1985 Cy Young winner could get was coaching his son's North Seminole Marlins Little League team. Now, in the seventh inning, blowing regularly into his balled right hand against the unseasonably cool weather, Gooden shed the age, the decay inflicted by cocaine and alcohol, and the rust accumulated from 18 months of inactivity.

Mariner hitters were noticing even more life on the ball as the game progressed. Alex Rodriguez had grown up a Mets fan in Miami, watching their games televised on WOR and idolizing Gooden. He thought to himself how funny this was, that he did not need a scouting report. He was seeing from 60 feet, 6 inches away what he used to see on his television. This was vintage Doc Gooden. "It almost seemed like he had a magical energy that took him back to his prime," Rodriguez says.

Gooden worked a perfect seventh and returned to the dugout wondering if his father was conscious enough at St. Joseph's Hospital in Tampa to know what was going on. In a hospital bed at Columbia-Presbyterian, just a few miles away in Manhattan, Gooden's best friend on the Yankees clicked on the radio one out into the bottom of the eighth inning. Cone's parents were visiting, and despite all of his money, he could not get a television with cable access in his private room to see the game. So to receive an update, Cone turned to John Sterling and Michael Kay doing the radio play-by-play and instantly felt a horrible emptiness. What? Dwight Gooden was five outs from a no-hitter, and he was not there to experience it.

Gooden struck out Bragg looking to end the eighth inning. He was now further than he had ever been with a no-hitter, having twice lost opportunities with the Mets in the eighth inning. He retreated to the dugout, his No. 11 fading from the view of a crowd now trying to will this improbable achievement. Gooden had hoped to wear No. 12, a nod to the 12-step program he felt had nursed him back. But his third baseman, Wade Boggs, possibly the majors' most superstitious player, refused to relinquish the number. So Gooden wore 11. Maybe this was the 12th step. Maybe it was perfect that a pitcher nicknamed "Doctor" would be such good medicine for a father in one hospital in Tampa, for a pal in another in New York, and for a team hungering to replace a seemingly irreplaceable ace.

"It was like a flashback night to Doc in his youth," O'Neill remembers. "Doesn't everyone dream of that? To for one day be able to go back in time to their best."

That had seemed impossible less than 4 weeks earlier. Gooden was crushed for six runs in three innings April 19 against Minnesota. That knocked him out of the rotation after three starts and made him think about asking for a trade. It was 2 days later that Stottlemyre began the reclamation project in the Metrodome bullpen, reasserting to Gooden how much confidence his pitching coach and manager had in him. Torre and Stottlemyre had seen enough hints of Gooden's old stuff in spring to believe there was a strong pitcher still inside that body. Could they get it out, and do it in time to save his spot on the roster, save his career, and—possibly—save their season?

Gooden recognized that Torre had expressed faith not only by reinserting him into the rotation when Cone went down but by doing so against the Twins again. Gooden rewarded his manager with six one-run innings that day, a first step back. Now Torre was showing even more faith. The bullpen was busy, but like his predecessor, Buck Showalter, the previous October, Torre—for a completely different reason—had no plans to summon John Wetteland against the Mariners.

Dwight Gooden took the mound in the ninth inning with 110 pitches in just his seventh start since his 18-month banishment. Florida's Al Leiter had thrown the first no-hitter of 1996 the previous week, but that was in an 11–0 rout of Colorado. This was 2–0, and the Mariners had Alex Rodriguez, Ken Griffey, and Edgar Martinez due up. Gooden got ahead of Rodriguez 1–2 but walked him to open the frame. Griffey followed with a corkscrew grounder that Tino Martinez fielded about 20 feet wide of first base. Martinez saw that Gooden would never beat Griffey to the bag, so he raced and then lunged headfirst, swiping the bag with an outstretched glove to just beat Griffey for the first out. Gooden issued his sixth walk, passing Edgar Martinez on a full count, and the first pitch to Jay Buhner was wild, sending both runners to scoring position. Seattle, despite no hits, was now a single away from tying the score.

Torre sent his pitching coach to the mound. Stottlemyre was prepared to pull Gooden if he offered; Wetteland was ready. But this was not Stottlemyre's desire. Stottlemyre told Gooden, "You've done a hell of a job here. No matter what happens, you have to go after this hitter." Gooden's legs were empty, his body having gone way beyond its limitations. He had started off with assistant trainer Steve Donohue focusing him to simply get through the early innings by saying, "Do this for your father." But with each hitless inning, Donohue told Gooden, "Do something special for your father." Now, though, Gooden had to clear his mind. He might lose not only the no-no but the game with a bad pitch. Buhner was a top power hitter, and so was Paul Sorrento on deck. The inspiration came from thin air. Yankee Stadium had derisively become known as the Halfway House that George Built, due to Steinbrenner's penchant for trying to revive the careers of addicts such as Steve Howe, Darryl Strawberry, and now Gooden. But here the Stadium was simply a great baseball cathedral again. There were 10,000 extra fans at the game, taking advantage of the free giveaway Steinbrenner had offered those who sat through the snow at the home opener.

That day Joe DiMaggio had thrown out the first pitch. This was better.

Gooden found his energy from the din, pumping a 2–2 fastball by a swinging Buhner. Two outs in the ninth. Gooden was now one out from becoming the first right-hander in 40 years to throw a no-hitter at Yankee Stadium. The last man to do it was Don Larsen in Game 5 of the 1956 World Series. A 16-year-old from Brooklyn named Joe Torre was in the upper deck that day. Now he was in the home dugout, a 55-year-old manager listening to bench coach Don Zimmer, who had played 17 games for those 1956 Dodgers, suggest walking Sorrento to get to righty-hitting Dan Wilson. Torre dismissed the idea of putting the winning run on base, even to avoid a righty-lefty confrontation at this moment.

Working from the first-base side of the rubber, Gooden threw two curveballs, a strike, and a ball. A high fastball made it 2–1. He had thrown 23 pitches in the inning, 133 for the game, and, dating to his start against the Tigers, had not allowed a hit in the last 48 official at-bats against him. At 10:18 p.m., Gooden reached back one last time—and to another time. Gooden's slider was up, but Sorrento was deceived enough to manage just a soaring pop up about 10 feet beyond the infield grass near shortstop. The ball was very high. High enough for Ruben Sierra, starting his first game of 1996 in left field, to race in toward the infield. High enough for Gerald Williams, starting for the injured Bernie Williams, to come forward from center. High enough for Andy Fox, the fourth-string second baseman who had just replaced fifth-stringer Robert Eenhoorn for defensive purposes, to shuffle over. High enough for Jeter, a rookie, to re-treat slightly onto the outfield grass and wonder if the ball was ever coming down. High enough for a man who in the not-too-distant past simply could not get high enough for his own satisfaction to lift his arms overhead and begin jumping on the mound before the ball nestled in Jeter's glove. The loudest roar yet filled Yankee Stadium.

His face shining with both sweat and a beaming smile, Gooden repeatedly pumped his fist to the crowd. Still wearing his glove, Gooden was carried off the field by Bernie Williams, Jim Leyritz, and Eenhoorn as the song "Simply the

Best" played over the sound system and the scoreboard read "The Doctor Is in the House."

In one hospital room, a teary-eyed Cone said, "I can't believe I wasn't there for this," and clicked on his television to watch the local news to see highlights and experience the joy in his friend's face. In another hospital room, the lifelong Cubs fan who had taught Doc Gooden how to grip his curveball was 10 hours away from heart surgery, a transistor radio placed near his ear, with no one sure if Dan Gooden had any idea what was happening in New York.

"To say it raised the spirits of the team would be a gross understatement," Sussman says. "It helped a team that was confused and searching for something positive. Here was a sense of redemption and hope for us all. This guy was really down, as low as you can get in the game and life. It was such a triumph that it gave the other 24 players belief they could rise up no matter how far down they had been."

New York now belonged to Gooden and the Yankees. Not long after Sorrento's pop out, Michael Jordan's Bulls eliminated the Knicks from the Eastern Conference playoffs. The Yankees were the biggest sports story in town, and Gooden was the most in-demand Yankee. Mayor Rudy Giuliani called the clubhouse to congratulate Gooden, and so did George Steinbrenner, basking now in being right about his personal reclamation project after absorbing so much abuse on the subject. All the morning shows called, wanting Doc to tell his drugs-to-riches story. But Gooden was on a 7 a.m. flight out of LaGuardia Airport the next day to Tampa, the ball from the final out in his carry-on bag. He had someone special to give it to.

In the fall of 1994, Gooden had received a letter from acting commissioner Bud Selig that cocaine had been detected in another urinalysis, and that his suspension for violating the substance-abuse treatment program was being extended to include the entire 1995 season. A baseball outcast, Gooden could always find support from his father. Dan Gooden assured his son at this lowest moment that he would pitch again in the majors and be better than ever. Gooden was not present when the surgery began, but he was there. From his gurney on the way to the operating room, Dan Gooden showed he was alert enough to hear the transistor radio the night before. "My son did it!" he told his family. "My son pitched a no-hitter!"

Dwight Gooden arrived in the waiting room with his wife, Monica, pregnant with their fifth child, to join family that included his nephew, Gary Sheffield. The good news came late in the morning. Dan Gooden's 3-hour double-bypass surgery was a success. He was still too weak to understand much, so Dwight Gooden decided to wait. Dan Gooden would receive a baseball the next day.

About the same time, David Cone left Columbia-Presbyterian Medical Center. He returned to his Manhattan apartment for a shower and a sandwich, and then by instinct—and against his doctors' wishes—put on a blue sports coat, tan slacks, and a red tie and headed to the ballpark. Just 5 days postsurgery, Cone's doctors thought their patient was still too weak for this physical and emotional expense. Cone didn't care. The leader in him fought the doctors. He felt it was important that his teammates see that he was fine and that he reassure the whole organization and even his own doctors by meeting the media.

There had been backlash following Cone's surgery that the doctors had used a radical and risky technique with the vein graft, sacrificing his potential long-term health in exchange for the possibility he could pitch again that year. Two pitchers from the Giants organization—Steve Soderstrom and Kevin Rogers—had had similar aneurysms, and no vein graft was used. Of course, Cone had favored this procedure—anything to pitch again, and pitch as soon as possible.

Cone moved slowly. His face was ashen, and he looked frail as he left teammates who were elated to see him but now had to dress for a game. He moved from the home clubhouse down the hall to an auxiliary locker room to face the media. Speaking with reporters, Cone was unable to hold his familiar game face, especially when discussing his absence at Gooden's no-hitter. He paused, his voice cracked, and, eventually, tears flowed. He defended his surgeons and vowed to pitch again. Already the discoloration was gone from his hand, the circulation had returned to almost normal, and his shoulder felt fine. Cone believed his doctors: that over the next 6 weeks the vein would integrate with the arteries in his shoulder, thicken, and grow strong enough to endure the rigors of pitching. So even though he could not yet lift his right arm overhead, he was already thinking 6 weeks and a day down the line, when he could pick up a baseball to begin the process back to the mound. There was no set path back from this type of surgery, Cone acknowledged, but he promised to blaze one. Sure, he had thought about the end, he told reporters, but now he was thinking of a new beginning.

The defiance in Cone, an asset that enabled him to stand 60 feet, 6 inches from trouble and believe he would always find the proper pitching response, led him to remind those assembled that he had pitched a complete game with an aneurysm in his shoulder. He was not regretful of all the innings and pitches. He was proud of them. Cone was reasserting to everyone who he was and that, because of that, he would be back. He seemed to be saying it as much for himself as anyone gathered to hear it. But his teammates heard it, too, and so did baseball New York. This trip was therapeutic for Cone and also for a flock of players just happy to see their leader again. "I expect to pitch this year, and I expect to pitch better than ever," Cone said. It was the kind of proclamation that in other forums would have been heard and then ignored as machismo blather by an athlete. But the 1996 Yankees were living the most unlikely of Hollywood scripts.

They had won through snow on Opening Day, through two interminable days at Camden Yards, through an 8–0 deficit at Comiskey Park, and now with a pitcher seemingly a decade beyond his expiration date throwing a no-hitter in place of perhaps the best pitcher in the AL.

David Cone was months away from playing again. But on the night of May 14, Dwight Gooden had reemphasized that for the 1996 Yankees no obstacle was too great.

7 | PERFECTLY AWFUL

"I remember going into Cleveland and thinking we had no chance. That is when we showed what kind of team we had."
—Mike Borzello, Yankee bullpen catcher

The Yankees were winning games and losing players. At one juncture in late May, the Yankees had nine players on the disabled list and a group of walking wounded that included Joe Girardi (back), Andy Pettitte (elbow), and Mariano Rivera (back). The injury epidemic threatened the Yankees' very ability to field a team, much less hold on to first place in the American League East. In spring training, Joe Torre had been pelted with questions about how he would divide seven starters into five spots. Now the rotation was a danger zone much like second base, where an eighth-year minor leaguer named Matt Howard was receiving playing time.

By the third week in June, three starting pitchers were on the disabled list. Melido Perez had yet to throw a pitch all season because of bone chips in his right elbow. David Cone was still closing in on being able to play soft toss as he navigated his way back from aneurysm surgery. Jimmy Key, disabled in May due to a strain in his surgically repaired left shoulder, had again been moved to the DL, this time with a calf strain. Scott Kamieniecki was supposed to provide depth but had performed so horrendously (11.12 ERA overall, 18 earned runs in his last $6^1/_3$ innings) that he was demoted to Triple-A Columbus, where he pitched so badly that he made himself a nonoption, despite the staggering needs of the parent club. The youngest and seemingly most durable starter, Pettitte turned 24 on June 15 and beat the Indians for his AL–high-tying 11th victory the next day, then was sent for a series of diagnostic tests to determine why he was feeling tightness in his left elbow. Dwight Gooden and Kenny Rogers, both George Steinbrenner ideas, were the only starters taking the ball without pain. Gooden, in particular, was thriving.

On April 4, what would have been the final game of a three-game, season-opening series in Cleveland had been washed away. It seemed innocuous at the time, just a rainout in the long season. Now it had created a crisis. That rainout was rescheduled as part of a day-night doubleheader on June 21 to initiate a four-game weekend series at Jacobs Field. Pettitte had been scheduled to start in the opener on Friday, but it was determined he had an inflamed elbow. He would not pitch before the series finale on Sunday, at the earliest. The Yankees were left to go on the road, against the majors' most lethal offense, and start rookies Brian Boehringer and Ramiro Mendoza in the doubleheader. The duo had combined, to that point in their careers, to post a 1–7 record with a 10.57 ERA. Boehringer had already faced the Indians in his lone 1996 start 6 days earlier and was creamed for six extra-base hits and six runs in five innings. The next day, June 16, the Chicago Bulls finished off the Seattle SuperSonics in the NBA final to cap a rousing year in which they went 72–10 in the regular season, and Pettitte felt the tightness in his left elbow.

Mendoza had suggested an outward calm by falling asleep at his locker before each start as clubhouse life buzzed by. He had encouraged management by winning his major league debut in the Yankees' house of horrors, the Seattle Kingdome. But in four subsequent outings after that, Mendoza surrendered 18 earned runs in $17\frac{1}{3}$ innings and admitted after his last start on June 17 that— pregame naps or not—he was feeling the pressure of replacing famous pitchers on the Yankee staff. Now he had to start in Cleveland on 3 days' rest.

To exacerbate matters, the Yankees were scheduled to go from Cleveland to Minnesota, where another doubleheader awaited with Boehringer and Mendoza lined up to pitch, both on 3 days' rest. The Yankees were staring at seven games in one 5-day stretch, four to be started by the two rookie right-handers. Joe Torre joked that the Yankees were not running out of starters just on the New York roster but at Columbus as well. But there was little laughter. The injury to Pettitte particularly unsettled the organization because he was so young and because he was so overtly disconcerted by the first real arm injury of his life. Pettitte could not straighten out his left arm and fretted that his career might even be over, although the team doctors kept assuring him that there was nothing structurally wrong.

The organization was so desperate for starting pitching that it briefly considered promoting Wally Whitehurst, who had not worked in the majors in 2 years and had just a week earlier been released from the Expo farm system. The Yankees sent a scout to watch 41-year-old Jack Morris in the Northern League, though he had not pitched in the majors since 1994. In May, the Yankees responded to the rousing success the year before of Japanese import Hideo Nomo by obtaining an orange-haired curiosity named Katsuhiro "Kats" Maeda from the Seibu Lions. They signed him to a $1.5 million bonus and compared him to Roger Clemens due to a fastball they claimed reached 98 miles per hour. In early June, the Yankees used their first-round pick to select Eric Milton out of the University of Maryland. Now it felt as if Maeda and Milton were just a few more injuries away from being summoned to the Bronx.

Torre, recognizing the stress posed by the Indian series, decided to take a few of his coaches golfing on an off day, June 20. His boss, however, saw nothing to relax about. George Steinbrenner convened a meeting in his office with Bob Watson and assistant GM Brian Cashman. Watson had been surveying the starting landscape and did not find much to his liking. Kansas City's Kevin Appier was the most appealing, but he was also expensive, and Steinbrenner already was not thrilled to have baseball's top payroll. Knowing Steinbrenner's impetuous history, rival GMs shot high, requesting either Mariano Rivera or his cousin, Ruben. Watson was refusing such demands. Steinbrenner actually had been in a foul mood for weeks, though Watson and Torre were learning there was little distinction between foul and normal. Beyond baseball, Steinbrenner watched as another major investment, the Nick Zito–trained Diligence, ran the worst race of his career at the 122nd Kentucky Derby. Diligence's ninth-place finish was unacceptable to the Boss.

But what really riled Steinbrenner was that the Yankees were going to his hometown of Cleveland, which had built the Indians a lush, new stadium, while New York City would not do the same for him. The Indians were playing before sellout crowds every game, with the organization enjoying the financial windfall of luxury boxes, among other modern, moneymaking amenities. Even worse for Steinbrenner, Peter Angelos's Orioles had received the same financial boost from Baltimore. The Orioles were on pace to outdraw the Yankees by nearly 1.5 million spectators. Steinbrenner instructed his media-relations officials to start the bizarre practice of including attendance rankings as part of the daily game notes, with headers such as "First in the standings, not in the stands." Just 15,614 had paid to see Dwight Gooden's first home start after his no-hitter, nearly 6,000 fewer than the Yankee Stadium average. The Yankee home average was just eighth in the AL, a fact Steinbrenner always slipped into interviews. It was a veiled way of suggesting no one wanted to come to the South Bronx, because in his spin it was too dangerous.

Steinbrenner wanted a new stadium built over the rail yards on Manhattan's West Side and was threatening to move his team to New Jersey when the Yankee Stadium lease expired after the 2002 season. He had an ally at City Hall in lifelong Yankee fan Rudy Giuliani, who was trying to tie a bid to the 2008 Summer Olympics to building Steinbrenner the West Side stadium. To emphasize his disenchantment, Steinbrenner ordered the layoffs of more than 20 game-day employees at the stadium, including 73-year-old Charles Zebransky, who had been guarding the clubhouse door since 1982. The players, who liked the upbeat, smiling Charlie, decided to chip in the $103 a game necessary to keep Zebransky on his post, an embarrassment to Steinbrenner.

The possibility of being humiliated at Jacobs Field only intensified Steinbrenner's wrath.

The Boss always worked from a starting point of gloom, so he anticipated a weekend sweep in Cleveland that would drop the Yankees from first place. At the June 20 meeting, he ordered Watson to call Torre. When it was discovered Torre was out golfing, Steinbrenner became even more infuriated. Steinbrenner associated golf with being on vacation, and he felt his employees should be on the clock every day, every hour, year round—25 hours a day in times of crisis. Watson buzzed Torre's pager, just after Torre hooked a ball off the fairway. Torre quickly returned the call, a potential ambush now under way. Squawking into the speakerphone, Steinbrenner challenged Torre: "It's the Boss. While you are in the fucking woods, we're here trying to figure out how to make your team better."

Without missing a beat, Torre responded, "How did you know my ball was in the woods? I haven't been able to keep it in the fairway all day."

The levity made even Steinbrenner chuckle. The stress was removed from the phone call; the mood even lightened back in the Boss's Bronx office. Torre then went on to acknowledge the obvious, that two inexperienced, mostly ineffective right-handers working before packed houses on the road was no way to face the Indians. But he told Steinbrenner that the club had manufactured ways to win all year through injuries and through a paucity of offensive power. The Yankees had won in Detroit on June 9, though they had started four rookies (Andy Fox, Matt Howard, Derek Jeter, and Ruben Rivera) for the first time in 5 years. Torre said he trusted his roster's resolve and promised Steinbrenner that his team would find a way to survive the weekend.

"That was the day I saw Joe's ability to defuse tension for the first time," Cashman remembers. "From then on I called what he did there Joe's Calm Bombs. He had this ability with his tone and his words to drop Calm Bombs at just the right times, and suddenly it was not as tense anymore."

Torre's Type B persona had surely been challenged even with the Yankees atop the division and a sense of destiny filling the clubhouse. And, when challenged, Torre had shown he could go Type A if necessary. In one game, Jeff Nelson was not thrilled to be removed and tried to convince Torre on the mound to leave him in. Torre, with his hand outstretched for the ball, said, "If you get to make the decisions, what the fuck am I out here for?" Nelson gave

Torre the ball and walked off the mound. The message was clear: Torre was not going to be shown up on the field by one of his own players.

But mostly Torre played to his strength, which was to soothe jangled nerves and to unleash Calm Bombs. On May 31, Ruben Sierra did not start in Oakland. This was particularly galling to the proud Sierra, since it was the A's who had traded the switch-hitter the previous July in a headache-for-headache transaction in which they obtained Danny Tartabull from the Yankees. Sierra had ripped Oakland GM Sandy Alderson upon his exit, and then A's manager Tony La Russa had decried Sierra as a "village idiot." Since Tartabull had found reason after reason not to go on the field much at home—faking injuries to avoid getting booed, in Showalter's view—Sierra became a necessary evil. But, at age 29, Sierra barely hinted at the young player he had been in Texas, who conjured comparisons to fellow Puerto Rican Roberto Clemente. Sierra's ego remained powerful as his game ebbed. He kept an undying belief that he was still a star player, despite a significant loss of speed and a near complete indifference to defense.

On September 14, 1995, angered that Buck Showalter had taken to regularly starting Darryl Strawberry as the designated hitter against righty pitching, Sierra ordered his agent, Jose Masso, to phone Showalter in the Camden Yards manager's office to complain. The call was not only an unprofessional breach of protocol but also an ill-timed distraction, coming with the Yankees playing what felt like a playoff game every day as they tried to claim the wild card. Showalter, who took the call with the media present, told Masso to contact Gene Michael and slammed the phone down.

Clean slate or not, different personality in the manager's office or not, Torre did not much care for Sierra, either. He disliked that Sierra was still griping that he could not get the number 21 worn by Paul O'Neill—the number worn by Clemente that Sierra had used in previous seasons. He disliked that Sierra kept carping about playing the field when it was clear that as a defender, his best position was designated hitter. And Torre did not like that Sierra stood far off the plate and unleashed an all-or-nothing swing that left him exposed to easy outs for any pitcher who could pelt the outside corner, especially when Sierra batted right-handed. And, just like with Showalter, there was the issue of playing time. Sierra had not homered in 88 at-bats going into May 31 and had not hit a homer batting righty all year. So with the A's starting southpaw Doug Johns, Torre put Ruben Rivera in left, Gerald Williams at DH, and Sierra on the bench. Sierra reacted by telling reporters, "I don't like people lying to me. He's been lying to me since spring training, when he said I was going to play the outfield. He said I was going to be the DH no matter what, and now I don't play. That's not telling the truth."

Before reacting and potentially ratcheting up hostilities, Torre always tried to imagine what motivated an outburst. This way, Torre felt, he could better understand the thought process that led to the problem and the path to resolution. Though furious, particularly about being labeled a liar, Torre simply called the word choice "unfortunate." He modulated his voice to serenely say he had made no such promises to Sierra. Besides, Torre explained, Sierra should take a look at the realities of his numbers and the defensive abilities of others and ask what he would do if he were the manager. Torre met with Sierra and actually posed those issues, explaining his thoughts in detail. Sierra nodded his head as if he understood and then said, "But why am I not playing?"

Torre tried again, and once more Sierra nodded in agreement and asked, "But why am I not playing?"

At that moment, Torre divorced himself from Ruben Sierra. He had authorized his former Angels broadcast partner and pal, Reggie Jackson, to work personally since spring training with Sierra, especially on the mental aspects of the game. There were no improvements. Appreciating the general bonhomie that existed in the clubhouse and sensing that "Sierra didn't get it because he just didn't want to get it," Torre privately told Watson to get rid of Sierra whenever possible. A week later in the lunchroom at Tiger Stadium, Watson first broached an idea with his Detroit counterpart Randy Smith—Sierra for

Cecil Fielder. Smith rejected the pitch, but lines of communication had been established.

Torre liked John Wetteland a heck of a lot more than Sierra. He admired that Wetteland never made excuses. As opposed to a cavalcade of players who had harpooned Showalter after his departure—notably Steve Howe, Pat Kelly, and Jim Leyritz—Wetteland never admonished the manager for refusing to use him in Game 5 of the 1995 Division Series against the Mariners, instead acknowledging how poorly he pitched in the series. And Torre appreciated that rather than feel threatened by upstart Mariano Rivera—as Sierra was feeling toward Ruben Rivera and Gerald Williams—Wetteland was mentoring Rivera through the transition from starter to reliever. Wetteland constantly counseled Rivera that a late-game reliever should never get beat with his second-best pitch in a game-deciding situation. He told Rivera that the key to life as a reliever was to think like a good cornerback and quickly forget a disappointing result, because another opportunity would come and come fast. "Wetteland groomed Mariano, and he had no problem with it," bullpen catcher Mike Borzello recalls. "He was a good guy."

He also was a good teammate. "Wetteland was the leader in the bullpen," Joe Girardi remembers. "He made guys pay attention. If we were on offense and a guy got a hit, if you didn't clap before the next guy's name was announced, he would hit you or spray you with the hose. There was a penalty. It made guys pay attention to the game."

None of that masked that Wetteland was miserable, and Torre knew this, too. On the eve of his arbitration in February, Wetteland had approved a $4 million contract with a $4.6 million option for 1997, but he never signed because the sides had agreed to try to negotiate a long-term deal. That figured to be no problem, since Wetteland's representative was Tom Reich. But, shockingly, Steinbrenner turned on his favorite agent. The Yankees paid Wetteland as if his salary were the $3.375 million he made in 1995. Reich filed a breach-of-contract grievance, demanding that his client be made a free agent instantly. Just before the grievance hearing, on May 17, Steinbrenner relented and began honoring the $4 million contract.

It was not just business that made Wetteland miserable. Wetteland was a hockey buff, playing in a roller league in the off-season. He would bring in his stick, ball up socks, and whack slap shots at the dodging young clubhouse attendants. Torre discontinued that practice. To relieve stress and retain muscle in his oak-tree legs, Wetteland Rollerbladed through the concrete concourses of stadiums, including the U-shaped alleyway beneath Yankee Stadium. Torre did not ban the practice totally, but he did tell Wetteland to diminish the daredevil speeds at which he whipped through turns and exiled Wetteland to areas away from the clubhouse. Torre could just imagine trying to explain to Steinbrenner that he lost his closer to a Rollerblade injury or, worse, lost another player when Wetteland barreled into him.

On June 13, reporter Danny Gallagher in the Toronto *Globe and Mail* quoted Wetteland complaining about the off-field distractions in New York and the handling of his contract. Wetteland indicated he had no desire to remain a Yankee after 1996. He initially claimed he had never even spoken to Gallagher, but when Gallagher made it clear he had a tape of the interview, Wetteland retreated. He said the interview reflected feelings that no longer existed. What had changed? Torre had recognized the melancholy state of his closer, brought Wetteland into his office for a chat, and dropped a Calm Bomb: "I know you are unhappy. I know you are mad at certain rules. But you have to get over it. People are counting on you." The call to a higher ideal struck Wetteland, and, as opposed to Sierra, he reapplied himself to finding a way to work within the team.

Ultimately, Wetteland emerged as a vital piece of the Yankees' winning Formula. He was not always pretty in his ninth-inning work, putting on runners and allowing homers. But he had a way of getting the final out before a tying run scored. He had run off 13 straight saves, including one in 10 consecutive appearances, as the Yankees headed to Cleveland. When Torre had placated Steinbrenner about facing the Indians, he was thinking about splitting the series, somehow fighting through two games with a lead after six innings and turning control over to his Formula, to Rivera and Wetteland.

The Yankees did have one advantage going into Cleveland. The Indians' fiercest hitter, Albert Belle, was suspended for the doubleheader for viciously bowling over diminutive Brewers second baseman Fernando Vina in the baseline between first and second. Belle initially received a five-game suspension, but it was lowered to three games, then two, by AL president Gene Budig through the relentless fight of the Players Association. In the previous 9 months, Belle had cussed out NBC's Hannah Storm during the World Series, chased and struck a trick-or-treater with his vehicle, cussed out a fan seeking an autograph, and purposely hit a *Sports Illustrated* photographer with a baseball.

Belle was the face of a particularly bad moment in baseball history. Marge Schott had agreed to relinquish running the Cincinnati Reds following remarks she made to ESPN casting Adolf Hitler in a positive way. Kirby Puckett, one of the sunshine faces of the sport, had been diagnosed with glaucoma that spring, a disease that would end his career. Dodgers center fielder Brett Butler was found to have throat cancer. Overweight ump John McSherry dropped dead on the field in Cincinnati on Opening Day. Mel Allen, the longtime voice of the Yankees, died in mid-June. And the resentment of the fans over the labor problems of 1994 and 1995 lingered.

Interestingly, fans and even other organizations that typically despised the Yankees actually found themselves liking this club. Torre had put a human face on a Steinbrenner-owned team. The Yankees performed with a workmanlike humility. Sierra was the only player who brazenly admired his home runs, rare as they were. And the team's struggle with injuries only brought an underdog patina to the ultimate overdog organization.

There was no moment when the Yankees felt more like an underdog—Belle or no Belle—than when the doubleheader began at the Jake on June 21. Between 1995 and 1996, Boehringer had filled in with the Yankees to make eight appearances, including four starts, and was 0–3 with a 13.10 ERA. He was over-matched against the Indians once again, leaving in the fifth inning, having put the Yankees behind 4–1. The lead was 5–1 heading to the eighth, and Cleveland was cruising behind ace Charles Nagy, who was pitching a four-hitter and on the brink of breaking a tie with Pettitte for the AL lead in wins. At that moment, the Yankees were 0–23 when trailing after six innings, the majors' only winless team in such situations. However, eight times in 1996, the Yankees had won when trailing by at least three runs. Torre's mantra was "chip away." Small bites will lead to big things. Good stuff will happen if you keep playing hard. In fact, in an attempt to take some of the onus off his inexperienced pitchers, Torre had changed the subject in recent days to how much concern he had with his offense mustering runs. It was a Calm Bomb of misdirection.

The Yankees began answering the challenge in the eighth, drawing within 6–4, fueled by RBI doubles from Tino Martinez and Sierra. That still left them down two runs in the ninth against Jose Mesa, who had 23 saves in 24 tries. But the Yankees loaded the bases with none out before Derek Jeter struck out to fall hitless in five at-bats. A Paul O'Neill RBI single made it 6–5. Martinez then hit a one-hopper to shortstop Omar Vizquel. A double play ends the game. Vizquel flipped to Carlos Baerga for the force at second, and Baerga threw to first. Martinez lunged headfirst, his hand striking the bag a millisecond before the ball hit Julio Franco's glove. Safe. The tying run was in. The 86th straight sellout crowd at Jacobs Field went quiet.

The Yankees again loaded the bases in the 10th inning, this time with two outs. To this point, Jeter had endured what he considered his worst game of the season. But of the many traits that Torre valued in Jeter—maturity, optimism, responsibility—there was none he respected more than the rookie's self-confidence. Torre, a superb hitter as a player, had spent a lifetime witnessing and experiencing the doubts that creep into even the best hitter's brain. Veterans such as Martinez and O'Neill stewed in self-doubt when a few fruit-less at-bats started to pile up, which of course tended to extend slumps. But Jeter, 5 days shy of his 22nd birthday, always behaved as if his next at-bat would remedy any slump. He acted as if he were playing pickup baseball with friends, remembering that this was a game and was fun. He radiated positive energy, and Torre thought that good not just for the shortstop but for the whole team.

Lefty Jim Poole went to 2–1 on Jeter before leaving a fastball up and over the plate. Jeter scorched it to center field for a single. Two runs scored. Wetteland relieved and for the third time in the past week surrendered a solo homer, this time to Jeromy Burnitz. But just like the previous occasions, he successfully closed out a game. The Yankees won 8–7. The mood in the clubhouse was euphoric. Torre was overjoyed. He had to use six pitchers with Mendoza waiting in the nightcap, but he had secured a win. The Yankees would not be swept in either the doubleheader or the series. Better yet, his club had offered further evidence of its resolve. Thirty minutes before the second game was to begin, Torre was told he had a phone call in his office.

"Where are you?" Ali Torre asked from Cincinnati, where she was visiting her family. Joe answered his wife but heard the ominous tremor in her voice. "Are you sitting down? I have bad news," she said. Immediately, Joe Torre knew his brother Frank was dead. Frank Torre had been feeling horrible for months and was in the hospital. He had been having trouble catching his breath, even when doing something as simple as fetching the newspaper on his front lawn in Palm Beach Garden, Florida. He had his gallbladder removed and a pacemaker put in, but nothing made him feel better. The last few times they had spoken, Torre had noticed his brother was giving up, that the discomfort and lack of mobility had removed Frank's fighting spirit.

"Rocco is dead," Ali Torre said.

"Rocco?" Joe Torre was in shock. His oldest brother?

Rocco's son Robert had just called Ali Torre with the news. Rocco had been watching the first game of the doubleheader on TV in his Flushing, Queens, home and saw his kid brother's team pull out a shocking win. He then collapsed and died of a heart attack in front of his wife, Rose. Rocco was 69, a retired New York City police officer. Due to their 13-year age difference, Joe and Rocco had not been very close during Joe's youth. But Rocco had become a fixture at

Sunday afternoon Yankee home games during the season, bringing bagels and good wishes for his brother.

After speaking to Rocco's now widow, Torre decided to manage the second game. Word circulated in the clubhouse about the death of Torre's brother. It was another moment in this 1996 season when a loss of a game would have been acceptable. But Torre was sending yet another message, this one about doing your job, even in tough times, even with the disabled list filled with a small team, even with a brother now dead. He had recently told his club not to fixate on who was missing but to recognize the quality of players still performing.

The Yankees scored seven runs in the first three innings against Julian Tavarez. Mendoza worked five innings and did not permit an earned run. Seeing an opportunity, Torre used Mariano Rivera for three innings. The Yankees won 9–3.

Reporters had been notified during the second game about Rocco Torre's death. But how do you broach this? Do you ask about a doubleheader sweep when a man has just lost his brother? Do you ask about death in a baseball clubhouse? Torre made the session easy. His head was down, his eyes reddened, but otherwise Torre was Torre as he dissected a day of both great wins and a tragic loss. The answers were forthcoming, long and insightful. He was disarming tension again, dropping another Calm Bomb.

"He made everyone else feel comfortable about the most uncomfortable situation you can ever imagine," says Jack Curry of the *New York Times*. Curry thought of Torre using this almost as therapy. Ali Torre explains that a baseball park was where Joe Torre always went for relief, where he had spent long hours to avoid a home with an abusive father. Joe Torre felt protected and relaxed at a stadium, and he projected those qualities to his players. When he had talked about this series to reporters, he had been the anti-Steinbrenner. He would not panic and remove Mark Hutton, Bob Wickman, or, especially, Rivera from the pen to make a spot start. The deep bullpen would support the young starters; the young starters would be asked just to do their best. The 1996 Yankees were about finding a way, Torre reiterated, and his serenity bled into the clubhouse.

Just a little over a year earlier, Torre had lost his job in St. Louis, and with it, he figured, the last opportunity to cocoon himself in a clubhouse. So just being in a stadium and having a team to manage made dealing with this kind of tragedy less overwhelming. Torre managed the following day, June 22, as well, when, amazingly, the Yankees rallied from a 5–0 deficit after five innings to win 11–9 in 4 hours and 10 minutes, the longest nine-inning game in the Indians' history. Sierra homered from both sides of the plate, which meant his first homer batting righty in 111 at-bats. Hutton became the latest Yankee to step out of the chorus and star. With no one else available to serve in long relief, the tall Australian went scoreless through the sixth, seventh, and eighth innings before Wetteland finished again.

On June 23, Wetteland's former Dodger skipper, Tommy Lasorda, managed his final game. The following day, Lasorda drove himself to the hospital, complaining of abdominal pain, when in fact he was suffering a heart attack. He officially retired 5 days later.

Lasorda and Don Zimmer had been Brooklyn Dodger teammates in the mid-1950s. Zimmer also managed on June 23, taking over in the second inning from Torre, who had to fly home for his brother's funeral the next day. Zimmer had actually known Frank Torre a lot better than Joe prior to joining the staff. He might see the two at the dog track in St. Petersburg and say hello. He had managed against Joe Torre but did not consider him a friend. So when Joe Torre called Zimmer in early November 1995 at his home in Treasure Island, Florida, Zimmer was surprised. He had been midway through his third season as Colorado's bench coach when he walked out of the dugout on June 6, 1995, in a game against Joe Torre's Cardinals, 10 days before Torre himself would be fired by St. Louis. Zimmer found communication with manager Don Baylor poor. So he simply left the bench, dressed, and headed home to Florida for what he figured was retirement. He told his wife, whose name was Jean but everyone called Soot, that he would make no phone calls to try to gain employment in 1996.

Zimmer had worked in professional baseball for 47 years, most famously as the manager of the 1978 Boston Red Sox, who blew a 14-game, mid-July lead in the AL East over the Yankees. He had managed four teams, and one of his former players with the Rangers, Buddy Bell, called during the 1995 playoffs. Bell was a coach for the Indians, and he felt he had a pretty good chance of being named Detroit's manager. If he did, Bell wanted Zimmer to be his bench coach. Zimmer told Bell to enjoy the playoffs, get the job, and call again at that time. But because the Indians went all the way to the sixth game of the World Series, plus new Detroit GM Randy Smith had to interview other candidates, including Buck Showalter, Bell did not nail down the Tiger job until November 9 — a week after Torre's Yankee press conference. Still, Zimmer figured Torre was calling in early November to inquire about a player he was familiar with that the Yankees had designs on obtaining. Torre asked about Zimmer's health and how retirement was going, then said, "How would you like to be my bench coach in New York?"

"I was shocked," Zimmer remembers. Zimmer had been a Yankee coach in 1983 and 1986 and had become fast friends with Steinbrenner, owing to their mutual love of horse racing. Zimmer also was pals from his Cub days with Steinbrenner confidant Billy Connors. Zimmer assumed this decision had been foisted on Torre from above and thought a forced relationship could not work.

Torre promised that this was his choice. Zimmer's history as a manager plus his previous experience coaching in New York made him ideal in Torre's mind. Zimmer remained circumspect. He called Connors and said he had no desire to take the job if either Connors or Steinbrenner had motivated the decision. Connors assured Zimmer that was not the case. As he did with Stottlemyre, Torre enlisted a man he hardly knew to a vital coaching area and ended up with not only an associate he trusted immediately but a dear friend as well. Zimmer ended up in the job of his life. At 65, he found a manager so comfortable in his skin that Zimmer could sit and make suggestion after suggestion without Torre ever feeling threatened. Quite the opposite; Torre loved Zimmer's counsel and found the cherubic man known as Popeye funny.

He also found him a great resource. Torre knew from the outset that this team would not be like the Bronx Bombers of the past. To Steinbrenner's chagrin, these Yankees lacked substantial power. Torre felt a need for a more National League–style approach, which is why early in the season Torre had awarded dinners to players who executed team-oriented little ball, such as advancing a runner with a grounder to the right side. It is also why before choosing Zimmer he had considered Chuck Tanner, whose Pirate teams Torre had admired for their base-path aggression. But perhaps no one in the majors was more associated with favoring strategies such as the hit and run or stolen base than Zimmer.

The Yankees stole just 222 bases from 1992 to 1995, by far the fewest in the majors. It reflected Buck Showalter's nature. With stopwatch and videotape, Showalter studiously pursued the perfect place for an advantage. For example, the White Sox were starting a lefty, Wilson Alvarez, on May 29, 1993, and Paul O'Neill will never forget that Showalter told his players to go on the pitcher's first move, and if they were picked off to just keep heading to second base because, he said, first baseman Frank Thomas hated to throw the ball. Sure enough, with two out in the fourth inning, Gerald Williams broke for second, Alvarez threw to first, and Thomas fired the ball into left field while Williams raced to third.

But that was not all Showalter had hatched for Alvarez. For weeks, Showalter had been plotting that if the Yankees' fastest runner, Williams, reached third base against Alvarez, he would have Williams steal home. He had noticed that even with a runner on third, Alvarez started with the ball in his glove chest high and his hand by his side, so as soon as Alvarez moved his left hand, by rule, he had to go through with his natural motion home or else it would be a balk. If a fast runner from third left as soon as Alvarez moved his hand, there was no way, Showalter determined, that he could deliver quickly enough to the plate to prevent a steal. In addition, as a left-hander with a deliberate windup, Alvarez had a blind spot behind him down the third-base line. The plan worked: Williams stole home, emphasizing Showalter's fanatic preparation. But that was the only time in 4 years the Yankees stole home, which underscored his restrictive nature that slowly choked the team.

Under Zimmer and Torre, the Yankees had already swiped home four times. Three weeks earlier in Oakland, the Yankees had stolen eight bases in one game, four by Gerald Williams. Yes, this team had Zimmer's imprint. As Jim Leyritz says, "Zimmer had the best job in baseball. He made all the decisions and got none of the blame."

Zimmer, though, was unquestionably in charge during the seventh inning of the finale against the Indians as Joe Girardi led off with a single against Jack McDowell. Funny, but there was no more talk about how the Yankees should have re-signed McDowell or kept Mike Stanley rather than obtain Girardi. Zimmer had been the strongest voice in the off-season about acquiring Girardi. In the second half of his rookie 1989 season for the division-winning Cubs, Girardi had been installed as the starting catcher by his manager, Zimmer. And Girardi had been selected by the Rockies in the first round of the expansion draft in 1992, and Zimmer was the bench coach. Zimmer thought of Girardi as the ultimate team player, defining himself by how a pitcher performed and by the final score of the game only, not personal stats. Zimmer always claimed Girardi was the kind of player you had to watch daily to see and appreciate the subtle skills—framing a pitch, getting a pitcher through a jam. From their National League days, Torre and Bob Watson liked how Girardi commanded a game from behind the plate, as well, and on November 20, 1995, he was obtained from Colorado for two minor league pitchers, Mike DeJean and Steve Shoemaker.

With Girardi on first, Derek Jeter batting, and the Yankees ahead just 3-2, Zimmer looked to add a run. Girardi had no homers so far in a year in which his cross-town counterpart, Todd Hundley of the Mets, would hit 41 to break Roy Campanella's single-season record for homers by a catcher. But Girardi would steal more than twice as many bases as any catcher in 1996, and on this occasion he swiped his seventh bag in seven tries, another sign of his headiness. What Girardi lacked in speed, he compensated for with reading situations, correctly divining when an off-speed pitch was coming to create a more favorable climate to attempt a steal. In the Showalter years, the Yankees had managed three steals overall from their catchers. Girardi's steal was the Yankees' 52nd of the season, two more than the Yankees had totaled the whole previous year for Showalter. Jeter walked. Andy Fox sacrificed the runners to scoring position. It was the Yankees' 22nd sacrifice bunt of 1996, two more than the Showalter Yankees had produced during the whole 1995 season. More NL ball. Wade Boggs tripled in two runs, and an O'Neill sacrifice fly made it 6–2. In the bottom of the inning, Carlos Baerga hit a two-run homer to knock out Dwight Gooden. Wickman walked Albert Belle. Zimmer summoned a lefty named Dale Polley, who was called up the previous day when the Yankees waived Steve Howe because he simply could not retire lefty batters anymore.

Polley, at 31, was the second-oldest rookie in Yankee history. He had spent 10 years and 339 games in the minors without having even a day in the majors. In 1994, demoted to Double-A, Polley quit baseball and operated a lathe in his father's machine shop in Georgetown, Kentucky, before returning in 1995 to be part of the Braves' replacement team during the lockout. He now joined a Yankee club that had David Cone and Joe Torre, two of the strongest player voices in the history of the union. Yet the 1996 Yankees worked rather seamlessly, in part because of the sense of family those two men helped establish in the clubhouse, and if Dale Polley could do what Steve Howe no longer could—deceive a lefty batter—then he was family. Polley's major league welcome was facing Jim Thome as the tying run. He struck out Thome with a curveball and then induced Eddie Murray to ground to Jeter. Now Dale Polley was there with Andy Fox and Matt Howard and Jim Mecir, unlikely heroes in cameo roles for the 1996 Yankees.

To begin the bottom of the eighth inning, Zimmer sent Gerald Williams in to play defense in left field for Sierra. With runners on second and third and one out, Kenny Lofton sliced a ball to the left-field corner. If Sierra were still in left, the ball would definitely have been a hit, the score tied, and, perhaps, Cleveland would have salvaged a piece of the weekend. Gerald Williams raced over and, with a do-or-die lunge for the ball, made a spectacular catch that robbed what would have been at least a two-run triple. Wetteland pitched a scoreless ninth, his third save in three tries over the weekend. The Yankees won 6–5.

The series George Steinbrenner had fretted Cleveland would sweep and that Torre had hoped to split had become a four-game Yankee party. The offensive star of the series was Sierra, who had eight hits and seven RBIs. The Yankees had swept a series in which they had used 13 pitchers, including two who were no longer even active when the series ended (Howe and Mecir). The only active pitcher who did not work was their top winner, Andy Pettitte, who was pushed back to rest his elbow and was upset about it because he was hoping to impress AL All-Star manager Mike Hargrove, Cleveland's skipper.

The Yankees won one game they trailed by four runs and another they trailed by five. They won both ends of a doubleheader started by Brian Boehringer and Ramiro Mendoza. They won amid Joe Torre's tragedy and with Torre having handed the managerial reins to Zimmer. They finished the year 6–0 at Jacobs Field and were 12–2 all-time at the stadium, the only opponent with a winning record there. That brought even more resonance to the previous October, when The Baseball Network schedule had created a Division Series in which the wild-card Yankees of Buck Showalter had to play the Mariners rather than the AL-best Indians. The Yankees were 15 games over .500, 4 games up on the Orioles. They were winning with small ball and with a cast deeper than an Altman movie. Torre had made the clubhouse a home, extinguished fires quickly with his Calm Bombs, and established a manner the Yankees were playing by—respectful, serious, all out—that was gaining them admirers.

So why was George Steinbrenner still so unhappy?

8 | THE IMPERFECTION
OF POWER

"There is no doubt about it, George likes home runs."
—*Joe Torre*

Joe Torre put a ball signed by all of his players, his cap, and the lineup card from the first game of the doubleheader in Cleveland, the last game ever watched by Rocco, into his oldest brother's casket.

While Torre attended Rocco's funeral, Bob Watson felt it proper to follow the team from Cleveland to Minnesota, just in case any issues arose. Watson was 6 miles from Darryl Strawberry, the distance from the Minneapolis Metrodome to St. Paul's Midway Stadium. A 10-minute drive. It might as well have been Earth to Pluto. Strawberry was tearing up the Northern League as a member of the St. Paul Saints, but Watson refused to even watch Strawberry. He finally grew so exasperated by reporters' persistent questions that he famously blurted his explanation: "He doesn't fit, he doesn't fit, he doesn't fit, he doesn't fit, he doesn't fit."

Yankee executives in New York familiar with life under Steinbrenner read the quote and were stunned. Of the many tacit rules under the Boss, one clearly was never—*never*—publicly reject a player Steinbrenner liked. Watson should have known better. He had been in many meetings in which Steinbrenner harrumphed, "We are not winning in Yankee style. These are not the Bronx Bombers." Strawberry's name had come up often at these meetings. He also knew Steinbrenner had ordered the signing of Strawberry the previous season against the protest of President Clinton's drug czar, Lee Brown, and was not fully supportive of one of Watson's first calls as general manager: to cut ties with Strawberry. The Yankees had a $1.8 million option for 1996, and Strawberry gave the team a 30-day extension so they could watch him play the outfield for the Santurce Crabbers in the Puerto Rican Winter League. But when the Yankees asked for a second extension in early December 1995, Strawberry refused, and Watson determined that the organization did not need a troubled player with questionable ability to play the outfield. Watson was equally concerned about how much Strawberry had left in a body damaged by years of cocaine and alcohol abuse, not to mention 5 years away from regular major league action. Watson's concerns had not changed, and he was quoted numerous times in numerous forums saying he had no interest whatsoever in Strawberry.

But Steinbrenner was now basking in the apologies of all those who had belittled his unpopular choices of Torre and Gooden. The glorious success of his manager and rehabbed starter elated Steinbrenner, who so badly wanted to be taken seriously as a real baseball man. His sense of entitlement expanded. What did his front office know? He could do this by himself. Nevertheless, it took even more of that eerie tonic of fortune and timeliness that so blessed the 1996 Yankees to fully explain how Strawberry came to the team.

Overshadowed by a terrorist truck bomb attack on the Khobar Towers apartment complex in Saudi Arabia that left 19 US servicemen dead, the Yankees returned from Minnesota to split a four-game home set with the Orioles from June 27 to 30. The 4½-game lead was the Yankees' largest at that point in a season in 16 years. But the Orioles had out-homered the Yankees five to one in the series and were ahead 120 to 67 for the season. Only the Twins and Royals had hit fewer homers in the American League than the Yankees. Steinbrenner just was not comfortable with Torre's National League style, especially not in this, the Year of the Homer. Maybe, Steinbrenner figured, the lack of the alluring long ball explained why attendance was off. This team simply did not have a Reggie Jackson, someone whose mere magnetism in the batter's box exuded can't-take-your-eyes-off-him power.

Marvin Goldklang had become one of Steinbrenner's limited partners not long after Jackson had helped the Yankees win a second straight title in 1978. He also owned the St. Paul Saints. Strawberry migrated to the Saints through a trail of misery and desperation. In a headstrong outburst after the Yankees declined his option, Strawberry departed Puerto Rico against the wishes of his agent, Bill Goodstein, one of the few remaining members of a tiny inner circle that still cared about him. Over the next 2 months, that inner circle would shrink further when both Goodstein and Strawberry's beloved mother, Ruby, died. Strawberry was more isolated than ever, feeling blackballed from the game and facing mounting legal troubles when, atop a 60-day home-confinement sentence for tax evasion, he also missed a deadline to pay $300,000 in overdue child and spousal support. That delinquency forced a court commissioner in Los Angeles to establish a July 5 trial date. Strawberry was 34 years old. He had questionable knees and a dubious back. He was an addict, a tax cheat, a deadbeat dad. He had 17 major league homers over the previous 4 years. He had left a few previous employers wishing they had never even heard his name. He was as big a risk as you could find in professional baseball.

Red Sox GM Dan Duquette, for example, was curious about Strawberry. His interest grew when his new catcher and Strawberry's 1995 Yankee team-mate, Mike Stanley, strongly endorsed Strawberry as a player and a person. But just the whiff of Red Sox involvement unleashed a media and fan backlash that moved Boston chief operating officer John Harrington to eliminate the Strawberry option. The St. Paul Saints, however, were Strawberry's kind of team. The comic actor Bill Murray was one of the owners. The team president was Mike Veeck, who, like his father, Bill, the onetime White Sox owner, favored fan-friendly theatrics at the ballpark. For example, the Saints had a pig named Tobias deliver fresh baseballs to the home-plate umpire. But to Strawberry, this was not a publicity stunt. This was his most recent last chance, and so the most important executive for him was Marvin Goldklang because Goldklang had ties to the Yankees.

Goldklang was leery at first about enlisting Strawberry, even for the puny $2,000-a-month salary. But Goldklang warmed quickly to Strawberry, finding him sincere about his sobriety and kind to everyone from teammates to fans. And Strawberry still had elite bat speed as he produced a Northern

League–leading 18 homers in just 29 games and a .435 batting average. Impressed, Goldklang told Strawberry, "Keep your life under control, and you will be back with Doc [Gooden] by summer." Behind the scenes, Goldklang was trying to make that happen with regular phone calls to Steinbrenner. So when the two men did see each other during the Oriole series in Steinbrenner's owner's box, the Boss knew what the subject would be, and his hunger for home-run power made him susceptible to Goldklang's pitch. "Okay, we'll bring him back," Steinbrenner told Goldklang, "but if he screws up, it's your ass."

"He looked into my eyes and asked for my word on Darryl being a model citizen," Goldklang remembers. Because this had to be a Steinbrenner decision, Goldklang contends, Strawberry almost certainly would not have been a Yankee if there had been no personal relationship between himself and the Boss.

Steinbrenner's choice left Watson publicly humiliated. He had to act as if he had changed his mind and actually wanted Strawberry. Watson had been working to meet Steinbrenner's demands for more power. Talks went nowhere with Oakland about Mark McGwire and a young lefty first baseman/third baseman he liked named Jason Giambi. That was fine with Watson because he had been preoccupied since spring training by Detroit's Cecil Fielder. In March, Tigers GM Randy Smith told Watson he was not trading the club's marquee player. In early June, just a week after Torre first asked Watson to purge Ruben Sierra, Watson met face-to-face with Smith in the Tiger Stadium lunchroom and broached a Sierra-for-Fielder deal. The Tigers were en route to a then-franchise record 109 losses, so Smith was more amenable to dealing his most expensive player, Fielder, who was due $7.2 million in both 1996 and 1997. But Smith wanted to rebuild, so he had no desire for Sierra.

A year and a half earlier—when Watson was still GM of the Astros and Smith was San Diego's GM—the two had arranged the largest trade in 37 years, a 12-player blockbuster in which Ken Caminiti and Steve Finley went to the Padres. The two men were linked further because Randy Smith's father, Tal, had been the Astros' president when Watson was named the first-ever African-American GM in major league history. Yet, with all of their ties, they could not find common ground. Smith asked Watson to also take another expensive contract in Chad Curtis. Watson refused. Watson agreed to include touted pitching prospect Matt Drews, but not Brian Boehringer, Jim Mecir, Ricky Ledee, or Gerald Williams. Blocked on Fielder, Watson obtained Mike Aldrete from the Angels on June 12 for Rich Monteleone. But Aldrete was a journeyman bench player, not anyone's idea of a slugger. So Watson simply had to accept the indignity of having Strawberry shoved onto the roster against his wishes.

"Joe [Molloy] and I were supposed to be running the club, but George was getting more and more involved," Watson says, looking back. "It made me think that this man has had a serious change of heart from October, when he said he was stepping back [as a sales pitch to hire Watson]. The Strawberry flap, though, was the first time I knew I was something less than the GM."

Still, Watson was not the most upset Yankee executive. In June 1980, as manager of the Mets, Joe Torre had advised his new GM, Frank Cashen, to take the best player available with the first overall draft pick and ignore talk of high school problems for the obvious top prospect. Cashen did take that phenom out of Crenshaw High, Darryl Strawberry. But Cashen had also been quite adamant in recent years that the drug addiction and downward spiral of Strawberry and Gooden, more than any other factor, had cost the Mets a dynasty. They won it all in 1986, but never again. Now, 10 years later, Torre was being told he would have to manage both men, not to mention the cranky Ruben Sierra. Gooden had not been much of a problem, to date, but why risk disruptions, Torre thought. He knew how fragile these types of players were. Just 2 days after he was released by the Yankees, Steve Howe had been arrested at Kennedy Airport for carrying a loaded .357 Magnum revolver in his luggage for his flight home to Montana.

"I was worried about the trouble associated with Darryl, and I told Bob, 'I don't want him; I like the makeup of my team,'" Torre says. But when it became inevitable that only one voice mattered in this organization, and that one voice wanted Strawberry, Torre went to a no-nonsense veteran and asked Paul O'Neill about playing with Strawberry in 1995. Torre was shocked when O'Neill reported that Strawberry was a great teammate who had caused no difficulties the year before, even when Buck Showalter shunned him late in the year and in the postseason.

The science-fiction thriller *Independence Day* was released on July 2, en route to becoming the largest-grossing motion picture of 1996. But the major theatrics of the week came on the actual Independence Day, July 4, when Steinbrenner presented himself a present for his 66th birthday, signing Strawberry to a contract that immediately enabled the slugger to pay off his back child and spousal support. Strawberry was assigned to Triple-A Columbus with the idea that he would join the team to start the second half of the season. But Strawberry homered three times in his first two minor league games, and Torre requested he be brought to Yankee Stadium to play on July 7, the game before the All-Star break. The Yankees opened the second half with four games in Camden Yards, and Torre hoped that by introducing Strawberry in New York, it would lessen the media storm around a Yankee-Oriole series. So Strawberry was promoted, and a seldom-used third-string catcher named Jorge Posada, who had been yo-yoing between New York and Columbus, was optioned back to Triple-A.

Two opinions about Strawberry formed around the Yankees right away. "He had a lot left," Joe Girardi says. Tino Martinez adds, "He was a great teammate." Despite all the drugs and drink and trauma, Strawberry simply could not destroy his body. In a cut-off T-shirt, you could see the name "Lisa" in script on his left triceps, a remnant of his destructive first marriage. But you could also see his left triceps, right triceps, and both biceps, bulging reminders that Strawberry still projected 6 feet, 6 inches of world-class might.

And then, as always, there was his swing. He might have found the Bible, but the door to the majors stayed open because Strawberry never lost that explosive arc that once made onlookers think they were watching the next Ted

Williams. Strawberry's must-see batting practices were a reminder that life, not talent, had derailed his Hall of Fame path. Teammates and opponents gathered around the batting cage to marvel at the distances Strawberry could reach. There was majesty to his shots, rainbows into the upper deck, lasers into the center-field black. "It was amazing how smoothly he hit the ball and it took off," Mariano Rivera says. "It was like he tapped it, and it went into the upper deck." Strawberry was instantly the most menacing presence in the Yankee lineup, regardless of the emptiness of his recent baseball career.

Just as O'Neill promised, Strawberry only enhanced the Yankees' excellent clubhouse chemistry. Strawberry without rancor abided by Torre's decisions, whether it was to use him in the outfield, as the designated hitter, or not at all. Sierra's playing time dwindled further with Strawberry around, but aside from his pal Mariano Duncan, the rest of the clubhouse had grown weary of Sierra's griping. Sierra was prone to telling any teammate who would listen about his career credentials. But that was in the past. This was 1996, and it was more and more obvious that Sierra could not help the club. This roster was too mature, too focused, to let Sierra infect it with discontent. And Strawberry was immediately part of that maturity, his seen-the-gutter wisdom helping no one more than Derek Jeter.

Jeter had played briefly at Triple-A in 1995 with Strawberry and liked him immediately. By midseason of 1996, with his instant success and youthful good looks, Jeter had become the heartthrob of New York. Later that summer, John F. Kennedy Jr. married Carolyn Bessette, and Jeter became widely known as the most eligible bachelor in the Big Apple. Perhaps nobody on the planet understood that quick rise in New York, and the lurking evils associated with it, quite like Strawberry. "He was like a big brother to me," Jeter remembers. "He was a guy who made mistakes and turned it into a positive by helping someone else."

The infighting Orioles actually needed, of all things, Strawberry's level-headedness even more than his bat. And, before the Yankees signed Strawberry, the Orioles were diligently courting him behind the scenes, hoping to reunite the slugger with his former Mets manager, Davey Johnson. "We were right there in the running," then Orioles assistant GM Kevin Malone recalls. "But his New York connection was just too much to overcome."

However, the fates of the Yankees and Orioles from 1996 forward were not determined by the signing of Strawberry on July 4. The key decision that would bring dynasty to one and misery to the other had been made 4 years earlier.

John McMullen had been a limited partner of the Steinbrenner Yankees from 1974 to 1979, and famously said of Steinbrenner's domineering style, "There's nothing more limited than being a limited partner of George Steinbrenner." Yet McMullen was enthralled by how owning a baseball team had turned Steinbrenner from just another millionaire into a celebrity. McMullen wanted into that society and purchased the Astros on May 10, 1979. He stormed in with a Steinbrenneresque flourish, signing Texas's favorite son, Nolan Ryan, to the first-ever million-dollar-a-year contract. Under McMullen, the Astros peaked in 1986, winning the National League West before losing a dramatic, six-game playoff series to the Darryl Strawberry/Dwight Gooden Mets.

That Astro core grew older, expensive, and ineffective together, and following the 1990 season, McMullen ordered a cost-reducing rebuilding program. Then GM Bill Wood oversaw a 12-month roster gutting, and the Astros finished with a National League–worst 97 losses in 1991, earning the first overall pick in the June 1992 draft. Hal Newhouser, the Hall of Fame lefthander, was an Astro scout in Michigan who was to turn 71 that May. He was ready to retire 2 years earlier, but he'd seen this skinny sophomore at Kalamazoo Central High, and this shortstop had so captivated him that he decided to stay on through Derek Jeter's draft class in 1992. Newhouser could not believe his luck that the Astros were so horrible in 1991 that they had no obstruction to draft this player.

As a senior, Jeter hit .508 and was 12 for 12 in steal tries. But more than talent stirred Newhouser's baseball soul. In the upper Midwest, high school seasons were abbreviated (Jeter had just 59 at-bats his senior year) because weather was cold and fields were of questionable condition. Yet it took only a few games—heck, a few innings—for Newhouser to see Jeter's intensity. Not in the habit of gushing, Newhouser summed up this player in his report to then Houston scouting director Dan O'Brien this way: "Derek Jeter gets it."

But John McMullen did not. He was, in many ways, the George Steinbrenner of the Southwest. In spring training 1992, not even 18 months after telling Bill Wood to rebuild, he impetuously reversed course. It was time to win again.

"McMullen felt we had to turn the timetable up," Wood recalls. "As a result, going into that draft, we were going to pick a guy that would be quick to the big leagues, as opposed to what we would have done if we were still in a rebuilding situation. Jeter very much was on our radar screen. Hal Newhouser was really strong for him. But we no longer thought we could take a high school player who would take a long time to reach the majors."

The Astros knew more about Cal State Fullerton third baseman Phil Nevin than any other draft eligible. Their West Coast regional scout, Ross Sapp, had managed Nevin as a high schooler for the Astros' scout team in Southern California. Sapp had been part of the 1963 Los Angeles high school champion Fremont High team that had future major league outfielders Willie Crawford and Bobby Tolan. Sapp pitched on that team to a catcher who was his best friend, a guy named Bob Watson. Watson was the Astros' assistant GM in 1992. He, Sapp, and most others in the organization agreed that Stanford outfielder Jeffrey Hammonds was the best draft-eligible player. But Hammonds had told the Astros in a predraft meeting that he had "a very—and underline *very*—strong preference to play on the East Coast. Let's say the message was delivered," O'Brien recalls.

To others, that message was sent in a less personal way. Though amateurs were not supposed to have agents acting as anything more than family advisors, Hammonds's representative, Jeff Moorad, sent letters to the Indians, Expos, and Reds, warning against selecting his client, according to executives from those clubs. Hammonds was from Scotch Plains, New Jersey, and Moorad wanted to steer him to a deep-pocketed East Coast team, the Orioles picking fourth or the Yankees selecting sixth in the June 1 draft. The Astros surmised Nevin needed 2 years of minor league seasoning, then could replace their third baseman, Ken Caminiti. So a day before the College World Series in Omaha, Nebraska, began on May 29, Sapp signed Nevin to a $700,000 contract. Newhouser, despondent that the Astros would not be taking the prospect of his dreams, retired and never worked in baseball again.

The Indians, selecting second, never wavered in their zeal for Paul Shuey's fastball and selected the University of North Carolina right-hander. In 1991, the Yankees had the top pick overall and drafted North Carolina schoolboy left-hander Brien Taylor. Advised by the precedent-busting Scott Boras, Taylor followed a prolonged and, at times, nasty negotiation by signing a draft record $1.55 million bonus. That deal further motivated teams to emphasize "signability," the need to know beforehand whether a desired player would agree at affordable dollars. The financially challenged Expos picked third, and their scouting director at the time, Kevin Malone, says his club loved Jeter. But Jeter had twisted his right ankle crossing first base on a snowy day in April of his senior season, an injury that hindered his play somewhat. That, Malone explained, worried Montreal. More troublesome, though, was that Jeter had a free ride to play for former Detroit Tigers star catcher Bill Freehan at the University of Michigan, giving him negotiating leverage. "We had to find someone who would be no trouble signing, and in our opinion we didn't know if we could afford Derek," Malone says. So the Expos, with $550,000 budgeted for the pick, surprisingly opted for Mississippi State University left-hander B. J. Wallace.

"We always had been high school oriented, but that particular year the emphasis was on money and signability," Malone remembers. "And even more than Jeter, Hammonds was the key to the whole draft. We felt Hammonds was our guy. But the letter . . ."

The Orioles had no such worries about signability or Moorad's letter. They were flush, thanks to the windfall from the opening of Camden Yards. In addition, they had an iron-man shortstop in his prime, Cal Ripken, so it was easy to bypass the skinny shortstop from Kalamazoo. Besides, under team president Larry Lucchino, the Orioles were successfully drafting college players in the first round: Gregg Olson in 1988, Ben McDonald in 1989, Mike Mussina in 1990, and Mark Smith in 1991. Former major leaguer Ed Sprague Sr. scouted the West Coast for the Orioles. His son, Ed Jr., had starred at Stanford on a team with Mussina, who later played with Hammonds. In 1992, Mussina, in his first full season, was already Baltimore's ace. So the Orioles chose Hammonds, whom they saw as a Marquis Grissom clone, and met his asking price of $975,000 — the second-largest bonus ever behind Brien Taylor.

Jeter was born in Pequannock, New Jersey, lived briefly in New Milford, New Jersey, and grew up in Kalamazoo. But for 12 straight summers he returned to his grandparents' home in New Milford, developing a love for the Yankees and a plan for his life. Before he was even a teenager, Jeter was telling family and classmates that one day he would be the starting shortstop for the New York Yankees. How amazing, then, that Jeter was unaware that the Yankees picked sixth. He had been told incessantly by friends, coaches, scouts, and media people that if Hal Newhouser did not get his wish with the top overall pick, then Gene Bennett was going to make sure Cincinnati tabbed Jeter with the fifth selection.

When Bennett, a special advisor to the GM, eyeballed Jeter for the first time, he instantly compared him to a player he had scouted and signed for Cincinnati with the fourth overall pick in the 1985 draft. Gene Bennett saw Barry Larkin. Larkin, like Ripken, was in his prime. He was the National League's best shortstop, 2 years earlier having starred on a World Series champion that had two other instrumental players scouted and signed by Bennett, Chris Sabo and Paul O'Neill. Bennett thought Jeter such a great athlete that he would play center field until Larkin retired. "I talked to Jeter's mom and dad about signing with the Reds, the whole ball of wax," Bennett recalls. "At the time, he would have been very happy to play for the Reds. He was our No. 1 guy."

Bennett knew then scouting director Julian Mock had seen Jeter play only once as a senior, and Jeter was nursing his twisted ankle and did not play well.

He also knew Mock fixated on tools, and University of Central Florida out-fielder Chad Mottola was 6-foot-3 and 200 pounds of power arm, power bat, and power legs.

Still, Bennett insists he firmly believed the organizational priority was Jeter, and when he walked in the draft room and heard Mottola's name being said into the phone, he initially thought it was a joke to rib him. "I laughed to go along with it," Bennett explains. "But then they came back on the speakerphone and said the New York Yankees were up. I said, 'That's the real thing.'"

Jim Bowden was elevated from director of player development $4\frac{1}{2}$ months later to become, at age 31, the majors' youngest GM ever. He served the Reds for $10\frac{1}{2}$ years in that capacity before being fired, and said with a laugh nearly a decade later, "I'm still working there if we take Jeter."

At the Yankees' draft headquarters, there was apprehension about their top choice reaching the sixth pick. Dick Groch was the Yankees' Hal Newhouser and Gene Bennett. He was Jeter's champion as their Michigan area scout. Groch worried somewhat about an "ugly" inside-out hitting stroke, "not the kind you want to see in an amateur player," he says. He, too, contemplated that Jeter might ultimately end up in center field: "I knew he was a player, but not what kind of player." However, it was 1992, and baseball had not yet demanded its shortstops and center fielders be offensive mainstays. There was something about how Jeter could still get on top of enough high fastballs, even with that funky swing, that made Groch believe he would hit in the majors. Bill Livesey, who ran the Yankee minor league system, had watched Jeter enough in batting practice while scouting him to see that "he could really get the bat around, and I believed that meant he would show some power in the majors."

Under Livesey's stewardship, the Yankees prized athletes and character in the draft, and in these areas, Groch saw all his reservations dissolve. "Forget baseball," he explains. "Just watch the athlete. It is the difference between going to a harness race at the county fair and the Kentucky Derby. That is what Derek had. His moves were easy, electric, refined."

Groch had also been intoxicated by Jeter's home life and intellect. The

Jeters' backyard fence was in right-center field at Kalamazoo Central High, and Groch recalls seeing the whole family pour out onto the field one day—his mother, Dorothy; sister, Sharlee; and father, Charles—to help Jeter take batting practice. In addition, Jeter ranked 21st in a class of 285 with a 3.82 grade point average and was a member of the National Honor Society. He had stable friends and, as then Orioles scouting director Gary Nickles recounts, "he was a coach on the field. He took charge. You just get a feeling for guys who think what is happening in the game is their responsibility."

The Yankee litmus test, Groch said, was in order: 1. Can the kid be a pro? 2. Can he be a major leaguer? 3. Can he be a Yankee? "The third question was most important," Groch says. And he had no doubt. When Livesey worried the day before the draft that Jeter might take the scholarship to Michigan, Groch had none of the reservations that froze Montreal's Kevin Malone. "He's not going to Michigan," Groch told Livesey. "He's going to Cooperstown."

Livesey was an easy convert. He had been part of a contingent of Yankee executives who had eyed Jeter during the shortstop's senior season. Uniformly they came to a decision. As June 1, 1992, approached, the Yankees liked the projectable, big body of Kenny Felder of Florida State University. A football background always juiced Steinbrenner, and so Ron Villone, a tight end/pitcher double letterman out of the University of Massachusetts, was considered. The Yankee scouts were split on Charles Johnson, the University of Miami catcher.

In the end, the Yankees distanced two players from all others: Jeter and Jeffrey Hammonds. It was just that even with Deion Sanders having fled the organization to return to football, the Yankees were already blessed with athletic center fielders similar to Hammonds throughout the system. Roberto Kelly was in the majors. Bernie Williams and Gerald Williams were at Triple-A. Carl Everett was working his way through A-ball. And readying to jump from the Yankees' Dominican program to the Gulf Coast League was the center fielder the Yankees already thought would be the best of the bunch, Mariano Rivera's cousin, Ruben.

As the draft neared, the Yankees believed Baltimore was not going to let Hammonds escape. The problem, the Yankees knew, was Houston with the first pick and the Reds at five. Because of that, the Yankees formed an alternative plan: Jim Pittsley out of DuBois Area High School in Pennsylvania. "We were very hopeful, but we were not very enthusiastic about Jeter being there," Livesey remembers.

But the Astros took Nevin, who failed to assume third base when Watson traded Ken Caminiti away in that 12-player deal with Randy Smith. By mid-season 1996, Nevin was trying to transform into a catcher for the Tigers. The Reds took Chad Mottola, who played briefly for the Reds in 1996 and then not again in the majors until 2000, never amounting to more than a Quadruple-A-type player. Paul Shuey never became the closer the Indians imagined, and B. J. Wallace never even played in the majors. Jim Pittsley was taken 17th by the Royals, the first high school pitcher selected in 1992, and was out of baseball by 1999. Hammonds had been the first member of the 1992 draft class to reach the majors, ascending the following season, and was the Orioles' Opening Day left fielder in 1996. But injuries, poor pitch recognition, and questions about mental fortitude undermined Hammonds, and on June 16, 1996, he was demoted to Triple-A Rochester.

"Jeffrey Hammonds had all the tools, but the passion for success was minimal," Malone explains. "He didn't seem to want to pay the price. He was happy being good enough. It takes a real commitment and desire to want to excel. It just wasn't that important to him. He made some money, but he had all the tools to be a big-time player. As we call it in the business, he didn't have the necessary makeup to be a star."

As Dick Groch promised, Jeter's makeup was off the charts. Jeter yearned to be great. So while Jeffrey Hammonds was not present at Camden Yards when the second half of the 1996 season began, Derek Jeter was.

Jeter fell behind Mike Mussina 0–2 with one out and Mariano Duncan on second base in the eighth inning. The score was 2–2 in the first game following the All-Star break. Hammonds might not have learned much about reading pitchers in the majors, but Jeter, despite being 3 years younger, was attentive. In his first two at-bats and in these first two pitches, he noticed he had received nothing but fastballs from the Orioles' ace. Jeter always thought fastball anyway; that was simply part of his aggressive nature. But even more than normal he dismissed any other possibility here because of Mussina's pattern. Sure enough, Mussina threw a high heater, and Jeter crushed a towering shot to left-center, 393 feet. As Bill Livesey had projected, there would be some power. Jeter's fifth homer of the year already matched his minor league high. It also gave the Yankees their winning 4-2 margin, though by the end of the night, the concentration of New York sports fans would be elsewhere. In the seventh round of a heavyweight-title fight at Madison Square Garden, challenger Andrew Golota was disqualified for continuous low blows against champion Riddick Bowe, setting off a chair-throwing melee in the ring and crowd that resulted in 17 arrests.

The next night, the Yankees won the second game of the series 3-2 when the unheralded trio of Gerald Williams, Joe Girardi, and Mariano Duncan keyed a two-run, ninth-inning rally against David Wells. That accentuated that the Yankees' team-wide effort was outdoing the star system employed by the Orioles. In the third game, Strawberry announced his return by homering twice to make a winner of Dwight Gooden in the first game they had played in together as teammates since September 23, 1990. A Girardi squeeze bunt that scored Strawberry—Joe Torre's style combined with George Steinbrenner's man—highlighted the sweep-clinching 4-1 victory.

The disgrace for Baltimore extended to the crowd, where Yankee fans had loudly invaded the park by the thousands, giving Steinbrenner for a few days what he so desired—a new stadium, albeit 175 miles south. During the finale, Orioles president Joe Foss gathered the media to urge the team's season-ticket holders to stop selling their seats to Yankee fans. John Wetteland saved all four games, moving his major league record for saves in consecutive appearances to 24. As the closer finished off Gregg Zaun on July 14, a majority of the crowd stood and applauded the Yankees' sweep. The Yankees improved to 56–33, a few percentage points better than Atlanta for the majors' best record. The division lead was now a major league–best 10 games. The Orioles were 46–43 and their problems went well beyond their record.

The Yankees had used 11 rookies in the first half and, most important, Jeter and second-year men Mariano Rivera and Andy Pettitte were already fully formed stars. They provided ready-made, inexpensive solutions in key areas and, vitally, were so good that they were beyond Steinbrenner's knee-jerk penchant for not trusting young players and demanding they be sacrificed for bigger names. They also fit the spirit of what Torre wanted. Jeter, Pettitte, and Rivera valued winning and, despite their quick success, espoused team over self. Jeter called his manager "Mr. Torre," and that exemplified an adult clubhouse. The shortstop of the Orioles, a month from his 36th birthday, was not quite so respectful of his manager.

The trouble that began brewing back when Davey Johnson pinch-ran for Cal Ripken in the May 1 loss to the Yankees at Camden Yards had only grown. One reason Orioles owner Peter Angelos had enlisted Johnson was to try to bring the cult of Ripken under control. But he was having no success with Ripken, his followers, or the team as a whole. Roberto Alomar, Brady Anderson, Bobby Bonilla, and Rafael Palmeiro infrequently ran groundballs out with any hustle. Alomar, who did not start the last game of the first half because of an injured finger, refused Johnson's request not to play in the All-Star Game. Bonilla, who was in the final season of the 5-year, $29 million contract the Mets had foolishly given him when they realized they had to replace Strawberry's power, was still taking potshots at Johnson. But the Ripken issue was most debilitating to the Orioles. In a Steinbrenner-type move in late June, Angelos asked his media-relations department to have reporters call him after he had read that Ripken said the team needed more time to "jell." Angelos told the Baltimore-area media, "The truth is the team is in desperate need of leadership on the field and in the clubhouse, and no one is more qualified to provide it than Cal Ripken.

If Cal accepted the challenge with as much zeal as he plays, there is no question the Orioles would reach their potential."

But it was not in Ripken's personality to lead overtly. He had an unwavering belief that he knew better than his managers and coaches what to do; in fact, Johnson had to stop Ripken from calling pitches from shortstop when his pal Chris Hoiles caught. Mostly, what Ripken believed without doubt was that the best Oriole team had his name in the lineup at shortstop every day. Johnson, however, thought that this iron-man ethos had gone on too long and that the graying Ripken's range had become limited. Johnson decided it would be incendiary in Baltimore to break Ripken's consecutive game streak. But with Jeffrey Hammonds gone and the Oriole player-development system mostly a wasteland, shortstop Manny Alexander stood out as the only way to inject youth into the lethargy of Baltimore's everyday lineup. Johnson hinted for months about moving Ripken to third base. Finally, the day after the Yankees left town, Johnson put Alexander at short, and, for the first time since June 30, 1982, Ripken started in a different position, moving to third. Ripken did not hide his disgust. And fighting Ripken in Baltimore was futile, a waste of time and energy. B. J. Surhoff says, looking back, "I don't think Davey handled us real well. Davey felt he needed to put his mark on the team."

It's amazing to remember that just a few months earlier, Johnson had come to his job as a World Series–winning player and manager, while Torre was one of the game's great losers. Yet, through the professionalism of his players and his honest communication, Torre could use rookie Andy Fox to play defense for Gold Glove third baseman Wade Boggs late in a game and not even stir a raised eyebrow in his clubhouse. Johnson learned he had none of the same cooperative spirit in Baltimore, especially with Ripken. At any point, Ripken could have embraced his manager and unified the club. Instead, the steely willpower that enabled Ripken to play day after day made him inflexible to believe that anyone knew what was better for the team than he did. His defenders among the fans and media and in the clubhouse only hardened in their support.

"It had always been Cal Ripken's team," Kevin Malone says. "Davey Johnson was determined to prove it wasn't Cal Ripken's team. And there were some undercurrents there, whose side you were on: Cal's or Davey's. It was uncomfortable."

Frozen out by Ripken and his formidable coalition, Alexander wilted. In six games as the starting shortstop, he had one hit in 18 at-bats and committed two errors. Davey Johnson put Cal Ripken back at shortstop. It took him 4 months to fully understand who was running the Baltimore Orioles and to recognize a fight that couldn't be won. Johnson surrendered in trying to make the 1996 Orioles his team.

With the sweep of the Orioles complete, the Yankees felt like a footnote throughout the remainder of the month. New York was aghast on July 17 when a Paris-bound 747, TWA Flight 800, exploded shortly after takeoff from JFK International Airport, killing all 230 people aboard, strewing debris along the Long Island coastline, and unleashing conspiracy theories that the Boeing jet was blown out of the sky by a missile. Two days later, spirits were somewhat restored when Muhammad Ali, his hand shaking from the ravages of Parkinson's disease, amazed a world audience by lighting the cauldron to open the Atlanta Olympics. Over the next 16 days, Michael Johnson set a world record in the 200 meters; Carl Lewis had a golden farewell by winning the long jump; and 18-year-old Kerri Strug became an American hero by nailing her landing on a vault despite a dislocated ankle, giving the US women's gymnastics team the gold medal. But the Summer Games—and the globe—were shaken early in the morning of July 27, when a bomb exploded in Centennial Park, killing one person and injuring 11 others. The world learned that Joe Klein was Anonymous, the initially secret author of *Primary Colors*.

Even a dramatic, historic moment from Darryl Strawberry did not have quite the same resonance. On July 28, Strawberry pushed the Yankees' lead over the Orioles to a season-high 12 games with a walk-off, two-run homer against Kansas City lefty Jason Jacome. It was the 300th homer of his career. It also was somewhat incongruous: Strawberry was not really helping the Yankees address their great shortcoming against lefty pitching, a deficiency known league-wide. The Red Sox moved Jamie Moyer from the bullpen to the rotation just to start against the Yankees. A Royals rookie named Jose Rosado won his first major league game on July 25, with $7\frac{2}{3}$ scoreless innings in a 7–0 Kansas City triumph at Yankee Stadium. It was the first time the Yankees had been shut out at home in 117 games.

The Yankees were feeling good about their chances of making the playoffs, but they saw where they could easily be exploited come October. The post-season was preprogrammed again, and the AL East champ was going to face the AL West champ. The Yankees already had well-established problems winning at either the Seattle Kingdome or The Ballpark at Arlington, and the Mariners and Rangers were vying for the AL West crown. If that weren't bad enough, Bob Watson deciphered the early maneuverings at the July 31 nonwaiver trade deadline: The AL West's two top teams were arming themselves for the Yankees. Seattle added Moyer and Terry Mulholland, who, along with Sterling Hitchcock and, especially, Randy Johnson, potentially gave the Mariners four lefties to start should they reach the Division Series. The Rangers obtained lefty reliever Mike Stanton from the Red Sox, and Watson was watching on TV on the night of July 31 as Texas' Darren Oliver permitted two runs in seven innings, and the Yankees fell to 0–5 in Arlington in 1996 and 15–16 when any lefty started against them.

That is why Watson worked so hard in the hours leading up to the midnight deadline to get a righty power bat. Ruben Sierra was no longer an option. Switch-hitter Bernie Williams was a superb righty hitter, but there was no fear quotient when he batted. Watson had been working on Fielder for the 2 days before the deadline and, of all things, the Yankees were having money issues. They had signed a $486 million, 12-year deal with Cablevision to air their games on the Madison Square Garden Network beginning in 1989. But David

Sussman, the longtime Yankee executive, says that created a myth that the organization was awash in cash. The truth is Steinbrenner received a good deal of the money up front, and those dollars were gone. The Yankees had won no championships in 18 years. They did not have a new stadium with multiple financial streams. Their attendance was middle of the pack. The Yankees were not the cash cow they would become. It was Madison Square Garden itself that was exhibiting deep pockets. In the past 10 days, the New York Knicks had signed free agents Allan Houston and Chris Childs and traded for Larry Johnson. The Rangers had signed free agent Wayne Gretzky.

So even when Randy Smith agreed to take Ruben Sierra as the price for receiving the Yankees' top pitching prospect, Matt Drews, the deal making was not done. Smith was willing to move Fielder because he had a big, young first baseman named Tony Clark ready to step in. But, he said, he had to have $1 million to offset some of the $11.7 million Sierra was due between 1996 and 1997. And Fielder was the majors' highest-paid player, owed $14.4 million between the two seasons. The Yankees decided the only way to get this done was if Fielder agreed to defer $2 million until 2000–01, which he did to escape last-place Detroit. Watson found George Steinbrenner at the Atlanta Olympics, where he was serving as a vice president of the US Olympic Committee, and received final approval for this trade. He then completed the deal with Smith. Seventy minutes before the trade deadline, Fielder moved from 29 games out of first place with the Tigers to 10 games in front with the Yankees. No wonder he smiled so broadly with the news. "I needed rejuvenation," Fielder said of his journey from hopelessness to first place. "I needed it to be fun again."

Still, the next morning, when Sussman informed the Yankees' chief financial officer, Barry Pincus, what a small group of team officials—Sussman, Watson, Steinbrenner, and assistant GM Brian Cashman—had done the night before despite the lack of cash flow, Pincus responded, "Are you fucking crazy? How can we afford this? The only way we can afford this is if Fielder eats the other players on our team."

Shortly after dealing for Fielder—and just before the midnight deadline—

the Yankees believed they had further solidified their fifth starter spot by dealing Steinbrenner favorite—but undependable—Mark Hutton to Florida for David Weathers. Gene Michael had authored positive reports on Weathers. The Yankees had also used a secret source, Mel Stottlemyre's son, Todd, who had been Weathers's Blue Jay teammate in the early 1990s. He gave a strong endorsement to his father. But the big trade, obviously, was Fielder. It removed the unhappiest and least productive member of the Yankee clubhouse, Sierra, and brought in a legitimate righty power threat. It also sent a resounding message through the roster, Girardi says, "that we felt the people upstairs were telling us all, 'We are going for it this year.'"

On August 6, it felt as if every element was in place for the Yankees as they opened a period in which they played 16 of 19 games at home. In midafternoon, David Cone threw off a mound for the first time in 96 days, a 58-pitch session so encouraging that Cone was now talking about returning even before a September 6 projection, and no one was disputing him. Fielder, who had already homered twice on the road, received a sustained standing ovation to greet his first at-bat at Yankee Stadium since the trade. And Strawberry responded to batting as low as seventh for the first time in his career by homering three times off White Sox starter Kevin Tapani. Strawberry began the game batting .213 after sitting out two previous games. But with advice from hitting coach Chris Chambliss to move a little off the plate, he produced a three-homer game for the first time in 11 years and 1 day, providing symbolic bookends to a time when Strawberry lived on the back pages of the New York tabloids as both superstar and bum.

With a little more than 6 weeks left in the season, life around the Yankees could hardly have been grander. Fielder and Strawberry were meeting Steinbrenner's mandate for more power. A T-shirt was hanging in every locker emblazoned with the team motto conceived by Mariano Duncan: "We play today, we win today. Dat's it." And the Yankee lead over the Orioles stood at 10 games. It was easy to dismiss that Peter Angelos had channeled Steinbrenner at the trade deadline and quashed GM Pat Gillick's deals of Bobby Bonilla to

Cincinnati and David Wells to Seattle, both of which would have brought back prospects and started the Orioles thinking about a future with younger, more well-rounded players. Just as Steinbrenner had pledged to Bob Watson, Angelos had told Gillick he would have autonomy to run baseball operations. But Angelos was a meddler by nature and said it was wrong to the fans packing Camden Yards to surrender with 2 months left in the season. There would be no trading of veterans.

So Wells stayed and won his third straight start on August 5, Bonilla knocked in a run for a fourth straight game on August 6, and the club seemed happier overall as Davey Johnson no longer tried to impose his will on the roster. He acquiesced to a set lineup that had Bonilla in right field and Ripken at shortstop. Still, there were just 41 games left. There hardly seemed enough time for the Orioles to do anything but perhaps make a run at the wild card. Life was so cheery around the Yankees that few noticed that Joe Torre had not been around to watch Cone's bullpen session. The manager had to be at the airport, having finally convinced his gravely ill brother, Frank, to leave his hospital in Florida for the world-renowned cardiac-care program at Columbia-Presbyterian Medical Center.

9 | THE PERFECT STORM

"It was the dumbest thing I've ever done."
—*Andy Pettitte on signing professionally with the Yankees*

Andy Pettitte had been selected in the 22nd round of the June 1990 draft, a selection process that exemplified the excellent evaluating eye of that era's Yankee scouting department. The Yankees also picked Ricky Ledee in the 16th round, Kevin Jordan in the 20th, Jorge Posada in the 24th, and Shane Spencer in the 28th. At Deer Park (Texas) High School, Pettitte had been pudgy enough to be the football team's center on offense and nose guard on defense besides throwing a fastball of 85 to 87 miles per hour. Wayne Graham, who would go on to college fame as the coach of Rice University, recruited Pettitte to San Jacinto (Texas) Junior College by telling the youngster he was a lefty version of another San Jacinto alum, Roger Clemens. Pettitte was seduced. He had grown up idolizing Clemens and decided not to sign with the Yankees out of high school.

In their 1 year together, Graham rode Pettitte about getting into shape. During the summer of 1990, Pettitte went on an orange juice and tuna diet, ran regularly in a sweat-inducing plastic top, and lifted weights seriously for the first time. He found he loved to work out hard and lost 16 pounds, dropping to 212. More important, with the additional strength, Pettitte increased the speed of his fastball and pitched at between 91 and 93 mph. Joe Robison, the Yankee area scout who had followed Pettitte in high school, stayed on him at San Jacinto and was stunned by the increased velocity. He also knew the clock was ticking. If Pettitte had enrolled at a 4-year college, the Yankees would have immediately lost his rights. But at a junior college, Pettitte fell into the category known within the game as a draft-and-follow. That meant the Yankees had 51 weeks from the date of selection to sign Pettitte, until 1 week before the 1991 draft, midnight May 25, 1991.

The Yankees were offering $40,000. But Graham told Pettitte that another high school lefty prodigy from the Houston area, Justin Thompson, who threw no harder than Pettitte did, was due to go in the first round in 1991 and reach six figures in a signing bonus. Robison continued to badger Pettitte, so on May 25, 1991, Pettitte and his father, Tom, decided to escape to his grandmother Jenny Martello's house in Baton Rouge. "It was fortuitous," Tom Pettitte remembers, "because Mr. Robison happened to be at a tournament at LSU in Baton Rogue."

Robison invited the Pettittes to his room at the Hampton Inn. A few agonizing hours passed, during which Robison disappeared to call minor league head Bill Livesey each time a new proposal was even discussed. Robison finally offered $55,000, telling the Pettittes it was as far as the organization could go because some kids out of California still had to be signed. "I finally got sick of the whole process, and I just picked a number out of thin air," Pettitte recalls. "I said, 'If you give me $80,000 right now, I'll sign.' Robison didn't blink, didn't make another phone call; he just said yes. I was mad—suddenly he didn't have to make another call. I should have gotten more."

That night, over pasta prepared by Grandma Martello, Pettitte signed. If Pettitte had just waited a few more hours, he would no longer have been Yankee property. That is why he looks back with resentment at the process; he believes that he would then have been one of the first players selected in the 1991 draft and signed for more than $200,000. But to the Yankees' great thrill, he was in the fold. He soon became part of what Mark Newman remembers as near-weekly discussions among the Yankee minor league brass about which young starter had the highest ceiling: Sterling Hitchcock, Mariano Rivera, or Pettitte. A pecking order was established by the start of the 1995 season. Rivera was in the minors, and Hitchcock won a battle for the Yankees' fifth starter job against Pettitte, who was sent to the bullpen. A relief slot was open only because to begin that year, major league rosters had been expanded from 25 to 28 players to compensate for the shorter spring training following the strike. Pettitte had lost again and did not like it. Assistant trainer Steve Donohue remembers how the mild-mannered Pettitte "might have been more pissed than I've ever seen him" about the decision.

On May 16, Pettitte was demoted to Columbus so he could continue starting. His stay lasted just 11 days. He was promoted to replace Jimmy Key, who would ultimately need shoulder surgery. That was fitting. At Columbus, while others sat on the bench during home games in 1994, Pettitte watched Key's starts off the satellite in the clubhouse. Like Key, Pettitte was a lefty who in the minors relied heavily on his changeup. So he studied Key. He was looking for ways to win in a major league future.

Tom Pettitte's early memories of his son are about Andy's intolerance for anything short of victory. Pettitte's strongest defender in the organization was Tony Cloninger, who had worked with him as the organization's roving pitching coordinator in 1990–91. Cloninger also sensed the left-hander's relentless desire to succeed. Gene Michael turned down many trade requests based simply on that relationship, saying, "Tony Cloninger influenced me on Pettitte. He once told me Pettitte is a mentally tough guy that has big inspirations to be better than Hitchcock. He wanted to pass him in the organization."

Upon being recalled to the rotation, Pettitte determined that this time he was never going to the minors again—he was going to convince the Yankees he was a keeper and better than Hitchcock. He did. In 1995, Pettitte won the most games by a Yankee rookie starter in 27 years and, vitally, showed his fortitude by going 5–1 with a 3.38 ERA down the stretch as the Yankees had to win nearly every day to secure the wild card. He was greatly influenced by Jack McDowell's toughness. McDowell was pitching with a strain in his upper back, and Pettitte was awed by McDowell's fortitude. "Talk about a competitor," Pettitte says. "That guy was willing to pitch through anything to win."

McDowell was gone in 1996 and so was Hitchcock, traded to Seattle because the Yankees believed Pettitte was the superior pitcher. McDowell, though, lived on with the Yankees in Pettitte. He admitted nearly a decade later that his elbow was never right after he volunteered to pitch in relief on May 1 against the Orioles, 24 hours following a failed start. The condition grew progressively worse. By mid-June Pettitte was in so much discomfort, he was worried his career was in peril, despite promises from the Yankee medical staff that he had no tears and was in no danger of worsening the injury. Still, the pain lingered, and Pettitte simply decided he would not give in to the discomfort and would find a way to win, just like McDowell would have. That attitude essentially saved the Yankee season during a mostly catastrophic August.

There were a few bright spots for the Yankees during the month. Darryl Strawberry hit those three homers, a reminder of the towering star he had once been. And on August 23 at Yankee Stadium, Mariano Rivera responded to John Wetteland's presence on the disabled list with a groin injury by serving nobly as setup man and closer against Oakland. Rivera came on with two out and one on in the seventh to face Mark McGwire, who led the majors with 43 homers. It was the greatest confrontation of power versus power that the 1996 season could offer: the swelling biceps of McGwire against the rising fastball of Rivera. McGwire was the go-ahead run and struck out on a 1–2 fastball. McGwire batted again in the ninth inning with the tying runs on base. There were two outs, and the Yankees led 5–3, when, with his 59th pitch of the game, another high fastball in a season of high fastballs, Rivera fanned McGwire once more.

However, the difference between the Yankees staying in first place or crumbling into second that August was a lefty who had a picture of Froot Loops' Toucan Sam taped over his baseball card in his locker, a self-recognition by Pettitte about the size of his nose. But it was the size of his heart that mattered most. From August 2 to August 30, the Ramones played their final show, Prince Charles and Princess Diana officially divorced, and the Yankees' lead shriveled from 10 games over the Orioles to 4. It was a period when panic, dissension, organizational missteps, and George Steinbrenner's cruelty blanketed the franchise. It also was a 28-game period in which the sore-armed Pettitte won four times, and the rest of the Yankee rotation combined for five victories. All four of Pettitte's victories followed Yankee losses. The rest of the rotation managed just two victories after Yankee losses during the same stretch. Overall for the 28-game phase, Pettitte was 4–1 with a 3.59 ERA, and every other starter was 5–8 with a 6.79 ERA.

Simply put, the youngest member of the majors' most expensive rotation was the most irreplaceable. David Cone, who was supposed to be the ace, missed a total of 4 months following his shoulder surgery. Rogers, who was slated to be the No. 2 starter, never fully gained Torre's trust nor displayed an ability to prevail over the New York pressure. Key twice landed on the DL as he tried to rediscover his precision and craft following shoulder surgery. Dwight Gooden, who spent $3\frac{1}{2}$ months rekindling 1985, finally succumbed to his workload and was as ineffective down the stretch as he had been at the beginning of the season. Melido Perez never pitched an inning for the 1996 Yankees or again in the major leagues. And Scott Kamieniecki's Yankee season lasted $22\frac{2}{3}$ ineffective innings. At $150,000, Pettitte made just $41,000 more than the major league minimum wage—31 times less than what Melido Perez earned not to pitch.

"We don't make the postseason without Pettitte, period," Torre reflected.

Pettitte was the lone Yankee to stay in the rotation all season. He depended upon a cutter refined by organizational pitching maven Billy Connors. He picked off a major league–high 11 runners with a deceptive move that he invented himself on the mound his father built in the family backyard. Tom Pettitte had helped teach his son to pitch by borrowing a book from the library that showed how Nolan Ryan gripped his various pitches. Mostly, though, Tom Pettitte imparted a work ethic to his son. He had been a police officer in Baton Rogue for 13 years before relocating his family to Deer Park, Texas, to take a job working the overnight shift as a chemical operator at a motor oil plant. Like his old man, Andy Pettitte was a grinder, and like Derek Jeter and Mariano Rivera, he walked into a veteran clubhouse unbowed. All three defined themselves by their zeal to win. They were young, yet almost immediately part of the winning DNA of the team.

Pettitte had certain traits similar to Paul O'Neill. He was a self-demanding perfectionist who belittled himself or erupted in anguish at failure. Wayne Graham had worked hard to get him to stop tearing up dugouts when he did not meet his own exacting standards and, instead, channel it back into work. As a result, Joe Girardi says, "Andy had an incredible ability as a young man to focus on just the next pitch, not the one before, not the one still to come. He could block out bad stuff."

And there was a lot of bad stuff in August 1996 for Pettitte to block out. On August 2, Rivera was rocked for four 10th-inning runs in a loss to Kansas City, and David Weathers was bombed in his Yankee debut start the next night. But on August 4, Pettitte ignored all of that to strike out a career-high 11 Royals in a 5–3 triumph. On August 12, Harold Baines hit a walk-off homer against John Wetteland at Comiskey Park for the second time in 1996, and the next day Weathers fell to 0–2 with an 11.17 ERA in three Yankee starts. But on August 14, the day Bob Dole was officially nominated as the Republican presidential candidate at the party's convention in San Diego, Pettitte assured the White Sox did not sweep the Yankees. He fanned nine in seven innings in a 3–1 victory. Coming off a 1–8 homestand, the Mariners nevertheless arrived in New York and expressed their continuing dominance over the Yankees by winning the first three games of a four-game series. The Yankees' overworked bullpen was being exploited. Wetteland was on the DL, and Torre was trying hard in the second half of the season to ease the abuse on the slender Rivera. But Rivera's dependability in the middle of the game could not be replicated. In the opener against Seattle, 50,724 fans participated in a gimmick associated with the dance craze of the moment by forming the largest Macarena line ever, and then watched as Dave Pavlas, Bob Wickman, and Jeff Nelson could not do Rivera's job, allowing three runs in a 6–5 Seattle win. Over the next two games, Rogers and Gooden lasted a combined $5\frac{2}{3}$ innings and permitted 15 runs, forcing the bullpen to pick up $12\frac{1}{3}$ innings. The Yankee lead over the Orioles was $5\frac{1}{2}$ games; the noose was tightening.

On August 19 at the Stadium, against a Mariner team that had just brutalized Yankee pitching for 29 runs on 42 hits over 27 innings, Pettitte was asked to prevent another sweep and save the bullpen. Deeply religious, Pettitte had been reading his Bible, seeking solace against his throbbing elbow. But a few days before this start, Pettitte had found comfort from an unexpected source. Torre's pal Bob Gibson told Pettitte that he still endured elbow pain. It was an occupational hazard from throwing a baseball with force over and over again during his Hall of Fame career. It eased Pettitte's mind to know the first significant pain in his arm was a normal part of the occupation.

But when Jay Buhner hit a three-run homer off Pettitte in the first inning, it was a here-we-go-again moment for the Yankees. Except, as Girardi noted, Pettitte had the skill to dispatch the negatives and hone in on the present, to focus on the next pitch. Pettitte permitted just one more hit—an Alex Rodriguez homer in the sixth—in a complete-game 10-4 Yankee victory. The Yankees won the next day in a rout over the Angels, 17-6. Brian Boehringer, who had been so horrible in earlier stints both in 1995 and 1996, won his first major league game with a brilliant 5⅓ innings of shutout relief. However, it was in relief of Weathers, who lasted just one-third of an inning and was smashed for five runs. His ERA soared to 14.81.

What climbed the most that month, however, was Steinbrenner's anger at Watson. The general manager had pursued Kevin Appier until he signed a 3-year extension with Kansas City. Watson wanted John Burkett, but the Rangers had a worse record than the Yankees and therefore had first waiver claim rights, obtaining the righty from Florida on August 8. Watson had checked into a myriad of places, including Philadelphia, to discuss Curt Schilling. The Yankees were so desperate, they even worked out a deal in mid-July with Jack Morris, though Gene Michael did not find the 41-year-old's stuff appealing while scouting him on the same Northern League team that Darryl Strawberry had played for just a few weeks before. But when Morris refused to make more than one Triple-A start, the Yankees revoked their offer. So the best Watson could muster for the rotation was Weathers, who was demoted on August 21 to Triple-A Columbus after four dreadful starts. So much for Watson's solution to the No. 5 starter slot.

And here was the horror show for Watson: He had not even made his most criticized trade yet.

Under the prodding of Steinbrenner, Watson had continued to tinker with the Yankee roster. The additions of Strawberry and Cecil Fielder had indeed made the Yankees more muscular, but not better. The Yankees had morphed into the Orioles. The National League game inspired by Torre and bench coach Don Zimmer had vanished. In its place, the Yankees waited around for home runs. They hit 40 homers in August, twice as many as they had hit in July and the third most in the American League. Yet the Yankees went just 13–17. All the modifications disrupted the underdog spirit and upbeat chemistry that had so roused these Yankees. But Steinbrenner was never going to take responsibility for any failures. Watson's predecessor as GM, Gene Michael, knew the condition well and used to joke that he would call his autobiography *I'm in Charge of Everything That Goes Wrong*.

From the outset of spring training, Watson and Torre had been obsessed with finding a suitable lefty reliever. Steve Howe, Paul Gibson, Billy Brewer, and, most recently, Dale Polley had proven inadequate. Watson recalled that as early as late July Torre was envisioning a playoff slate that could include such lefty mashers as Boston's Mo Vaughn, Baltimore's Rafael Palmeiro, and Atlanta's Ryan Klesko. Torre asked management for a way to counteract such potential opponents. Brian Cashman canvassed the Yankees' lefty hitters, Wade Boggs, Tino Martinez, and Paul O'Neill. The list of available candidates included Detroit's Mike Myers. But the unanimous opinion favored Milwaukee's Graeme Lloyd, a 6-foot-7 Australian whose size enabled him to conceal his slider during his delivery. Lefties had hit just .210 against Lloyd to that point in 1996. The endorsements of his players combined with his manager's yearnings convinced Watson it was worthwhile to overpay to obtain Lloyd. He initially asked his counterpart, Milwaukee's Sal Bando, to accept Bob Wickman even up for

Lloyd, and then countered with Gerald Williams for Lloyd. Bando wanted both, imagining Williams as his starting center fielder and Wickman, perhaps, as the closer.

The Yankees were in a trickier position to trade Williams, even though Derek Jeter's best friend on the team had regressed to all of his swing-at-everything problems and was now in a deep slump. Their top prospect was outfielder Ruben Rivera. But the immature Rivera had infuriated Torre by sulking when he was demoted June 15. He exasperated the whole organization on July 19 when, after being caught stealing in a Triple-A game against Norfolk and being ejected for arguing the call, Rivera simply left Cooper Stadium without permission. The organization suspended him for seven games for insubordination, and, when he returned to Columbus, Rivera continued to brood and struggle on the field. Watson did not want to reward bad behavior, and Torre did not want to inject that attitude into his clubhouse. So to offset losing their defensively valuable fourth outfielder, Williams, and to avoid having to promote Rivera, the Yankees agreed to conclude the trade if the Brewers included outfielder Pat Listach.

The deal was consummated on August 23, and, in a personification of how chaotic the Yankee roster shuffling was in this period, Joe Girardi introduced himself to Lloyd on the mound in the seventh inning by asking the lefty reliever what kind of pitches he threw. Lloyd struck out the lone batter he faced, Oakland's Jason Giambi. Mariano Rivera followed Lloyd, and that was the game in which he whiffed McGwire twice. That was the last happy moment for Watson and the Yankees during the regular season when it came to that trade. Three days after the transaction, Listach had to be disabled with a fracture in his foot that was incurred when he was still a Brewer but went undetected by initial X-rays. Three days after that, Lloyd faced four Mariners in the Kingdome, retired none, had his Yankee ERA swell to 53.90 in five appearances, and revealed after the game that he had taken a cortisone shot into his aching elbow 9 days before the trade and felt there was no life in his arm. It was another medical issue the Yankees knew nothing about.

The Brewers claimed they had done nothing wrong. They nevertheless agreed to pay the rest of Listach's 1996 contract and send the Yankees two additional players, ineffective reliever Ricky Bones and infield prospect Gabby Martinez—who, it was learned, had been sent home from his minor league team due to a charge of spousal abuse. On some level, the Yankees had to be thankful to get even that compensation. After all, the acting commissioner of baseball was Bud Selig, a living conflict of interest because he also happened to be the owner of the Milwaukee Brewers. But Steinbrenner was not placated. Day after day and several times a day, the Boss reminded Watson of this failure, often belittling him in front of other team employees. "They pulled your pants down, Bob," was a regular putdown, or "Bob, you were a good player, but you are a horseshit executive." Steinbrenner told Watson he was not to be trusted to complete even the simplest front-office endeavors by himself. One of Steinbrenner's favorite threats was to tell one of his executives, "You are on the bubble," meaning he could go either way in keeping or firing the executive. Steinbrenner ended nearly every diatribe against Watson by reminding his GM that he was on the bubble.

The abuse had been steady almost from the moment Steinbrenner hoodwinked Watson into accepting an offer to be the Yankee GM. Steinbrenner told Watson he would be left alone to run baseball operations. But in November, Randy Velarde surprised the Yankees by spurning their retention offers to sign a 3-year contract with the California Angels. Watson was just finishing Thanksgiving dinner at home in Houston when he was phoned by Steinbrenner and called "a fucking idiot for letting our best second baseman go to the Angels." Steinbrenner told him that vacation was over. He was to report immediately back to Tampa; and, until further notice, he was not allowed to speak to player agents. "That was the first time I saw the full wrath of George," Watson remembers.

Yet the storm grew worse. Then executive VP/general counsel David Sussman says, "It was an incredibly difficult, tense period. George was all over Watson. From George's perspective, his New York baseball people had been bamboozled. Lambaste is too gentle a word. The quality that is missing from that word is the relentlessness George has when he fastens on something that has gotten under his skin. He felt screwed. He felt his baseball people had let him down. If he had to call every 15 minutes to get that point across, so be it."

Thus, when Pettitte started on August 30 in Anaheim, the Yankees were at their lowest point of the year—and not just because they had a season-worst five-game losing streak and the Orioles were now four games back. All the feelings of destiny that had enveloped the Yankees in the first 4 months of the season had vanished. The Yankees had arrived in Southern California after being swept three games in Seattle, bringing back all the pain of being swept out of the Kingdome and the playoffs the previous October.

Maybe nothing had really changed except for the cast of characters. Lloyd was the losing pitcher in the first two games against the Mariners. In the finale, Seattle skipper Lou Piniella again ordered one of his pitchers, Tim Davis, to buzz Paul O'Neill. It was the continuation of a grudge match that went back to their time together as manager and player with the Reds. In that time, O'Neill did not learn what Piniella wanted: how to become a pull-hitting power force. But Piniella did learn that O'Neill hated to be brushed back, and for four seasons now, a period covering both Piniella's term with the Mariners and O'Neill's with New York, Seattle pitchers had been using O'Neill for target practice. This time O'Neill snapped. He glared into the Mariner dugout at Piniella and ignited a brawl by getting into a fight with catcher John Marzano. Piniella called O'Neill a crybaby; Mariano Duncan defended his former Reds and current Yankee teammate, O'Neill, by describing Piniella as "the biggest fucking jerk I have ever met in baseball."

The incident should have unified and recharged the wobbly Yankees as they moved to California. Instead, on August 29, Wally Whitehurst, the Yankees' 10th different starter on the season, was gone after one inning. Lloyd then had his infamous four-batter effort and deflating postgame admission about cortisone. Before the game the next day, August 30, word circulated in the Yankee clubhouse, spread mostly by a disenchanted Jim Leyritz, that the Yankees had obtained third baseman Charlie Hayes from Pittsburgh for minor league

pitcher Chris Corn. Leyritz, as always, was already annoyed that he was not getting regular playing time, and the addition of a righty-hitting third baseman was
going to cut further into his role. But it was the regular third baseman, Wade
Boggs, who was most disturbed.

Boggs had no homers against lefty pitching and just a .259 average. Hayes's
addition was yet another attempt to get more pop against southpaws. The
Yankees were just 2–9 in games started against them by a lefty, with nine straight
losses, since Fielder had been acquired to solve that shortcoming. But Hayes
also had an option on his contract for 1997. Boggs, who obsessed on his statistics, saw his full-time play jeopardized. He told reporters, "I'll get 3,000 hits
somewhere." Aware that Joe Torre had made reference to the 38-year-old being
"tired and his bat slow at times," Boggs yelled sarcastically to one of the clubhouse boys, loud enough for the media to hear, "Hey, can you get somebody
to carry my bats onto the field? I'm a little tired."

All the roster changes were finally eating into what had been enchanting
clubhouse fraternity. It was just one more element that Pettitte carried to the
mound that night. Pettitte pitched to his personality—understated, almost
boring. He did not dominate because he did not have dominating stuff. He allowed eight hits in eight innings. But his expertise was poise when the inevitable
hits did come. He was a boxer who did not flinch. He stranded five runners
through three innings, striking out Chili Davis and Garret Anderson with runners on first and third to finish off the third inning. He accumulated a season-
high 130 bullpen-saving pitches, and Torre credited the lefty's "stomach" with
the way he handled pressure. When the season had started, the Yankees would
have been pleased had the reserved Pettitte merely repeated the 12–9 record
and 4.17 ERA that had enabled him to finish third in the AL Rookie of the Year
balloting in 1995. But, as it turned out, the Yankees needed more—much more.
And Pettitte gave it to them. This victory improved Pettitte to 19–7. There was
now Cy Young talk in the air.

The Yankees, though, were not nearly over their problems. They needed ex-

ernie Williams emerged from his shy cocoon to become a star, flourishing in the 1996 postseason and here enjoying a clubhouse dousing after he excelled in the Division Series against the Rangers and childhood pal Juan Gonzalez. *(Photo by Charles Wenzelberg/NY Post)*

*T*he most powerful force on the 1996 Yankees was the relief formula of Mariano Rivera handing off to John Wetteland. Here Wetteland wraps up the Division Series (his left arm is around catcher Joe Girardi) as a smiling Rivera (in dark warm-up top) is fittingly the first to greet him out of the dugout.

(Photo by Charles Wenzelberg/NY Post)

▶ The Yankees were not completely sold on Derek Jeter in the spring training of 1996, but the safety net was removed when Tony Fernandez (background) fractured his elbow. The precocious Jeter removed all worry by winning AL Rookie of the Year and becoming a cornerstone to the dynasty.

▼ Wade Boggs was terrified of horses, but he could not contain his joy and saddled up in the euphoria after the Yankees won the World Series over the Braves.

(Photo by Charles Wenzelberg/NY Post)

(Photo by W. A. Funches Jr./NY Post)

(Photo by Nury Hernandez/NY Post)

◀ Jeffrey Maier brought his black Mizzuno glove to Game 1 of the ALCS, changing the course of Derek Jeter's fly ball and the series.

▼ Many influenced the championship roster, including GM Bob Watson (far left) and George Steinbrenner's confidant Billy Connors (drink in hand). But no one was more responsible for the talented, professional group than former GM Gene Michael (striped shirt).

(Photo by Charles Wenzelberg/NY Post)

*I*n October 1996, Joe Torre got the World Series title he had chased his
entire life and Frank Torre got a new heart, a combination that made the
Torres of Brooklyn New York's first family. *(Photo by Charles Wenzelberg/NY Post)*

◀ Booed in February at the Fan Festival, Joe Girardi heard the loudest cheers of all when he connected for the go-ahead RBI triple off Atlanta's Greg Maddux in the clinching game of the World Series.

▼ No one on the Yankees talked a better game than Jim Leyritz. And no one delivered a bigger hit in 1996 than this one: Leyritz connecting for a three-run game-tying homer off Atlanta's Mark Wohlers in World Series Game 4.

*T*ino Martinez, Wade Boggs, and Paul O'Neill were valuable imports who delivered seriousness to the clubhouse and left-handed excellence to the lineup. *(Photo by Charles Wenzelberg/NY Post)*

◀ Dwight Gooden accentuates his journey from humiliation to euphoria as he is carried off the field following his May no-hitter of the Mariners.

▼ No Yankee celebrated more at the Canyon of Heroes victory parade than Kenny Rogers (atop the float), though no Yankee did more to damage their chances of winning in October 1996.

cellence from the son of another blue-collar employee who worked the grave-yard shift. They needed David Cone.

After the disappointment in the Kingdome at the end of the 1995 season, Cone hibernated for a few weeks, churning over the miserable loss and trying to re-gain life in his exhausted body. When he emerged, he decided to use free agency to find a more permanent playing home. He had wearied of the "hired gun" label that came with moving teams four times in 36 months. A fellow named Pat Gillick had executed the first of those moves. Gillick had left Steinbrenner's em-ploy in 1976 to become Toronto's GM and in 1982 preyed on the Boss's impa-tience by getting him to include as part of a Dave Collins–Dale Murray swap a first-base prospect named Fred McGriff. After the 1989 season, Gillick trans-formed the Blue Jays from a strong team to one capable of winning titles when he made a daring trade. He swapped McGriff and Gold Glove shortstop Tony Fernandez to San Diego for RBI machine Joe Carter and a young player whose burgeoning skills were being hidden in noncontention on the West Coast: Roberto Alomar. To galvanize the first of Toronto's two championship clubs in 1992, Gillick made a late-August swap, sending Jeff Kent and Ryan Thompson to the Mets for a righty overflowing with competitiveness, mettle, and stuff. David Cone was available only because the Mets were in the midst of a downfall vividly portrayed in the book *The Worst Team Money Could Buy*.

The Yankees had originally wanted Cone after the 1992 season as a free agent, but the righty decided to leave Toronto to go home to Kansas City when Royals owner Ewing Kauffman gave him a $9 million signing bonus. The re-building Royals traded Cone at the start of the 1995 season to the Blue Jays. Toronto, recognizing its glory days were gone, decided to deal the free-agent-to-be near the trade deadline. The Yankees had looked elsewhere for rotation help, mainly because Jimmy Key was done for the season. Cone would have been the winning pitcher in the clinching game of the 1992 World Series for the Blue Jays had Tom Henke not blown a save against Atlanta in the ninth inning. Instead, Key won in relief. Like Cone, Key left as a free agent after that title. The Yankees' first free-agent choice that off-season was Greg Maddux and then Cone. They ultimately settled for Key, who turned out to be a superb Yankee.

Toronto made it clear to the Yankees that it was going to take an elite pitching prospect to land Cone. However, then GM Gene Michael told his counterpart, Gord Ash, that as desperate as the teetering Yankees were, he was not making Sterling Hitchcock or Andy Pettitte available as requested. However, Michael was willing to build a package around the well-regarded Marty Janzen. In a scenario that had unfolded often in Michael's tenure, he found himself at odds with minor league head Bill Livesey. Buck Showalter used to regularly point out that Livesey's name backward was "yes evil." The consensus of the New York office was that Livesey had a brilliance for unearthing talent, but that he had a bad personality and turned childish, vindictive, and obstinate when he did not get his way. And Livesey did not want Janzen moved. George Steinbrenner inserted himself as the tiebreaker into what had evolved into a nasty confrontation between the Tampa and New York offices. The Boss told neither faction what path he would follow when he took over trade negotiations directly with Toronto president Paul Beeston. "No one knew what was going on," Brian Cashman recalls about the blackout period that followed. Steinbrenner ended up including Janzen as the key component of a three-prospect trade that brought Cone to the Yankees, bumping a young righty named Mariano Rivera from the rotation.

Unlike the experience with Maddux following the 1992 season, Cone was clearly the Yankees' top free-agent choice after the 1995 campaign. He was more than that, however—he was their obsession. The Yankees also targeted Roberto Alomar, the best free-agent position player on the market. The Orioles' wish list began with those two players, as well, unleashing the competitive animosity between Steinbrenner and Orioles owner Peter Angelos that served as the backdrop to the 1996 season. Angelos was the lone maverick owner who did not field a replacement team during spring training of 1995, a gesture that mattered to union loyalist Cone. It also helped the Orioles that their GM was now Pat Gillick, who had obtained both Alomar and Cone in his past. Davey Johnson, who managed Cone as a Met, was now the Orioles' skipper.

Still, Cone's first choice was the Yankees. After a drawn-out process with the Yankees that Cone's representative, Steve Fehr, termed "strange" because the team kept dancing around a firm proposal, Cone reached an oral agreement in mid-December on a 3-year, $19 million offer extended by Watson. Fehr remembers Watson acting "sheepishly" with his next phone call, when he lowered the offer at Steinbrenner's behest to $18.55 million without providing a reason. Infuriated, Cone turned to Gillick. The Orioles bid $17.75 million on December 20, and the sides were within $500,000, all of which was tied up in deferred payments with no interest. Because the Orioles were in the midst of finalizing a 3-year, $18 million accord with Alomar, Angelos said he needed to mull over the numbers and would call back.

In another of those astonishing bits of timing that impacted on the future of the Yankees, Steinbrenner called Fehr from a pay phone at a Tampa hospital to return the original offer, plus add a no-trade provision and include two option years that made the total guarantee $19.5 million. Of course, he blamed Bob Watson for the miscommunication that caused the initial offer to be lowered. Angelos later explained to the *Baltimore Sun*, "What I should have told [Fehr and Cone] was 'hold the line,'" rather than hanging up and providing a passageway for Steinbrenner to sneak in and grab Cone.

"I was very close to being an Oriole, within a few hours," Cone says. "The Yankees backpedaled. The deferred money the Orioles were talking about was pretty ludicrous over 3 years in the scheme of things—a couple of hundred thousand dollars. That little discrepancy held up talks and enabled Steinbrenner to come back and get me. The deal with the Orioles could have been done before the call from the phone booth if the Orioles had not haggled over deferred money."

Still, the Yankees were now unsure what Cone would do, and they had already lost control of Jack McDowell by deciding not to offer him arbitration. They called agent Scott Boras frantically to inquire about Kevin Brown, Ben McDonald, and Kenny Rogers, all of whom had not been on their radar until that point. Losing Cone would be unacceptable; losing him to the hated division-rival Orioles would be intolerable. "I have ruminated often on the course of baseball history if David signs with the Orioles rather than the Yankees," Fehr says.

One more twist occurred early on the morning of December 21. Cone's pal, Mets closer John Franco, was aware of the negotiating intrigue and recommended to management that the Mets try to nab his friend. Mets GM Joe McIlvaine made an 8 a.m. stop at Cone's East 56th Street apartment to see if he could reunite the righty with the Mets to serve as ace and guru to the Generation K starters. He offered 2 years, and Cone asked, "Haven't you been reading the papers?" alluding to the well-documented, 3-year tenders already made by Baltimore and the Yankees. McIlvaine, after consulting with Mets owner Fred Wilpon, returned to the apartment in the afternoon to bid $14.7 million over 3 years. Besides being significantly lower than the offers of the Yankees and Orioles, the Mets also would not provide Cone with a no-trade clause throughout the contract, a necessity for him to shed his image as a hired gun. More irritating to the pitcher, McIlvaine spent a good deal of time inquiring if Cone was a media leak during his 6 years playing for the Mets.

Annoyed by that, but still having the strongest pull to stay in New York, Cone accepted a Yankee offer that could, if the options kicked in, pay him $29 million over 5 years. Now in 1996, as the Yankees' division lead dripped away, Cone felt obligated to that contract. He was paid to lead this staff, and he worked each day with that in mind, to distance himself from surgery and get back on a major league mound again and earn his money. He started by playing catch with Yankee team physician Stuart Hershon, MD, and slowly graduated to two starts for Double-A Norwich at Thomas J. Dodd Memorial Stadium. It was supposed to be three. On August 26, Cone made the second minor league start on the same day the Mets fired Dallas Green and promoted Bobby

Valentine to manage. The Generation K crew of Jason Isringhausen, Bill Pulsipher, and Paul Wilson, which Joe McIlvaine had hoped Cone would mentor and that had so frightened George Steinbrenner into believing New York would again be a Mets town, all had injured their arms and needed surgery. Cone, meanwhile, was demonstrating the success of his own controversial surgery, allowing one unearned run over six innings to the Hardware City Rock Cats and topping out at 91 mph in his 83 pitches. He informed Yankee officials to scrap the plans for a third start. "I just have a limited number of bullets; let's not waste them down here," he told Watson.

Besides, the plummeting Yankees needed Cone, and Cone needed the Yankees. The collapse in the 1995 Division Series, that split-finger fastball in the dirt to Doug Strange, still haunted Cone, motivating him. Cone always sought such inspirations. As a kid in Kansas City, Cone watched his father develop rheumatoid arthritis working early mornings as a mechanic in the freezers of a meat-processing plant. He was determined not to end up in such circumstances. His father had been his demanding basketball coach, football coach, Little League manager, and inspiration. The sound Cone most associates with his youth is that of the garage door opening at 3 a.m. and his father heading to work. Still, his father spent plenty of late afternoons squatting at Budd Park, acting as a catcher to teach the youngest of his three sons to pitch. Father also taught son to use all the slights as energy to defeat the naysayers. And David Cone knew there had been plenty of naysayers who thought he would never pitch again in 1996.

Cone took that to the mound with him on September 2, Labor Day, in Oakland, when he was slotted back into the rotation. Cone told everyone from the outset that this was not a feel-good story. He was at the Coliseum to be David Cone — to be dominant. He was holding himself to the highest standards, even if there was a 7-inch scar that ran from beneath his right biceps to his armpit. And there was no time for him to ease back into his job anyway. The idea that Cone would return to the roster for a couple of low-pressure September starts in preparation for the playoffs was gone, having disappeared with the Yankees' substantial division lead. This was no longer a laboratory or a second spring training. It was now vital that Cone pitch well.

The Yankees had lost the night before in Anaheim. Chuck Finley had beaten the Yankees for the fourth time in four tries in 1996. And Kenny Rogers had pitched so tentatively, his ERA swelling to 5.00 overall and 11.64 in his last four starts, that Torre said he was moving the lefty to the bullpen for at least one rotation turn. In the off-season, the Yankees had brought both free-agent lefties, Finley and Rogers, to Tampa, putting Finley up at the Hyatt and Rogers at Steinbrenner's Bay Harbor Radisson, not even a mile farther down the Intercoastal. The organizational vote was 12–3 in favor of Finley, including strong support by Torre, who knew Finley well from his time broadcasting Angels games. But, according to a person who worked for the Yankees at the time, Scott Boras convinced Steinbrenner that Watson had reached a verbal deal with his client Rogers, and the Yankees were concerned that he might sue. "It was bluster," the Yankee employee says. "But George felt he had to bail out Bob. He lashed into Bob something fierce. It was ugly." Boras denies ever threatening to sue. Rogers also made a face-to-face appeal to Steinbrenner to ignore the talk that he was a hick intimidated by New York and the Yankees. The Boss was charmed. Rogers received his money, $20 million over 4 years. But he did not fulfill his role as the No. 2 starter to Cone, so that intensified the pressure on the No. 1 starter. That was fine with Cone.

As a surprise and for inspiration, Cone's wife, Lynn, had set up tickets behind the Yankee dugout for 62-year-old Ed Cone, who had flown in from Kansas City for this start. Ed Cone had attended plenty of his son's games but always sat in the family section, usually behind home plate. He had never sat behind the dugout. So inning after what became no-hit inning, Cone returned to the bench and for the first time as a major leaguer locked eyes with the man who had taught him to pitch. It was corny, and David Cone loved that too.

Cone held nothing back. Though he had not pitched as a major leaguer for 122 days, Cone used his entire repertoire, arm-anguishing sliders and split-finger fastballs included. He was his inventive self, owner of the most diverse library of pitches in the majors. He struck out Oakland catcher Terry Steinbach two times, on both occasions dropping down to the side to whip what he called his Laredo slider, so named because he delivered the pitch from down south. His teammates could not believe the precision, the command, and the array. This was a guy who had not pitched a major league game since May 2. He had not lost his stuff or his game face. Cone had a Jekyll-and-Hyde quality. Off the mound, his face was placid, his mien welcoming, his tone friendly. But at first pitch a seriousness invaded his face, a don't-fuck-with-me wall was erected. It was work time for Ed Cone's son. His eyes hollowed and blotches of red illuminated exertion or ire, standing out on his otherwise pale skin.

"Once the game began, there was never any messing around with David," Bernie Williams recalls. "But that day was even more special. He was on a mission. There was something in his eyes. He sat in the dugout, and he was in his own little world."

A's starter Ariel Prieto finally allowed one run in the sixth and three in the seventh, and what remained to be determined was how far Joe Torre and Mel Stottlemyre would let their surgically repaired ace go with this no-hitter after establishing a 100-pitch maximum. The seventh inning ended with Charlie Hayes robbing Mark McGwire of a single with a diving stop at third, and Williams reaching over the center-field wall to pull back what would have been a Geronimo Berroa homer. The no-hitter was preserved. Back East, watching on television in awe and pride on this holiday weekend, were the four doctors who had spent 3 hours hunched over Cone's right shoulder on May 10: vascular surgeons George Todd, MD, and Alan Benvenisty, MD; orthopedic surgeon Louis Bigliani, MD; and team physician Dr. Hershon.

Cone was at 85 pitches on this sunny afternoon. Ed Cone told fans sitting nearby that if they left it up to his iron-willed son, "they'll have to use that tractor over there to pull him off the field." The father was right. The night before the game, full of anxiety about his team and himself, Cone had resolved to pitch well enough and long enough to just get the ball to Mariano Rivera. That was not enough anymore for the dogged Cone.

Torre appreciated what a wonderful story this was, made all the more poignant because Dwight Gooden had pitched a no-hitter after stepping into the injured Cone's rotation spot. Now Cone was back to take the charmed baton just as his pal Gooden was running on fumes. Still, Torre decided 1 day—albeit a great day—was not worth risking everything ahead of the Yankees. So David Cone, who just 4 months earlier had worried that he might lose his hand, maybe even his whole arm, departed after seven no-hit innings. Rivera pitched a perfect eighth inning, but with one out in the ninth, the lefty-swinging Jose Herrera swatted a grounder that trickled off Charlie Hayes's glove. Derek Jeter backhanded in the hole and fired to first just as Herrera arrived with a headfirst slide. Umpire Larry McCoy ruled safe, and even almost a decade later Jeter says, annoyed, "Out. You have to call him out." It was the only hit by Oakland in the Yankees' 5–0 victory. Cone was disappointed yet appreciative. Torre and Mel Stottlemyre were merely looking out for the best interests of both him and the team. There was still a lot of baseball to play, and, having reintroduced himself to the pennant race, even David Cone saw the irony of it all—he was a hired gun again.

Two days later, on September 4, New York was astonished as a cramping Pete Sampras survived a stomach virus that caused him to puke on the court; the heartbreak of losing his coach and dear friend Tim Gullikson to a brain tumor; and a 4-hour, 9-minute battle against Spaniard Alex Corretja to win a US Open quarterfinal match in Flushing Meadows. Three thousand miles away, the gutsy Pettitte followed another atrocious outing by Gooden by striking out six of the first eight A's he faced en route to becoming, aptly, the first 20-game winner in the AL since one of his oracles, Jack McDowell, in 1993. No Yankee had won 20 games since Ron Guidry in 1985. More impressive, Pettitte was now 13–3 following Yankee losses. The team felt great to have Pettitte work with such ferocity all season, better yet to have the pugnacious Cone back.

The lead over the Orioles was four games. But it wasn't safe, and neither were the jobs of Joe Torre and Bob Watson.

10 | THE PERFECT RESOLVE

"Joe, if you blow this thing, they'll never let you forget it. You'll have to live with it the rest of your life. You'll be another Ralph Branca."

— *George Steinbrenner to Joe Torre on a conference call in August, when the division lead was still eight games over the Orioles*

The problem with the powerful devotion to David Cone and Andy Pettitte was that when they lost, the pain was more traumatic throughout the team. On September 7, rapper Tupac Shakur was fatally shot while leaving the MGM Grand in Las Vegas after watching Mike Tyson knock out Bruce Seldon in the first round, and David Cone lost to the lowly Blue Jays. Pettitte lost the next day. The winning starters for Toronto were Paul Quantrill, who was 4–13 with a 5.29 ERA and pitched only because American League ERA leader Juan Guzman needed an emergency appendectomy, and Erik Hanson, who had a 5.87 ERA. It was yet more signs all was not right with the Yankees. They were 23–30 since sweeping those four games at Camden Yards to open the second half, a sweep that was supposed to leave the Orioles out of contention, at least for the AL East title.

George Steinbrenner had menacingly paced around the clubhouse following the September 8 loss to Toronto. He departed in an obvious rage but refused to comment to the media. Joe Torre no longer needed to hear Steinbrenner to know what he was thinking anyway. After all, a month earlier, when the lead was still pretty substantial, Steinbrenner was full of both dread and cruelty when he used the forum of a conference call to the manager's office to liken Torre to Ralph Branca, the historical face of baseball collapse. Torre had grown up a rarity, a New York Giants fan in Brooklyn. Torre was a joyous 11-year-old on

October 3, 1951, watching on television when Bobby Thomson homered off of the Brooklyn Dodgers' Branca, culminating the Giants' historic charge from 13½ games back on August 11 to the pennant. Torre went to his first World Series game that year at the Polo Grounds to see Joe DiMaggio's final Yankee team win what would be the third of five straight titles.

Steinbrenner did not sense another Yankee dynasty incubating in September 1996, however. He sensed collapse. Only seven teams in history had blown a lead of at least 12 games. One of them was the 1978 Red Sox, who led the Yankees by 14 games on July 20. That infamous Boston club had been managed by Don Zimmer, who now sat beside Torre every game as a daily reminder to Steinbrenner of the worst possibilities. Steinbrenner had become convinced his 1996 Yankees were going to join that legion of all-time chokers and, worse than that, allow the team owned by his nemesis, Peter Angelos, to win the AL East. So Steinbrenner did what he always did in such times: He began assigning blame.

For much of the season, Watson actually had Steinbrenner follow his chain-of-command request to relay problems with the manager through the general manager rather than hounding Torre. It was a magnanimous and ultimately painful gesture by Watson, who ended up absorbing even more of Steinbrenner's abuse. Watching pieces of the division lead seemingly disappear daily removed Steinbrenner's shackles as far as assailing Torre, yet what lingers in the memory of Yankee players is how unruffled Torre remained during this dismal stretch.

Serenity was Torre's nature, but he was finding even more perspective these days. He either visited or talked by phone daily with his brother, Frank, who was now on a transplant list at Columbia-Presbyterian, hoping a heart would arrive in time to save his life. Frank always tried to change the subject from his dire situation to see if he could offer advice and support to his kid brother about the Yankees' shrinking lead. Torre, however, did not need much of a lift. He still thought he was managing the team of his life, though he recognized that the confidence was draining from his players.

There were 20 games left in the season. The Orioles had won on the Yankee off day, September 9, so the lead was 2½ games when Torre gathered his squad for a 20-minute meeting on September 10 in the claustrophobic confines of the visiting locker room at old Tiger Stadium. Five times Torre emphasized, "We are going to win this thing." Torre had seen some behavior recently that hadn't thrilled him, notably Wade Boggs's snide comments after the acquisition of Charlie Hayes. But, in general, he still admired the unity of the club enough to tell the players that this was the most selfless team he had ever managed. Torre stressed that the togetherness and grittiness that had bolstered the team into first place were advantages it had over the Orioles that would not disappear and, instead, would keep it ahead.

Torre was trying to transfer his conviction and calmness to his players. He believed that relieving tension from the clubhouse and allowing players to concentrate on playing was a manager's most vital role. Mariano Duncan ended the revival meeting the way he had been ending all of the Yankee meetings for a while now, with his team motto: "We play today, we win today. Dat's it." The good vibes lasted 30 Dwight Gooden pitches, long enough for him to surrender four runs in two-thirds of an inning. No player had more exemplified the sense of destiny that hugged these Yankees over the first 4 months than Gooden. A Hollywood producer was so enamored with Gooden's nowhere-to-no-hitter story that he was planning a movie about Gooden's life. There was talk Denzel Washington might play the lead. Steinbrenner had ordered Gooden to stop discussing the project during the season, claiming this distraction, and not a dead arm, was causing his downfall. Whatever the reason, it was obvious now that there would be no happy ending for Gooden in 1996. By early September, no player more embodied the thinning sense of destiny than Gooden.

For the Yankees to have a happy ending, others would have to be destiny's darlings.

Even with the perspective offered by time, Derek Jeter still says, "Ruben Rivera was as good a player as I've ever seen. Ruben could do everything. It was just that Ruben was a little immature." The child in Rivera had caused his problems with Yankee management. As Rick Down remembers, "We used to talk about Ruben Rivera being a six-tool player, and the sixth tool, the one between his legs, got him in trouble."

But those other five tools, at least in 1996, were Rivera's life preserver. When Pat Listach went down with his foot injury, Steinbrenner overruled his executives and ordered Rivera summoned to the team to serve as an extra outfielder. Torre did not like seeing Rivera again, but he could not ignore his value, regularly using the athletic 22-year-old to pinch-run or to play defense late in games. The Yankees led just 9–8 in the opener in Detroit when Torre sent Rivera in to play right field in the bottom of the ninth inning. He removed Paul O'Neill, who had been laboring with a hamstring injury for 2 weeks. Bobby Higginson smacked a John Wetteland pitch toward the right-center-field gap with one out, the tying run on second, and the go-ahead run on first. With his body extended and his glove scraping the grass, Rivera made an astounding backhand grab. So a guy named Ruben whom Torre did not want on his team helped the Yankees win the series opener. The same was true the next night.

Upon arriving with the Tigers after being traded for Cecil Fielder, Ruben Sierra had told the Detroit media that the Yankees did not care about him: "All they care about over there is winning." Amen, thought Torre and his players. Sierra had been so tied up in his personal battles, believing that he should play the field every day despite skills inferior to other players, that he lost the big picture. On the worst-in-the-majors Tigers, however, Sierra was in left field with the score tied 3–3 in the seventh inning and two out. For the second straight night, the Yankees' division lead was in jeopardy of falling to 1½ games, when O'Neill sent a routine fly to left field. Sierra moved in and to his right, looking up into a steady rain. He lifted his glove and, at the last instant, lurched forward, only to have the ball fall untouched as two runs scored. The Yankees won 7–3.

"It is corny to say destiny, but Ruben dropping the ball after we traded him, come on," Jim Leyritz says, looking back.

Still, all was not copacetic with the Yankees. In the September 12 *New York*

Times, Bob Watson was quoted by beat reporter Jack Curry as saying, "We have the highest payroll in the history of the game. If we can't hold a 12-game lead, then the leadership is responsible. The pilots crash the plane, not the passengers. Joe and I are the pilots. We're the ones who are responsible." Watson also reacted to a column in the *Bergen Record* that had an unnamed source in the Yankee organization saying the GM would not be back in 1997. Watson assumed the source was Steinbrenner and told *The Times*, "It doesn't surprise me to the point that he would do this. It surprises me that he would leak to someone without telling me. He's a very volatile man. But I would think he would be enough of a man about it to come to me."

Yankee executives were split by Watson's motives for slamming Steinbrenner. Some thought Watson was looking to provoke Steinbrenner into firing him so he could escape the abuse while still being paid for 1997. Others believed Watson had finally snapped under the unending duress inflicted by the Boss. How else to explain a veteran baseball man publicly assuming that Steinbrenner was the "source" on a story?

Steinbrenner reacted predictably by taking shots at the staggering GM. Torre also reacted predictably. His team had righted itself with two startling victories in Detroit and had been in first place for 4 months. Yet Watson, not only Torre's supervisor but his friend, said the manager also should be fired if the team did not win the division. He had unnecessarily thrown Torre into the quicksand beside him. Torre forgave Watson, citing his harrowing job. Torre also acknowledged that Steinbrenner was in charge and could do whatever he wanted.

No matter how much insanity broke out around him, Torre remained unfazed. For the most part, his players followed that composed lead. But they could not completely ignore the vanishing lead, despite their manager's calm exterior. Tensions did rise on occasion. On September 12, the Yankees routed the Tigers 12–3 in the series finale, with Bernie Williams driving in eight runs. But during a six-run top of the sixth, Jose Lima plunked Derek Jeter with a pitch in the upper back following four straight hits, including homers by Hayes and Andy Fox. The Yankee bench was sure it was done on purpose, out of frustration by Lima. In the bottom of the inning, Jeff Nelson twice buzzed Tiger hitters and was quickly visited by pitching coach Mel Stottlemyre.

In a desperate battle to hold the division lead, Stottlemyre, Torre, and Don Zimmer agreed they did not want Nelson risking a suspension, and Stottlemyre ordered Nelson to desist. That infuriated Mariano Duncan, who had taken on a role of leadership with the Yankees, mainly because of his ebullience and non-stop chatter. But also because he had old-school genes, Duncan's cheery exterior could dissolve quickly into fury if he saw a violation of the established way the game should be played. Duncan would get in the face of a teammate who was just going through the motions, not running out grounders or not hustling on defense.

Duncan loved that despite his tender age, Jeter was old-school as well. Much to the rookie's appreciation, Duncan became an older brother and, at times, protector. Lima's pitch was the ninth time Jeter was hit that year, and Duncan felt not enough was being done to defend Yankee hitters, notably Jeter. As soon as the Yankees returned to the clubhouse after the victory, Duncan angrily confronted catcher Joe Girardi, and the clubhouse was so small that everyone in the room could hear the second baseman's scorching words. He screamed that Jeter needed to be protected, and Girardi calmly responded that this was not the point of the season to ratchet up hostilities. Duncan called Girardi "a piece of shit" and Zimmer jumped in to defend his favorite player, telling Duncan, "He's not a piece of shit, you're a piece of shit." Duncan turned on Zimmer, yelling, "What are you, his fucking father? Get out of my face." Other players stepped in, and calm was restored before reporters were allowed in for postgame interviews.

Still, there were 17 games left in the season. The Orioles were 3½ games back. The pressure was not abating.

Steinbrenner's hatred of the Orioles was deep-seated and dated to Edward Bennett Williams's ownership of the team. Williams enlisted an attorney from his law firm to serve as his right-hand man with the Orioles in 1979, and Larry Lucchino and Steinbrenner immediately disliked each other. Their expletive-filled jousts were main events at owners' meetings. Steinbrenner felt Lucchino was always trying to get into the Yankees' ample pockets. Lucchino found Steinbrenner a boor who did not care about the overall health of the game. What irritated the Boss and increased his rampaging stadium envy even more was that Lucchino was the driving force behind the building of Camden Yards. Lucchino left the Orioles in 1993 when Angelos bought the team, and Steinbrenner seamlessly transferred his animus to Angelos.

Steinbrenner was agitated further that Angelos was being hailed for the decision to overrule his GM, Pat Gillick, and block the trades of Bobby Bonilla and David Wells. That judgment had served as a catalyst to the Oriole turn-around. Instead of tearing down the veteran core, Baltimore instead added to it by obtaining Eddie Murray and Todd Zeile, stocking the Orioles with nine regulars who each reached at least 20 homers in 1996. On September 15, in a 16–6 rout of the Tigers, the Orioles hit five homers to give them 243 on the season, erasing the 1961 Yankees' record of 240. The symbolism was clear as the Orioles closed the gap on the Yankees' division lead.

In reality, Murray's greatest value was not his home-run power as much his might in the clubhouse. Murray had a hostile relationship with the media, but he was always known as a good teammate and proved to be a unifying force for the splintered Orioles. In addition, Armando Benitez and Alan Mills had come off the disabled list, and Terry Mathews had been obtained from the Marlins, solidifying what had been a porous bullpen. Also, manager Davey Johnson had decided to solve the club's fifth starter misery by doing away with a fifth starter in early August. Finicky ace Mike Mussina did not like the disruption of his set patterns and the burden on his arm of being in a four-man rotation, but he arrived to the opener of the final series of the season between the Orioles and Yankees on September 17 having gone 6–1 since the change, reaching 19 wins with four starts left in his season.

Mussina and David Cone were the scheduled starters in an opener that had been threatened all day by rain. Torre had been pleasantly surprised before the game when Darryl Strawberry entered his office and told him not to worry about his feelings; that it was in the team's best interest to start Tim Raines in left field. Torre appreciated the gesture as another sign that Strawberry really had changed from selfish young man to elder statesman. But Torre knew he was starting Raines anyway, since Raines was the latest player to thrive at an opportune time to help the Yankees. Like Gooden and Strawberry, Steinbrenner brought Raines to the Yankees against his baseball officials' wishes. Tom Reich had arranged both his client's acquisition from the White Sox and a 1-year contract extension for Raines that amounted to a gift from Steinbrenner to his favorite agent. Why give Raines a contract for 1997 when that was the due date for elite outfield prospect Ruben Rivera's full-time arrival? Raines fractured his thumb in spring training, returned to play regularly for a month, and then suffered a hamstring injury that kept him out from late May until mid-August. There were members of the front office who were suspicious of how long it took Raines to heal and used to joke derisively that George's signing was off playing golf in Florida with the Yankees' money.

Raines did not have a starting job when he returned, but he never whined. In fact, Tim Raines was always in a good mood, playfully needling teammates. When Paul O'Neill was in one of his water-cooler-busting tirades during a hitting slump, Raines was the one Yankee who could ease the dugout anxiety with a joke that inevitably defused O'Neill. That day-in, day-out cheerfulness, win or lose, elated no one more than the positive Derek Jeter, who would come to call Raines his favorite teammate.

Raines was from a small town outside of Orlando and had aspired to be a football star. But the Expos drafted him in the fifth round in 1977, and he saw the potential for longevity in baseball. Early in his pro career, Raines noticed how veterans mistreated the farmhands and resolved never to be that way. A strength of the Yankee clubhouse was the absence of such divisions.

It had not been like that earlier in the decade, when Mel Hall seemed to be on a personal vendetta to destroy Bernie Williams, who arrived with thick glasses and reticence to the Yankee clubhouse. Hall taped "Mr. Zero" to the top of Williams's locker to signify that he meant nothing to the team. One day Hall nearly brought Williams to tears by saying "Zero, shut up" every time Williams tried to speak. The more Williams tried, the louder Hall interrupted with repetitive chants of "Zero."

Hall imitated Williams's base-running mistakes during batting practice. One time Williams pulled up on a ball he should have caught, thinking it was right fielder Jesse Barfield's play, and raised his hands in confusion. For the next few days, in front of Williams, Hall ran up to Barfield, stopped, and threw up his hands. Buck Showalter and Gene Michael knew that Williams had a future with the team and Hall did not. And Showalter and Michael probably did nothing more important for the 1996 Yankees than the arduous dirty work of clearing all the problems out of the clubhouse, such as Hall, and establishing a community of seriousness that Joe Torre inherited.

Still, within that fraternal population, no veteran made Jeter feel more part of the clubhouse fabric than Rock Raines, who would good-naturedly tease a bad haircut or questionable fashion choice, offer sage counsel, or simply outdo even Jeter's seemingly unlimited optimism. Jeter felt blessed to have a locker adjacent to Raines. "I knew I would be a guy who could influence him and make him feel at home," Raines says. "I talked to him a lot and made him laugh a lot. I was the one guy he could talk to, at least when I wasn't hurt. I was the one who gave him respect before the others."

By September, however, Raines's value finally extended to the field. He celebrated his 37th birthday on September 16 by hitting two homers and driving in six runs at SkyDome to lift the Yankees to a 10–0 rout of the Blue Jays. The victory assured that the Yankees entered the home series against Baltimore with a three-game lead. It also motivated Strawberry to impress Torre with his selfless office visit.

Torre was not quite as thrilled with his next visitor. For 90 minutes before the start of the biggest series of the year, George Steinbrenner planted himself in the manager's office. He turned it into the nerve center as club officials tried to determine if a game could be played through inclement weather that night and how the Yankees would proceed should there be a postponement. It was more a frayed-nerve center. Steinbrenner believed he was projecting leadership at times like this as he barked orders at security staff, front-office employees, coaches, and manager. But it was all rather unsettling, a feeling that only expanded over the course of the night.

The game should never have been started, since it was raining steadily at first pitch. Cone threw 19 pitches in the top of the first. Mussina threw 16 in the bottom half and had two out and two on when umpire crew chief Joe Brinkman ordered the tarpaulin put on the field. The teams waited around a ridiculous 2½ hours, when it became clear there would be no letup in the miserable weather.

By the time a postponement was announced at 10:46 p.m., open hostility had broken out in many quarters. Steinbrenner said Brinkman was told by the Yankees not to start the game. Brinkman said no such conversation ever took place. The AL office revealed that it was the Yankees who had been pushing all day to play the game and avoid a doubleheader. Enraged, Steinbrenner stalked the press box and returned to a favorite punching bag, belittling AL president Gene Budig for being at a charity function in Kansas City rather than at this marquee series.

The animosity that existed on the ownership level between the Orioles and Yankees spilled over to the players. On July 12, when a Yankee-Oriole game was rained out at Camden Yards, Baltimore officials had asked the Yankees to play a split doubleheader so the Orioles could get the benefit of two gates. The Yankee players asked for $5,000 each ($3,000 more than the normal fee), along with a considerable charitable donation. The Orioles refused and ended up playing a single-gate doubleheader on July 13. Now, with the Yankees asking for a split doubleheader, Oriole players fired back by refusing Steinbrenner's desire to get two gates. Steinbrenner retaliated by letting his players know the resolution—a single game the next night and a twi-night doubleheader on

September 19. Yankee personnel left the stadium, while the Orioles remained in uniform and uninformed.

But beyond the bickering was a bigger issue that impacted on the AL East race. There was concern that the warmup and the need to pitch the first inning knocked the surgically repaired Cone out of this seminal series. Mussina was younger and healthier, but he had been operating against his will in the four-man rotation. He had done enough first-inning work to put his availability for this series in doubt as well. Cone did not hesitate. He said he would pitch in the doubleheader. Mussina said he would, too. But who knew what they had to give in their arms.

The first time the Yankees and Orioles had met in 1996, they played the longest nine-inning game in major league history, followed by a 15-inning marathon. Now they had hardly played at all and still were as compelling as ever.

In the pregame on September 18, Steinbrenner again tried to overshadow this vital series. He told reporters that Torre, whose 2-year contract covered 1997, would manage the Yankees in 1997. The major news was that Steinbrenner, still bitter about the shots Watson had taken at him in the media, refused to say his GM would also return, although Watson's contract covered 1997, too.

Nothing Steinbrenner did before the opener could truly eclipse Orioles-Yankees. They played a gladiator game, evoking skill and fortitude. Andy Pettitte had taken a line drive off his left kneecap in his previous start at SkyDome, when he won his 21st game of 1996. But there he was leaving the mound to a standing ovation from 40,775 fans with one out in the ninth inning, having pitched excellently yet again, though the Yankees trailed 2–1. Despite a doubleheader the next day, Torre summoned Mariano Rivera, who normally protected leads, to preserve the one-run deficit. Torre wanted this game that much. Paul O'Neill opened the bottom of the ninth by drawing a walk off closer

Randy Myers, and Ruben Rivera pinch-ran. Cecil Fielder also walked and, with one out, Davey Johnson lifted Myers in favor of Alan Mills, who was in the midst of a streak of retiring 18 straight batters. But Bernie Williams grounded a game-tying single up the middle, and Mariano Rivera pitched a perfect top of the 10th inning, making Torre's choice all the wiser. Rivera faced five batters in this game and retired them all. Jeter led off the bottom half of the 10th with a single. For the first time since he came to the Yankees, Charlie Hayes executed a sacrifice bunt. Jeter moved to third on a Tim Raines groundout. That brought up Ruben Rivera for his first at-bat of the game with two out and the winning run 90 feet away.

There are many reasons the Yankees held first place for such a long period over the Orioles, but perhaps none was bigger than the fertility of the Yankee farm system, compared with that of Baltimore. In the 1960s and 1970s, no team did a better job of developing talent than the Orioles, whose farm system provided the backbone for 16 seasons of 90 or more wins from 1964 to 1983. Baltimore won the World Series in 1983, which was Cal Ripken's second full season. But Ripken was the last impact-position player developed before the system went fallow, and the Orioles had not been to the postseason since that year. The Yankees, conversely, had spent the latter half of the 1980s and the early 1990s developing one of the majors' strongest farm systems, thanks to four men in particular: Bill Livesey, Brian Sabean, George Bradley, and Mark Newman.

Livesey and Sabean were masters at finding talent. They had a flock of loyal scouts that stayed together for a long time, so the group was in accord on what Livesey and Sabean preached. They wanted their scouts to take risks and scour the world for talent. They emphasized winning in the minor leagues. They thought knowing how to win was a vital tool that should be stressed up and down the system, and that games should be played to win, not to build prospects' stats. They favored size and athleticism. Livesey, in fact, devised a blueprint for how tall he thought a player at each position should be. Visitors to the Yankee minor league complex might think they were watching a basketball tryout because the players were so big and agile. "When I first came to the organization in 1989, I came from the Reds, and I was in awe of the athletic ability and size and strength of the players," says longtime Yankee minor league coach Gary Denbo.

Bradley and Newman brought organizational skills to complement the scouting acumen of Livesey and Sabean. Bradley arrived in 1988, and his good nature and coalition-forming skills instilled a greater collaborative spirit to the tension that had developed between scouting and player development, in large part because of Livesey's inability to see any way except his way of doing business. Bradley inspired a sense of community to an organization run by a dictator like Steinbrenner. He knew the human value of having an engraved nameplate on a minor league coach's locker, rather than a piece of tape with a name in magic marker. He made sure scouts had their expenses paid on time. He also made a series of hires of industrious, intelligent coaches and executives, none more important than Newman. Newman had a law degree and had been the head coach at Old Dominion University from 1981 until joining the Yankees in 1988. He used both disciplines to influence the Yankee system.

"Newman was great at taking everyone's input and then making a decision on how we would do things," remembers Mark Weidemaier, a Yankee minor league coach and instructor from 1989 to 1991. "He would say, 'Gentlemen, I am not saying this is the best way or the only way, but I am saying that when we reach a decision and leave this room, it is the Yankee Way, and that when you begin coaching, do not deviate with the players.'"

That is how the Yankee Way was born—in a laboratory of ideas. Yankee personnel would take out a stopwatch to determine the quickest way to turn a double play. There would be hours-long discussions on, for example, what a standard lead from a base was and from which foot and part of the foot you measure. A decision was made to put two coaches at every level, so the manager managed from the dugout rather than the third-base coaching box when his team was batting. When a player was promoted up the ladder, the videotape of the player hitting and fielding was sent up with him, so the new manager could familiarize himself with the player.

Newman gathered insights from 15 others and in 1989 compiled the 500-page Yankee System Developmental Manual. If you wanted to know how many degrees to turn on a cutoff play, it was there. This became the bible from which Yankee minor league officials taught, creating a uniformity and culture of seriousness at every level. The Yankees were also blessed to have recruited a group of diligent minor league coaches and managers such as Brian Butterfield, Gary Denbo, Rick Down, Trey Hillman, and Glenn Sherlock. Buck Showalter was already in place but epitomized the breed, and perhaps cared even more because he had spent his entire minor league career as a Yankee. Being a Yankee mattered to him. He infused a generation of minor leaguers with his sense of purpose and with the gravity of wearing the pinstripes. "A lot of people killed Buck Showalter, but he ingrained the Yankee Way into us," Jim Leyritz says.

In the late 1980s, the Yankees took over the facility on Himes Avenue in Tampa from the Cincinnati Reds, renovated it, and created a state-of-the-art locale. Yankee officials encouraged minor league coaches to move to the area, helping the Yankees to become the first team to keep their facility open year-round for use by their major and minor leaguers. Derek Jeter, for example, moved to Tampa and spent the winter months speeding up his development.

The last key element in the rise of the Yankee farm system was George Steinbrenner's suspension from August of 1990 to March of 1993. Although there was always a sense of his continued covert influence, Steinbrenner was unable to impose himself in his more familiar, overbearing manner. For those years, a greater calm existed in promoting players such as Scott Kamieniecki, Pat Kelly, Gerald Williams, and, especially, Bernie Williams and giving them a chance to develop. There was not a frenzy to trade prospects for a stab at immediate gratification.

"People say you can't rebuild in this town," Brian Cashman says, looking back. "That's bullshit. We did. George had to be banned, but we got great dividends. That came from completely rebuilding when Stick [Michael] and Buck were here. George would not have allowed rebuilding because of his competitive nature."

By 1996, Sabean had fled the organization to work for the Giants, Bradley had been fired after losing a power struggle with Gene Michael, and Livesey had been fired in September 1995 over power and money issues. Newman was the only main official who remained, but the philosophy and diligence of the executives lived on. Jeter, Andy Pettitte, Mariano Rivera, and Bernie Williams were homegrown products that were flourishing, and Jim Leyritz was a useful ingredient. Andy Fox and Ramiro Mendoza had popped up from the minors to offer key assistance during the 1996 season. David Cone, Cecil Fielder, Charlie Hayes, Joe Girardi, Tino Martinez, Jeff Nelson, Paul O'Neill, Tim Raines, and John Wetteland had been obtained using players developed on the Yankee farm following the gospel of the Yankee Way.

"The Yankees were architects for a lot of ways to build an organization," says J. P. Ricciardi, a coach in the Yankee organization from 1982 to 1984, and later the Blue Jays' GM. "They took high-risk guys in the draft who would be tough to sign. They did on-base percentage before it was in style. They had their tentacles everywhere in the world. And they made great trades."

The culmination of all the great work done in this period manifested, the Yankees believed, in the most talented player they had developed, perhaps since Mickey Mantle. A kid named Ruben Rivera.

Still, Rivera was not a completed product when he stepped in against Alan Mills as the Oriole-Yankee opener neared its climax. If there was one factor beyond his immaturity that had stunted Ruben Rivera's growth, it was his inability to identify a slider from a righty pitcher. That was Mills's best pitch. If Joe Torre had another extra outfielder available, he would have pinch-hit rather than feed Rivera to Mills. But Torre had used Darryl Strawberry earlier in the game.

The righty threw five straight sliders. Rivera lofted the fifth, on a 2–2 pitch, just beyond the leaping efforts of second baseman Roberto Alomar in the 10th inning. Sometimes a division race can come down to this, the ball eluding Alomar by an inch, maybe not even. Suddenly the trade of Gerald Williams, the injury to Pat Listach, and Steinbrenner's overruling nature had a positive outcome. It had allowed Ruben Rivera to make the most important defensive play of the season in Detroit and deposit this ball into right field against Baltimore. Jeter scored the winning run in a 3–2 victory, and the Yankees engaged in their most enthusiastic celebration yet, emptying out of the dugout to smother Rivera. The lead was back to 4 games with 12 to play. And the Orioles were back to being the Orioles.

After the game, Randy Myers complained about getting pulled out of the save situation by Davey Johnson and having fallen into a ninth-inning time share with Mills. Just a few weeks earlier, Myers had been critical of Mussina for being selfish and complaining about being part of a four-man rotation. Now Myers, one of Johnson's few staunch supporters dating from their days together with the Mets, had abandoned the Orioles manager. Mussina lasted just two innings in the doubleheader opener on September 20, and the Yankees roared to a 9–3 victory. That lessened the pain of Cone allowing six runs in five innings in the nightcap. Mariano Rivera took the loss when he was strafed for three runs in one-third of an inning in a 10–9 Oriole triumph.

The Yankees had accomplished their mission, however. They had won two games in this series while taking three more off the schedule. They had proven once again their superiority over the Orioles, winning the season series 10–3 and essentially ending the division race. Greg Norman was going to remain the biggest sports choker of 1996, having blown a six-shot lead over Nick Faldo on the final day of the Masters in mid-April. The Orioles were a confident 9–2 that day, a first-place team. Now they were 4 games back, with 10 to play. After all the worry of August and early September, it was now just a matter of time until the Yankees wrapped up their first division title in a full season since 1980.

That time came on September 25, at home against the Brewers in the opening game of a doubleheader. The Yankees scored 14 runs in the first two innings, and so the final seven innings were a long celebration. It seemed so right that Cone was the starter and the winner that day. "If you told me 2 months ago that David Cone was going to pitch the clincher, I would have said, 'You are out of your mind,'" Torre said. Torre's only important decision was which pitcher to let finish the game and savor being on the mound for the clinching out. With expanded rosters after September 1, he could have picked a disposable arm to mop up. But Torre thought it only fitting that designation go to a player who had made the full journey from spring training to this magic moment. Torre also saw this as a chance to give a boost to a player who would find honor in the event. He was already managing for October. Torre chose the talented but erratic Jeff Nelson, who induced Fernando Vina to fly to Bernie Williams in center, uncorking a confetti-strewn celebration.

The Yankees had taken a punch and righted themselves to secure the division, winning 11 of 15 games. In retrospect, Joe Girardi would say that the plummet of August was good for the Yankees because it forced them out of a coasting mentality and into a high level of play for the postseason. The summertime collapse and recovery reasserted to the group that they could rebound when situations looked grim.

In the postgame clubhouse, Torre was told a congratulatory phone call was awaiting him from the man who a few weeks earlier had likened him to Ralph Branca. Torre had not forgotten, so when he picked up the phone as the manager of the AL East champion Yankees, he said to George Steinbrenner, "Hi, Bobby Thomson here."

Torre had more serious matters to talk about after clinching the division title. Just as he did in spring training, he made it clear that the goal was a championship; anything short of that was unacceptable. So in the waning days of the schedule, he prepared his team for October, resting regulars and gathering the last dollops of information to shape a 25-man postseason roster. On September 28, Andy Pettitte faced his idol, Roger Clemens, in what the Rocket correctly suspected was his final game at Fenway Park as a Red Sox. He took a fistful of dirt from the mound as he departed. That was the day that Dwight Gooden learned from Torre that he would not be on the Division Series roster. Gooden's lost confidence, lifeless fastball, and 13.78 ERA in his final 11 starts made him too much of a liability. Ten years earlier, Clemens and Gooden had been the flame-throwing main event when the Red Sox and Mets played for the 1986 World Series. A decade earlier, Doc and the Rocket were the most dominant arms in the game.

In 1996, that distinction belonged to Mariano Rivera, who finished his regular season on September 28 by striking out Nomar Garciaparra and Bill Haselman with the tying runs on base to end the eighth inning of a 4–2 Yankee win. Rivera began spring training as an excess part. He wound up the most important player on this division winner. He was a closer, even if he rarely pitched in the ninth inning. He was a counterbalance to a season of runaway offense. In a year when the most runs in major league history were scored, Rivera went 8–3 with a 2.09 ERA, held opponents to a .193 batting average, and broke Goose Gossage's Yankee relief record of 122 strikeouts by fanning 130 in 107²/₃ innings. Most amazingly, of the record 4,962 homers spanked in 1996, Rivera allowed just one, to Baltimore's Rafael Palmeiro on June 28.

Rivera's spot in the bullpen was obviously not the one in question for the playoffs. The final decision came down to one lefty slot, Dale Polley or Graeme Lloyd, and one righty job, Dave Pavlas or David Weathers. Torre's decision was to take Lloyd and Weathers, the faces of Bob Watson's most miserable trades. On September 24, Watson had been forced by Steinbrenner to file an official protest with the AL office, asking that the Lloyd trade be reversed. So, essentially, the Yankees had just put on their playoff roster a pitcher they were hoping would be taken off their regular roster and given back to Milwaukee. AL president Gene Budig said he would hear the case on October 28, the day after Game 7 of the World Series was scheduled. The Yankees assumed they would not be participating in a World Series if Lloyd or Weathers was needed much in October anyway. The Yankees did figure their road to a championship had been enhanced when Texas held off Seattle to win the AL West. At one juncture in mid-September, the Rangers lost 9 of 10 games and, in that short spurt, watched a nine-game lead over the Mariners fall to one game. It looked as if Seattle would use a dynamic close to its season for a second straight year to reach the playoffs. That would have meant the Yankees were staring at Edgar Martinez and the Mariner team that owned them in another first round. But Texas righted itself to win the division.

The Rangers were a better matchup for the Yankees but posed problems similar to Seattle. Texas had a bludgeoning offense and a stadium at which the Yankees could not win. That year the Yankees were 1–5 at The Ballpark in Arlington, having been outscored 44–15. The Yankees were just 3–10 at the facility since it opened in 1994. Like the previous season, the best-of-five series was set up so that the Yankees would host two games before the next three were scheduled at the home of the West champion.

The luck of the draw again seemed to work against them. The Yankees, after all, were 6–0 at Jacobs Field in 1996, but the AL Central champion Indians had drawn the wild-card Orioles in the first round. So the pressure was intense on the Yankees to do just as they had done in 1995 and win the first two games at home. In John Burkett versus David Cone, the Yankees believed that they had an overwhelming advantage in Game 1. Also, like the Mariners the previous year, this was the first time in the Rangers' 36-year history (the first 11 in Washington as the Senators) that they were in the playoffs. The Yankees thought they should have an edge in composure as well.

But Game 1 proved disastrous. Torre decided to start Darryl Strawberry over Cecil Fielder as the designated hitter, and Strawberry went 0-for-4, failing in three at-bats with runners in scoring position. Derek Jeter, who had handled the pressure of the regular season exquisitely, stranded a total of six runners in the game. The Yankees had one hit in 12 at-bats with runners in scoring position, and, stunningly, that allowed Burkett to pitch a complete game. The

Rangers acquired Burkett from Florida 9 days after the Yankees obtained David Weathers from the Marlins. So Steinbrenner found yet another avenue to fume at Watson. Why did he obtain the useless Weathers from Florida, rather than Burkett?

Most disturbing for the Yankees was that Cone, who was supposed to be the big-game guy, had allowed a three-run homer to Juan Gonzalez and a two-run shot by Dean Palmer in the fourth inning to set the tone for a 6–2 Ranger triumph. The only Yankee highlight of Game 1 was, surprisingly, authored by Graeme Lloyd. Before the series had even begun, Torre's postseason wisdom was questioned because he had included Lloyd and his 17.47 Yankee ERA on the roster. Torre always said a manager has to consult his gut, and his gut told him Lloyd was better than the dismal numbers, with more weapons than Dale Polley.

The fans did not agree. The largest gathering ever at the refurbished Yankee Stadium, 57,156, made Lloyd the only Yankee booed during pregame introductions. The fans greeted him with thunderous disapproval when the lefty took the mound in the seventh. But Lloyd was cheered off the field when he retired three straight Rangers on groundouts in seven pitches. It was rare lefty success when facing the Rangers. Southpaw starters were 14–25 with a 6.56 ERA against Texas in 1996, and the Yankees had three lefties in a row now scheduled to start: Andy Pettitte, Jimmy Key, and the emotionally fragile Kenny Rogers. Plus, the Rangers had done what even Seattle could not do the year before: win a Division Series game at Yankee Stadium. Game 3 and, if necessary, 4 and 5, scheduled for The Ballpark in Arlington, lurked even more ominously now.

The large crowd at Yankee Stadium had not included the first-term governor of Texas. George W. Bush told a TV station in his home state, "I don't want to go to Yankee Stadium. I would have to arm myself." New York mayor Rudy Giuliani reacted with irritation, citing crime statistics for how safe his city had become. Karen Hughes, Bush's spokeswoman, said the governor had merely spoken in jest, and this was a misunderstanding. Bush had given up ownership of the Rangers to become governor, and he certainly planned to attend the games at The Ballpark in Arlington to watch his beloved team.

By the time the third inning of Game 2 was complete, it was looking more and more as though Bush was going to be on hand to watch a major league team from his state win a playoff series for the first time. Gonzalez had a solo homer and a three-run homer off Pettitte. During the regular season, Gonzalez had mashed Yankee pitching for 20 hits in 37 at-bats with 5 homers and 16 RBIs. Now he had 3 homers and 7 RBIs in his first seven Division Series at-bats. Juan Gonzalez was the Yankees' worst nightmare, the Edgar Martinez of 1996. The Rangers led Game 2 4–1 and were six innings away from a Yankee Stadium sweep—six innings from going up two games to none before a single game had been played in Arlington.

The Yankees had used a franchise record–tying 49 players in 1996, none of them named Tony Fernandez or Melido Perez. Pat Kelly hardly played, and David Cone and Tim Raines played far less than expected. The Yankees dealt with the trauma of Cone's aneurysm and the carnival-like arrival of Strawberry. Joe Torre had one brother die and another brother awaiting a heart transplant. The Yankees stared down infamy by surviving their late-season swoon, and they endured the nefarious machinations of Steinbrenner.

Yet at 9 p.m. on October 2, the Yankees were at their bleakest moment of this trying, thrilling season.

11 | THE PERFECT TEAM

"The Yankees really weren't our big concern when the playoffs began. We thought we were better than them. We were more talented and had more veterans. We were looking at the Baltimore-Cleveland series more than our own."

—*Rangers reliever Mike Stanton on his club's mind-set as the Division Series began*

To fully appreciate the Yankees' Division Series plight, you have to remember who they were as the fourth inning began in Game 2. They had not won a playoff round in 15 years. They had just 12 months earlier lost three straight games in Seattle to erase a two-game Division Series lead. Because of that, they were roundly viewed as chokers.

Joe Torre and the Washington Senators had joined the major leagues full-time in 1961. The Senators, now the Rangers, had finally won their first playoff game. Torre was still waiting. There was no history of the Rangers being unable to beat the Yankees in October. On the contrary, they had a one-game lead in this series, a three-run lead in Game 2, a dominant home-field advantage lurking, and the most frightening hitter on the planet in Juan Gonzalez. At this moment, a dynasty for the Yankees was inconceivable. Instead, the reputations of a team and its manager were on the brink of absorbing irreparable harm. Stanton's cockiness is better understood through this lens.

But Game 2 was going to last quite a while—long enough for Torre's image to be buffed and his team to exhibit a late-game poise that would become its October trademark. Torre determined before the first pitch to treat Game 2 like a must-win elimination contest. He could not imagine the Yankees winning three straight in Texas. So whatever was necessary to produce a victory, Torre was willing to do. That included rectifying his own misjudgment in starting

Darryl Strawberry in Game 1. Strawberry had experience against Game 2 starter Ken Hill from his National League days, but the same was true about John Burkett. Those numbers, though, were from another lifetime, when Strawberry was as imposing as Juan Gonzalez. Strawberry's poor at-bats in the opener could not be ignored. So Torre inserted Fielder as the designated hitter, and in the bottom of the fourth inning the Detroit import boomed a home run to left and the Texas lead shriveled to 4–2.

Through four innings Andy Pettitte battled himself, not just Juan Gonzalez. He walked 6 of his first 18 batters. Then Torre made another crucial decision. He spent an entire season watching Pettitte weather early bombardments to work deep into games, giving himself and the team a chance to win. So Torre invested in Pettitte, not retrieving the ball until there was one out in the seventh. Pettitte did not allow another run and finished by retiring five straight Rangers. He would not earn his 14th win after a Yankee loss, but the positive length of his outing contributed to a Yankee victory. With the righty might of the Ranger lineup—Ivan Rodriguez, Gonzalez, and Dean Palmer—awaiting to hit for a fourth time, Torre thought it necessary to insert not only his best righty reliever but someone capable of changing momentum. And there was no one on his roster more capable of changing momentum than Mariano Rivera.

It further illustrated Torre's desperation. From the middle of May until the end of the regular season, a span that covered 47 appearances by his most reliable reliever, Torre had used Rivera just twice when the Yankees trailed. He summoned Rivera on August 26 against Seattle just to get the righty work. He also went to Rivera on September 18 in the final series against the Orioles to take over from Pettitte and preserve a 2–1 deficit in the ninth inning. The Yankees rallied to win that vital game. The idea was the same here. Torre knew he could not afford to cede any more runs to the Rangers, and Rivera was his ultimate stopper. Rivera struck out Rodriguez on three pitches and induced Rusty Greer to ground out.

In the bottom of the seventh, with runners on second and third and one out, Torre again shunned how he might have managed in June or July. He had spent so little of his life in the playoffs yet instinctively had the most essential element nailed. Each game at this time of year is so precious. A playoff game could change quickly and take the series with it in a new direction. Thus, it was not a time to worry about bruising feelings. You managed only to win that day, no longer psychologically nursing players through the laborious season. So with lefty Dennis Cook on the mound, Torre pinch-hit Charlie Hayes for Wade Boggs, a five-time batting champion. Hayes lifted a sacrifice fly, and the Yankees were within 4–3. "You try to manage the game and not the name, especially at this time of the season," Torre said afterward.

Rivera buzzed through the Rangers again in order, and in the bottom of the eighth inning, Bernie Williams led off with a single. Williams had earned the nickname "Bambi" early in his career because, especially on the bases, he could look as confused as a deer in the headlights when deciding where and when to move. But in a decisive burst, Williams shocked the Rangers by tagging to take second on a fly to left by Tino Martinez. That put him into position to come home when Fielder rewarded Torre's judgment once more with an RBI single that tied the score. Fielder was 2-for-3 with a homer, two RBIs, and a walk. Torre did not hesitate to send Rivera out to pitch a third inning; the Rangers had to be held scoreless. A year earlier, Buck Showalter hadn't trusted his eyes—hadn't believed what he saw—as Rivera mowed down the Mariners in the postseason. Torre, though, had marveled for a full year at Rivera's excellence. Rivera went three-up, three-down in the ninth. He had faced eight Rangers in all, retiring every one of them in a mere 25 pitches. Mostly, he had achieved Torre's mandate. Mariano Rivera had changed the momentum of Game 2, providing the scoreless cover for the Yankees to rally to knot the score.

Still, tension washed over Yankee Stadium. The 57,156 in attendance recognized the value of this game as John Wetteland, another reliever shunned in the waning minutes of the Showalter regime, followed Rivera with two shutout innings. In the top of the 12th inning, Torre used four relievers—Graeme Lloyd, Jeff Nelson, Kenny Rogers, and Brian Boehringer—to get three outs. Rogers threw four straight balls to Will Clark to load the bases in his first relief appearance since 1993, even more proof that Rogers was not useful to Torre. Boehringer, though, got Palmer to fly to right as rain began to fall. The Yankee pitchers, Andy Pettitte and six relievers, had now thrown the equivalent of a complete-game shutout since the third inning. Yet with Rivera and Wetteland out of the game and only Boehringer and David Weathers left from the pen, Rangers general manager Doug Melvin thought his team would win, if only they could get through the bottom of the 12th, which Derek Jeter led off.

There had been questions after his lousy Game 1 about Jeter's stomach for the postseason. Torre never even considered that Jeter might be overwhelmed by this milieu. Jeter was certain to be named American League Rookie of the Year for what he did on the field. Yet Torre's lasting impression was formed from what he saw off the field. All year, Jeter had exemplified a high baseball IQ for such a young age, especially when it came to baserunning. He was the antithesis of Bernie Williams—he was aware and decisive. But on August 12 in Chicago, Jeter broke one of the cardinal rules of the game when he tried to steal third base as the tying run with two out and Fielder batting. You never steal third with two out unless you are 100 percent certain to make it. You certainly don't try in the late innings with a renowned RBI man up and your team trailing. Jeter was thrown out and knew instantly he had committed a bonehead play. He knew just as quickly how furious Torre was. Still, when he returned to the dugout, Jeter sat right next to Torre. It was his way of telling his manager that he was accountable, that he would accept any reprimand associated with such an egregious mistake and not run away or hide. Torre was defused. Although he hated the blunder, Torre loved Jeter's recognition and, more important, his willingness to own up to it. How many veterans would do that? Torre thought appreciatively. He tousled Jeter's head and said, "Get out of here."

Torre reasoned his young shortstop would not go into a cocoon of self-doubt following his poor opener. Hadn't Jeter been the Yankees' best hitter in

September, batting .356 as the Orioles closed in? Hadn't he generated a 17-game hitting streak during that month, the longest by a Yankee rookie since a guy named Joe DiMaggio went 18 in a row in 1936? Hadn't he looked into the manager's office on the way out of the clubhouse following Game 1, as he so often did, and playfully advised his battle-worn skipper to get a good night's sleep because the most important game of Torre's life was the next day? The kid was the same as ever, Torre decided, not even worth talking to before Game 2.

Jeter, in fact, was incredulous that reporters thought his opener was anything more than a bad game, like any bad game that happened occasionally. He was not cowed by the playoffs. Jeter told the media that sitting on the bench as an inactive player during the previous year's Division Series as nothing more than a cheerleader was much more nerve-racking than actually playing. Jeter welcomed the magnitude of these games, yearned for them with all of his athletic desires.

The year 1996 was a coming-out party for two steely-nerved young athletes. Earlier that day, 20-year-old Tiger Woods shot a first-round 70 at the Las Vegas International en route to his first PGA Tour title, not even 2 months after his unprecedented third straight US Amateur win and the announcement he was turning pro. That night, 22-year-old Derek Jeter put an exclamation point on his declaration that he lived for these moments by opening the 12th inning with a single off of Stanton, his team-high third hit of Game 2.

Tim Raines began his at-bat trying to lay down a sacrifice and instead drew a walk, making it first and second. That brought up Hayes in what had been Boggs's spot in the order. In spring training, Hayes found it ridiculous how much Pirates manager Jim Leyland made everyone practice bunting. A rotund but durable player, Hayes was the type who went through the motions during bunting drills, figuring it was not his role. He had, after all, only eight sacrifice bunts in 941 major league games entering spring training of 1996. But now, as

Willie Randolph flashed the sign to sacrifice, Hayes silently thanked Jim Leyland, who had demanded his players' attention by preaching that the day would come when the skill to bunt would be necessary. In this situation, Hayes knew he had to steer the ball to make sure the third baseman charged and fielded.

In Game 1, third baseman Dean Palmer had made the defensive play of the game, diving to stop what likely would have been a two-run, tempo-setting, first-inning double by Paul O'Neill off John Burkett. Now he charged Hayes's expertly placed bunt as Texas second baseman Mark McLemore moved over to cover first. The Rangers had played error free over the first 20 innings of this series—no surprise, since Texas's 87 errors were the fewest in the majors, four fewer than the second-place Yankees. But the rain that fell in the top of the 12th made Hayes's bunt slick. Palmer did not grip it well and bounced a throw about 5 feet in front of McLemore. The ball skittered down the right-field line as Jeter loped all the way home from second base, touching home plate at 12:36 a.m. on October 3 and igniting a joyous, relieved celebration by the Yankees, who were 5–4 winners.

A year earlier, in a much heavier rain, Jim Leyritz had won a Game 2 at Yankee Stadium at 1:22 a.m. with a two-run homer off Seattle's Tim Belcher. The Yankees celebrated hard that night, as well, having taken a two-games-to-none lead. They never won again in 1995. They needed just one victory in the Kingdome and failed. So while feeling their season was resuscitated with this victory, the Yankees knew what awaited them. They had to win twice in a place they thought of as Arlington Cemetery.

And they were going to have to win with their owner in a complete frenzy. George Steinbrenner, 44 years older than Derek Jeter, was not proving as impervious to the tension of the playoffs as his rookie shortstop. For Game 1, Michael McGorry, a friend of Texas backup catcher Dave Valle and Ranger assistant GM Omar Minaya, had volunteered the luxury box of his Wall Street firm, S. G. Cowen & Co., for the Ranger wives so they could avoid being abused by the crowd. Valle and McGorry had known each other since playing in

Queens for a Catholic Youth Organization baseball team managed by a Flushing detective named Rocco Torre. The luxury box was down the third-base line, next to the Yankees limited partners' box, and word advanced to Steinbrenner that the women next door were cheering. Late in the Yankee loss, Steinbrenner arrived "in an absolute fury," McGorry remembers, and said the women were blocking the view of other fans. He told McGorry that his company had lost the right to use the box. "He only did it because he was angry the Yankees were losing; it was just bad sportsmanship," McGorry says. "He just lost it."

The Ranger wives were back in the stands for Game 2. As for Yankee wives, Steinbrenner banned them from the team charter to Texas because spouses had traveled to Seattle for the playoffs in 1995, and the Yankees had lost.

The wives were not the only ones Steinbrenner did not want to see on the charter. The Boss was sitting on the bus that was to carry Yankee front-office officials, the manager, and coaches to Newark Airport about 90 minutes after Game 2 had ended, around 2 a.m. Reggie Jackson, a member of Steinbrenner's special advisory board, entered the crowded bus, and Torre slid over to invite his pal to sit beside him in the first row on the passenger side. Steinbrenner was in the seat directly behind them, and Torre says he thought it ticked the Boss off that Jackson was sitting a row ahead of him. But bad will had been brewing for a while, in part because Jackson wanted to be listened to on, among other things, player personnel. Steinbrenner was in a phase when he had no use for Jackson. Talking loudly enough to be heard throughout the bus, Steinbrenner began assailing Jackson, inquiring in a nasty tone about who had given him permission to be on this trip. Jackson responded by asking if Steinbrenner wanted him to leave. The Boss said no, but he belittled Jackson by saying that in the future he needed Steinbrenner's permission to go anyplace with the team. At that point, according to a club official who was on the bus, "Reggie just snapped. He could have used an insanity defense if he were charged with anything because he completely lost control." Jackson got into Steinbrenner's face and began screaming that he would not accept being treated "like an animal anymore."

"It was like the worst umpire confrontation ever from Lou Piniella and Billy

Martin. That is how in George's face Reggie was," the club official added. "Instinct took over for George, like someone playing dead in front of a grizzly bear, because he just stood down and let Reggie go off. It was the smartest thing he ever did. Everyone on that bus thought Reggie was going to hit him if George said one more word."

Torre, Mel Stottlemyre, Willie Randolph, and Gene Michael restrained Jackson. Steinbrenner continued to simmer, but not about Jackson. He had been laying into his executives during the first two games. He was angered that the Orioles had already won two games against Cleveland, out-homering the Indians 4–2 to gain control of the Division Series. He was incensed that his front office had been so sure that Baltimore's power would not translate into more tightly contested playoff matchups. But the Orioles had scored 17 runs in two games.

Meanwhile, Juan Gonzalez was on a tear right before his eyes. For the second straight year, a player leveling the Yankees was being dubbed with a Spanish version of Jackson's nickname, Señor October. Last year it was Edgar Martinez, now Gonzalez. This was the kind of power hitter for which Steinbrenner lusted. Gonzalez was going to win the AL Most Valuable Player award off of his 47 homers and 144 RBIs regular season. Now he had three more homers in the playoffs.

Steinbrenner fumed about why one of his executives could not find someone like this.

Juan Gonzalez was from Vega Baja; Bernie Williams hailed from the adjoining town of Puerto Rico, Vega Alta. In the spring of 1985, when Gonzalez was 15 and Williams 16, they played together for the champion Sabana Hoyos team in the Mickey Mantle League. A Yankee scout named Roberto Rivera watched a center fielder with long arms and long legs and wrote in his reports to his bosses back in New York that he was sizing up the next Dave Winfield. The scouting director, Doug Melvin, did not see that in Williams. He had run track in high school, specializing in the 200 and 400 meters, and Melvin immediately appreciated Williams's speed and proper running form, his hands open and pumping like blades cutting the air. The kid was nice, respectful. Even as a teenager, Bernie Williams looked you in the eyes and pondered a question studiously.

His game was raw, however, and he had a way of disappearing into his own world—what his teammates would later dub playfully "Bernie World." Sometimes the scouts in Puerto Rico looked into the outfield and saw Williams playing air guitar instead of staring intently toward the infield. Williams was just a righty batter then, and his ability to hit at a big-league level had to be really projected, Melvin recalls, because there was not much power. "But scouts have dreams," Melvin says. "And Roberto Rivera dreamed with this kid."

At the time, the Padres had the strongest tentacles in Puerto Rico, having signed the Alomar brothers, Roberto and Sandy, Carlos Baerga, and Benito Santiago, among others. Rivera fretted that if the Yankees waited until Williams's 17th birthday, September 13, 1985, when he was legal to ink his first pro contract, another club, probably San Diego, would swoop in beforehand to sign him. So Fred Ferreira, the Yankees' international scouting head, hatched an idea to hide Williams in the United States. Williams's mother was a schoolteacher and not an easy convert to the idea of her son leaving the island for several months, much less playing professional baseball as a career. "I really had to sell her, and it wasn't easy," Ferreira says, looking back. The Yankees persuaded Williams's parents on the necessity of adjusting to American culture and learning better English before their son started playing full-time the following year. There was a baseball academy in Cheshire, Connecticut, a 20-minute drive from Melvin's home in Branford.

But Rufina Williams was not the only person Ferreira had to sell. He had to convince George Steinbrenner it was a worthwhile investment to put up a 16-year-old all summer in Connecticut. Williams, fearful of feeling lonely in a strange place, called Ferreira the day before he was scheduled to fly to the States and asked if he could bring a friend. "I didn't want to ask Mr. Steinbrenner about a second guy," Ferreira recalls. "So I told Bernie that I thought it might be too much of a distraction and expense for his pal to come along." The friend was Juan Gonzalez. That is how close the Yankees were to having both young-sters under their watchful eye.

Williams stayed in the dormitories of a baseball academy in Connecticut, occasionally eating dinner at Melvin's home and falling hard for his wife's straw-berry shortcake. In September, Williams returned to Puerto Rico. At a Howard Johnson's restaurant in San Juan, Rivera cried when informed by Melvin and Ferreira that the club would offer only an $8,000 signing bonus. Rivera said he could not take such a small sum to Williams's parents, not after his mother had initially fought so hard against her son relocating. The next day the offer was increased to $16,000, and Williams was a member of the Yankee family.

It was Melvin who decided he had to leave the organization, having grown weary of the 152-mile daily round-trip from his Connecticut home to Yankee Stadium. Melvin had pitched four seasons in the Yankee minor leagues in the late 1970s, signed by then scouting director Pat Gillick. After retiring as a player, he had risen in the Yankee hierarchy from batting practice pitcher to scouting director. Melvin was from Chatham, Ontario. His Canadian roots and long association with Gillick, who by 1986 was the Blue Jays' GM, convinced George Steinbrenner that Melvin would try to get to Toronto. So the Boss had his then GM, Clyde King, block that possibility. It turned out worse for Steinbrenner. Melvin was hired by Steinbrenner's sworn enemy in Baltimore, Larry Lucchino, and served nearly a decade in the Oriole organization before becoming the Rangers' GM for the 1996 season.

Melvin was sitting in his box at The Ballpark in Arlington in the first inning of Game 3 when, with two out, the 16-year-old boy he had once hidden near his home proved that he had indeed developed power. Bernie Williams homered to right field off Darren Oliver to give the Yankees a 1–0 lead. With two outs in the bottom of the inning, Williams displayed the sprinter's grace that Melvin had once so admired, racing with those long strides before leaping at the outfield wall to pull what would have been a homer by Rusty Greer off of Jimmy Key back into the park. That prevented a tie score and Williams's friend from the sandlots of Puerto Rico from batting in the first inning.

Juan Gonzalez, however, did bat in the fourth inning and hit his fourth homer of this series to tie the score at 1–1. In the fifth, Ivan Rodriguez doubled in a run to put Texas ahead 2–1. There had been a tryout camp run by the Rangers in the mid-1980s in Puerto Rico when Williams, Gonzalez, and Rodriguez were all on the field together. Now Gonzalez and Rodriguez, also from Vega Baja, were excelling in the first-ever playoff game in Arlington. The Rangers had so captured the imagination of the region that they were the top sports attraction in the football-crazy state, though the Friday night lights were on all over with high school football games in play.

The Yankees, meanwhile, were feeding the joy at The Ballpark by playing in such a sloppy fashion. Charlie Hayes, starting in place of Wade Boggs against the lefty Oliver, was picked off second base in the third inning. Williams was picked off first in the fourth inning. Jeter failed to cover second base on a Kevin Elster steal in the fifth inning, allowing Rodriguez to bat and produce his RBI double that moved the Rangers into the lead. After the inning, Torre walked over and, loud enough for everyone to hear, told Jeter, "Get your head in the game." Torre was angry with Jeter for the mistake. But he also realized his rookie shortstop was tough enough to be singled out for everyone to get the same message.

Torre had gone so far as to install Jeter as the leadoff hitter because the Rangers were starting a lefty, but also because he recognized Jeter would embrace the responsibility. The lefty, Darren Oliver, carried a four-hitter into the ninth inning with Jeter due to bat first. The Rangers were three outs away from taking a two-games-to-one lead in this best-of-five series. The Yankees were three outs away from handing their season to Kenny Rogers. But Oliver had completed just one game in 37 career starts. Mike Stanton said there was a sense in the bullpen of uneasiness that Rangers manager Johnny Oates was going to try to get Oliver through the top of the order again. Oates had finished up his playing career as a backup catcher and teammate of Bob Watson on the 1980–81 Yankees. In 1982, he managed the Yankees' Double-A affiliate, Nashville, to the Southern League title. The Sounds won the decisive game over Jacksonville in the 13th inning when Buck Showalter scored the winning run. Now Oates, like Showalter a year earlier, was afraid of his bullpen. Jeter had seen nothing but fastballs from Oliver and guessed what was coming again, generating his second hit of the game, a single to right. He went to third on a single by Tim Raines. Only then did Oates call upon his designated closer, Mike Henneman. Williams clocked the first pitch to right for a game-tying sacrifice fly. Cecil Fielder grounded weakly to third, allowing Raines to take second. Oates then eschewed bringing in the lefty Stanton to face Martinez, though he had struck out Martinez in Game 2. Instead, Oates had Henneman walk Martinez to set up a righty-righty matchup against Mariano Duncan.

Duncan was a talisman. He had been to the playoffs five times in 11 seasons with four different teams. He was perpetually enthusiastic—infectiously so, like Tim Raines. He was brought to the Yankees to be nothing more than a utility man. He blossomed into the regular second baseman, batting a team-best .340, despite being one of the least patient hitters in the majors. Duncan was the definition of a first-ball, fastball hitter, and Henneman wanted to capitalize on that free-swinging approach by getting Duncan to chase a first-pitch forkball. But Henneman left the pitch up, and Duncan stroked it to center field for a go-ahead single, only the Yankees' fourth hit in 27 at-bats in this series with runners in scoring position. They were doing just enough to win. John Wetteland, as was his wont, got into trouble by walking the leadoff man in the ninth but retired the next three hitters to save the victory for Jeff Nelson, who had delivered an imperative three innings of shutout relief. It was the first reward back to Torre for letting Nelson be on the mound for the division clincher. The Yankee bullpen had not allowed a run in $12^2/_3$ innings in this series. For the 13th time in 1996, the Rangers had blown a game when leading with three outs to go. The battle lines of this Division Series had been drawn.

The Yankees had a much more trustworthy bullpen than the Rangers did, and they too had gotten a pretty darn good player off the Sabana Hoyos Mickey Mantle League team of 1985.

The Yankee minor league system had a policy in the late 1980s and early 1990s of determining whether players had an aptitude for switch-hitting. Bernie Williams's predecessor in center field, Roberto Kelly, had shown no capacity to hit lefty, so the plan was quickly scrapped. But Williams, a natural righty, showed enough bat speed hitting lefty to extend the experiment. Carlos Tosca, a coach on Williams's first pro team in the Gulf Coast League in 1986, remembers Williams fighting his shyness to ask Tosca to pitch him batting practice after every game so he could work on his lefty stroke. The Yankees were co-tenants at their facility in Sarasota, the Ed Smith Complex, with the GCL Rangers. So Williams shared a clubhouse with Sammy Sosa, Kevin Brown, and a skinny outfielder he knew really well, Juan Gonzalez. Fred Ferreira said the Yankees just did not have the money in their budget to sign Gonzalez, who received $75,000 to join the Ranger organization in May 1986. Gonzalez was lean and agile enough back then to play center field, next to Sosa in right, in what was the first pro season for both.

After what also was his first pro season, Williams returned to play winter ball back home in Puerto Rico for Caguas and was further encouraged by his manager, Tim Foli, to keep working on his lefty stroke. Williams thought it was a good idea, too, a way for him to further capitalize on his speed. In 1987, Williams began the year by batting just .155 in his first 25 games at Single-A Fort Lauderdale for manager Buck Showalter, failing to get any hits left-handed before he tripped over first base and separated his right shoulder. Williams still has a ridge on the shoulder, a memento of the injury.

That was not the most important thing that lingered. Williams used the same term for suffering his injury in 1987 that Derek Jeter would about hurting his hand in 1993: "a blessing in disguise." And Williams also thanked the same man as Jeter. But rather than defense, Brian Butterfield worked every day to help Williams hone his lefty stroke while the two were together with Rookie Level Oneonta. He tutored Williams with extra soft toss and batting practice before and after every game. Bernie Williams worked so hard because, though he was just 18, he felt he was at a crossroads in his life. He was taking premed classes at the University of Puerto Rico in the off-season. He was majoring in biology and had always thought about going into orthopedics, a dream his mother had strongly wanted him to follow. Williams was internally debating his commitment to full-time baseball, so he decided at this moment that he would immerse himself in the game and self-impose a mandate: "I was going to become a switch-hitter or quit baseball," Williams says, looking back. "And the truth is, failing at that challenge was not a possibility to me. I had never failed at anything in my life, and I was not going to let this be the first. I decided, *I'm going to be a switch-hitter.*"

In 25 games for Oneonta upon his return, Williams hit .344. The extra work in Brian Butterfield's factory paid off. The following season at Single-A Prince William, he won the batting title, hitting .335. "That put me on the map," Williams says. It also motivated him to return home that year and tell the dean of his department: "Maybe I could do both things at once, but I have a passion for the game and, right now, I am not doing a service to either. I am mediocre at both." Williams says, "The dean told me to do the baseball thing. He told me the window of opportunity was a lot shorter in baseball. He said the door would always be open there for me back in school."

Ten years later, Williams had not returned to college. But he was leading off the fourth inning of Division Series Game 4, batting lefty against Texas starter Bobby Witt. The Yankees already trailed 4–0. Torre had lifted his starter, Rogers, after just two innings and two runs because he sensed the lefty was a nervous wreck against his former team. The Rangers had tried to re-sign Rogers the previous off-season with Doug Melvin, offering 4 years at $17.5 million, which was roughly equivalent to the $20 million Rogers ultimately accepted from the Yankees because Texas had no state income tax. Rogers also lived in Arlington, just a few miles from the stadium. Rogers explained that he moved on to the Yankees because "I wanted to play for a winner," a comment that so annoyed the Rangers that in spring training they had posted a newspaper clip with the quote in their clubhouse for motivation. Now they had exacted real vengeance against Rogers, who was furious for being lifted so quickly. Brian Boehringer allowed two runs in the third inning, one of which came on Juan Gonzalez's fifth homer in four games. Gonzalez tied Ken Griffey and Reggie Jackson for the most homers in a playoff series. So Williams's single off Witt hardly seemed like a response to Gonzalez. But, despite the big deficit, Williams challenged the elite arm of Ivan Rodriguez and stole second, triggering a three-run inning in which the Yankees batted around. Lefty Dennis Cook retired Wade Boggs to end the onslaught, but because Williams was leading off the fifth inning, Johnny Oates inserted righty Roger Pavlik to make Williams bat from his weaker left side again. Williams worked the count full and crushed a 428-foot homer into the Ranger bullpen in right-center field, tying the score and honoring all that extra work that Carlos Tosca and Brian Butterfield had undertaken with a shy teenager.

In the bottom of the inning, with runners on first and second, no outs, and Gonzalez at bat, Torre summoned David Weathers. At that moment it was harder to conceive of a bigger mismatch in baseball. Gonzalez had batted 14 times against the Yankees in the series, to date, and homered on five of them. Weathers was a pudgy fellow with braces whose claim to fame at that moment was that he was going to be part of the case to get Bob Watson fired; Steinbrenner had taken particular glee during Weathers's struggles to point out that his general manager had acquired a pitcher the Boss had never even heard of. It all looked even worse when Weathers fell behind 3–1 to Gonzalez. But Torre had not put Weathers on the playoff roster cavalierly. When Weathers returned from his Triple-A banishment in mid-September, he was used exclusively in relief, and his sinker-slider repertoire was better suited for this role. He had allowed just one run out of the Yankee pen in seven relief appearances covering seven innings. He had followed his fellow maligned import, Graeme Lloyd, in the Game 1 loss and retired all six batters he had faced, including Gonzalez on a fly to center.

In this spot, Torre figured he just could not have Gonzalez challenged with more fastballs, Boehringer's weapon of choice. Torre thought Weathers's slider gave the Yankees their best opportunity to defuse the Ranger cleanup hitter. Gonzalez chased a slider down and away to run the count full. Weathers threw another slider, and Gonzalez, feeling the weight of carrying an entire team, chased a pitch that broke severely off the plate. Strike 3. Weathers then induced Will Clark to bounce a sinker into an inning-ending double play.

At that moment, this series was effectively over; the Yankees would not have to face a decisive Division Series Game 5 on the road for a second straight year. Weathers completed a journey from invisible to invincible with, amazingly, three shutout innings, just as Nelson had done the day before. "The biggest relief appearance of the series," Wetteland said of Weathers. Mariano Rivera and Wetteland combined for three more scoreless frames, Wetteland again working in and out of trouble by striking out Dean Palmer to end the game and the series with the tying runs on base via two walks. Cecil Fielder continued to make Torre's decision to reinstitute him into the lineup look brilliant with his second RBI single of this game, this one in the seventh inning, putting the Yankees ahead.

And, in the ninth inning against Stanton, Williams homered from his natural right side. It would mark just the second time in playoff history that a player had homered from both sides of the plate. The other time came in Game 3 of the Division Series in the Kingdome a year earlier off lefty Randy Johnson and righty Bill Risley. Ruffina Williams's son had done it then as well. The Yankees lost that game, the first of what would be three in a row. This time Bernie Williams made history in a Yankee win, their second straight in a place where the Yankees made new history, a place where they exorcised their Arlington demons. In the postgame celebration, teammates mobbed Williams, pouring champagne over his head and screaming "M-V-P, M-V-P." It was certainly a long way from Mel Hall.

The Yankees had come from behind to win three straight games, victories made possible by a bullpen that allowed one earned run in 19⅔ innings. Yes, Rivera and Wetteland had been as impeccable as ever. Rivera had faced 15 batters in the series, walked one, and retired the other 14. The Yankees were now 87–1 on the season when leading after eight innings because of this dynamic duo. But the bullpen was proving to be more than just Rivera and Wetteland. The winning Yankee pitchers in this series were named Boehringer, Nelson, and Weathers, and even Lloyd had provided his superb outing in the Game 1 loss. The Rangers batted just .104 after the sixth inning.

Gonzalez had indeed been great. But unlike Junior Griffey, whose five homers were supported by the brilliance of Edgar Martinez, Jay Buhner, Tino Martinez, and Randy Johnson with the 1995 Mariners, Gonzalez was alone. He hit five of the Rangers' six homers and produced 9 of their 16 RBIs. The Yankees were mentally tougher than in 1995, their bullpen so much better. And they were a team rather than a Juan-man band. Williams had helped neutralize the impact of his childhood pal, while Jeter's star continued to grow. Jeter batted .412 against the Rangers, rebounding from his dismal Game 1 to score the 12th-inning winning run in Game 2, trigger the winning ninth-inning rally in Game 3, and drive in a run in Game 4. Fielder and Hayes validated their acquisitions, and Duncan and Raines underscored the depth of this Yankee roster. The way this series had played out had the Yankees using the "F" word liberally. But they were not the only team that now believed Fate was on its side.

The Orioles were projecting an extra layer of toughness after a season in which that quality had been questioned. They had weathered all their internal problems to win the wild card and had just manhandled the team with the majors' most victories, eliminating the 99-win Indians in four games. Plus, they had overcome an additional distraction to reach the AL Championship Series for the first time in 13 years. On the final Friday of the regular season, September 27, Orioles star second baseman Roberto Alomar had taken a called third strike and argued heartily with home-plate ump John Hirschbeck. The dispute continued even with Alomar in the dugout. Hirschbeck ejected Alomar. Davey Johnson and Alomar raced onto the field, with the manager trying to stay lodged between his player and the umpire. But Alomar got close enough to spit in the umpire's face. It was an act both disgusting and disrespectful, yet not even Alomar's worst offense.

In postgame comments, he said, "I think he got problems with his family after his son died. I know that's something real tough in life for a person. I don't know, he just changed personality-wise. He just got more bitter." Hirschbeck's 8-year-old son, John Jr., had died on March 7, 1993, of a rare brain disorder called adrenoleukodystrophy, and his 9-year-old son was living with the disease. Upon hearing the comments through the media, Hirschbeck bolted into the Oriole clubhouse to try to confront Alomar, which he failed to do. But Alomar had made himself into the most hated man in baseball, even more despised than Cleveland's Albert Belle. The furor elevated when AL president Gene Budig handed out just a five-game suspension to Alomar that did not begin until the following regular season. The umpires threatened to strike the postseason unless Alomar was handed a harsher sentence, one that began immediately with the playoffs. Twice the Commissioner's Office needed court intervention to return the umpires to work during the four Division Series. Alomar was booed at his every appearance at Jacobs Field. Yet he had emerged the Orioles' hero, tying Game 4 with a two-out RBI single in the ninth inning and winning the game and the series with a 12th-inning homer.

That set up an ALCS date with the Yankees that had Torre wondering about the fairness of it all. The wild card was just in its second season, and Torre thought it unjust that the Yankees could beat the Orioles all year to win the AL East, taking 10 out of 13 games from them in the regular season, and still not have eliminated Baltimore. Instead, the Yankees' season came down to a best-of-seven series against the Orioles.

The Yankees knew not to make too much of their regular-season dominance over Baltimore. What did the Rangers' 5-1 success over the Yankees in

Arlington mean come playoff time? What did it mean that the Orioles had 11 fewer wins during the regular season than the Indians did? David Cone, Dwight Gooden, and Darryl Strawberry were refugees from a 1988 Mets team that had won 10 out of 11 from the Dodgers during the regular season, but those Davey Johnson Mets lost the NL Championship Series in seven games to Los Angeles. So, as Orioles manager, Johnson had enough ammunition to convince his players to dismiss the regular season, especially since his current relievers, Roger McDowell and Randy Myers, were part of that 1988 Mets team, as well. Besides, it was fitting that this is where the AL season ended after George Steinbrenner and Peter Angelos began going dollar for dollar, man for man, and ego for ego in the off-season. The Orioles eyed David Cone, Mariano Duncan, and Kenny Rogers, who all went to the Yankees. The Yankees mulled over Roberto Alomar, B. J. Surhoff, and David Wells, who all went to Baltimore. Both teams changed managers and general managers, Johnson briefly flirting with the Yankees. The final AL report card for all of this maneuvering and counterattacking was, as it should have been, Orioles versus Yankees in the ALCS. "This was meant to be," Johnson said.

Johnson's team immediately gained a tactical advantage when the opener became the first ALCS game rained out in a quarter of a century. Joe Torre decided to start Andy Pettitte rather than David Cone in Game 1 because the Orioles' lineup was weaker against lefty starters. But that was only part of the reason. Torre determined Pettitte was durable enough to start Games 1, 4, and 7, which allowed the Yankees to bypass Kenny Rogers. The rainout, however, eliminated an off-day between Games 2 and 3. The first five games of this series would be played on 5 consecutive days, ending any chance to use only three starters. However, by pushing back the opening two games, the Orioles were able to rearrange their rotation to have David Wells start the second game in the Bronx on full rest, rather than have to wait until the third game in Camden Yards. Wells was the majors' most dominant starter at Yankee Stadium, having gone 9–1 with a 2.85 ERA and a .218 batting average against there.

Wells's acquisition by the Orioles from Cincinnati on December 26, 1995, had sent Steinbrenner into a tizzy. "You are letting our enemies get stronger," the Boss yelled at Bob Watson. When he had heard about the potential for a deal, Steinbrenner had tried to muscle his way between Baltimore and Wells but failed. "That is when we turned our attention to Kenny Rogers and Chuck Finley," Watson recalls. Now the Yankees were downright scared to use Rogers in the ALCS. The Orioles had worked it out so that Wells could pitch twice at Yankee Stadium if the series went six games. But he certainly was going to start Game 2, which again placed tremendous strain on the Yankees to win the opener.

The Yankees scored two early runs in Game 1, gift wrapped by miserable Oriole defense. Baltimore flexed its long-ball prowess, capitalizing on homers by lefties Rafael Palmeiro and Brady Anderson to gain a 3–2 lead off Andy Pettitte. He had allowed just one homer to a lefty hitter previously all season, Texas's Rusty Greer on April 14. B. J. Surhoff's sixth-inning sacrifice fly made it 4–2. With one out in the seventh inning and Wade Boggs on first, Bobby Bonilla had a Bernie Williams drive to right go off the heel of his glove for a double as he slammed into the wall. Bonilla bruised his left shoulder on the play, and Oriole starter Scott Erickson was knocked out of the game in favor of Armando Benitez. Cecil Fielder was intentionally walked to load the bases with two out. Darryl Strawberry had his first meaningful moment of the postseason, taking a full-count fastball from Benitez for ball 4 to force in a run: Orioles 4, Yankees 3.

Jeff Nelson had grown up in the Baltimore suburb of Catonsville, Maryland, cheering for the Oriole teams of the 1980s that included Cal Ripken Jr. and Eddie Murray. Now Nelson worked a perfect eighth inning during which he retired both men. So the Yankees had what they wanted: a battle of the bullpens.

Still, they trailed by one run when Benitez struck out Jim Leyritz to open the bottom of the eighth.

The Yankees needed a hero, and that could have been the next batter, Derek Jeter, who already had two hits and a stolen base. Or maybe the hero could be a 12-year-old from Old Tappan, New Jersey, seated in Box 325, Section 31, Row A, Seat 3, who played center field on his Little League team.

12 | THE PERFECT
CATCH (ALMOST)

*"We had beaten the Indians, who had the best record in the league. And we had Game 1
of the ALCS won except for a certain kid. Till today, no one wants to admit it was the
wrong call."*
—B. J. Surhoff

Jeffrey Maier knew his tickets for the American League Championship Series
opener were in right field, but when he arrived at Yankee Stadium to see they
were in the first row, he was instantly glad that he had taken his black Mizuno
glove along with him. Just a few years earlier at Shea Stadium, at the first game
he had ever attended, Maier thought he might have caught a foul ball by
Atlanta's David Justice if he just had his mitt. He vowed never to come unpre-
pared again. And Maier believed he had a legitimate shot at a ball. He was
young, but he already considered himself a student of the game he loved. He was
so rabid about baseball that his bar mitzvah the previous weekend had been
themed Jeffrey's World Series, and he sat at the place of honor, the Yankee
Table, named for his favorite team.

Maier was so attuned to the nuances that he imagined a lefty slugger such as
Brady Anderson, Rafael Palmeiro, or Tino Martinez could reach where he was
seated, since Box 325 was 30 feet inside the right-field foul pole. Each time a
muscular lefty hitter batted, Maier went on full alert. But his father had also
told him on their frequent visits to Yankee Stadium that a righty hitter against
a righty power pitcher could reach the right-field seats as well, so Maier positioned himself to be able to move quickly when Derek Jeter came to bat against
Armando Benitez with one out in the eighth inning.

It was probably wishful thinking by a kid about his favorite player. Jeter did

235

have two hits in Game 1, but both were infield hits. With his inside-out swinging approach, Jeter often delivered hits to the opposite field—usually singles that bounced in front of the right fielder. But against Benitez, Jeter did not have to do all of the work. Benitez just might have been the hardest-throwing reliever in the AL. His fastballs never zipped at anything less than the mid-90s in miles per hour, most carrying even more oomph than Mariano Rivera could muster. Thus, when Jeter reached out to sock a 94 mph 0-1 heater on the outside corner, the ball had extra lift and carry. Jeter worried only that the ball had such elevation that it would not travel far enough to clear the fence about 325 feet away. So, as always, he ran hard, thinking about reaching second, at minimum, as the tying run. The altitude of the ball also provided time for a flock of fans in right field to scramble into the walkway that separated the seats from the outfield wall. The hunt for a souvenir was on, and Jeffrey Maier had worked his way to the front of the pack.

In the previous game played at Yankee Stadium, Game 2 of the Division Series, Juan Gonzalez had hit a drive down the left-field line. A fan reached from foul territory across the foul pole to grab the ball. The umpires ruled home run. That play was still fresh enough that near the conclusion of the standard pre-ALCS meeting between the umpires, managers, and key front office executives, the umpire scheduled to work right field in Game 1 asked about locking down the area just beyond the fence. "Me knowing I'm going to be in right field and knowing the history out there, I made the comment to [director of Yankee Stadium operations] Sonny Hight, 'What are we going to do there?'" remembers Rich Garcia. "He said, 'Don't worry. We'll take care of the whole thing. We won't have anyone hanging over the railing.'"

There was more security personnel overall, except the priorities had shifted. Roberto Alomar, the No. 1 villain in sports, was in the house, and the Yankees and Major League Baseball security were on high alert to defend against miscreants jumping onto the field or throwing items such as bottles or batteries. The possibility of someone simply reaching onto the field diminished in importance. The recent incident between Alomar and umpire John Hirschbeck normally would have worried the Orioles about getting a fair game called by Hirschbeck's brethren. But it was common knowledge that the umpires had no love for the Yankees. Nobody sent more tapes of disputed calls to the league office or made more irate phone calls about the quality of umpiring than George Steinbrenner. During Game 2 of the 1995 Division Series at Yankee Stadium, Steinbrenner had summoned reporters to a press-box-level video room to detail what he perceived as missed calls during a larger attack in which he questioned the integrity of the umpires and AL president Gene Budig. The Boss disparaged a rotating system that left "the best umpire in the league . . . in left field. Is that crazy?"

Steinbrenner was talking about Rich Garcia. Now Garcia was in right field for this ALCS opener. He was not scheduled to work the plate, as Steinbrenner would have liked, unless there was a Game 6. In his 22nd year as an AL umpire, Garcia was known as fiery but also excellent and committed to his craft. But he had a problem here: What to do?

"People might not understand this," Garcia explains, "but your whole career you work home plate, first, second, and third base. You are not umpiring the right- and left-field lines except for in the playoffs. Technically, no one can teach you how to work those areas. No one has enough experience at it to do that. You have all these experiences, how to get the proper angle when you umpire. For example, when you umpire first base and the ball is hit in the air down the line, you turn and move to get the proper angle to make the call. The ball is going past you. But when you work the line, the ball does not go past you as quickly, and the worst thing you can do is move. My theory in umpiring is to take as many plays from the same position as possible so you have seen it before, seen it before, seen it before. In right field, you have not seen it before."

Unfamiliar with the play, Garcia did not stand on the line, instead hustling to follow the arc of Jeter's ball, moving toward the wall to get as close a look as possible at the play. His quest was to get a great angle to see if right fielder Tony Tarasco trapped the ball against the wall or not. He recalls being unconcerned about a fan interfering because "Sonny Hight had promised me that no one would be allowed in that area." The defensively deficient Bobby Bonilla was out of the game now because of the bruise he had suffered smacking into the wall while chasing Bernie Williams's double an inning earlier. Tarasco, a far superior fielder, had replaced Bonilla and was positioned with his back against the wall, his left hand raised in anticipation of the pop of the ball in his mitt. But the popping sound came an instant too soon, and there was no thud of ball striking mitt. Something was wrong. "To me," Tarasco said afterward, "it was like a magic trick because the ball just disappeared out of midair."

Tarasco immediately pointed toward the stands, where fans were now scrambling for the ball. To his horror, he saw Garcia spinning his raised index finger to signal a home run. Garcia had rushed so hard toward the play that he had moved too close to the fence, losing depth perception. Neither Tarasco nor Garcia witnessed Maier laying his small body atop the tiny restraining wall, leaning over the fence, and, with his black glove, scooping the ball into the crowd. "I know this sounds a little crazy, but I don't even remember going downstairs or going to the wall," Maier says, looking back. "It was almost like I was in the outfield in Little League. Everything was blocked out. It was just like I was trying to catch a fly ball. I thought it was a home run. I didn't realize at that moment that I was involved in a play."

Maier failed to make a catch, but he had made sure that Tarasco did not, either. The ball disappeared into a mosh pit of frenzied spectators. Tarasco kept pointing toward the fans as he ardently argued with Garcia and was soon joined by manager Davey Johnson, Benitez, and a slew of Orioles. Over and over on replay, while the dispute continued, fans across the world saw on television replay what Garcia had missed: that the ball was not going to clear the fence without Maier's intervention.

Had Garcia noticed Maier's action, he could have invoked Rule 3.16, which covers spectators interfering with balls. In such cases, the umpire gains sole jurisdiction to "impose such penalties as in his opinion will nullify the act of interference. . . . If spectator interference clearly prevents a fielder from catching a fly ball, the umpire shall declare the batter out."

After the game, Garcia watched film of the play and publicly conceded his gaffe. The ball, he agreed, would not have cleared the fence. But, Garcia says, he still thought the ball would have struck the top of the 9-foot-high wall anyway. So, he figured, he would have ruled a double and not an out, even with an unobstructed view. Almost a decade later, Garcia had not changed his opinion on either count. "It was a mistake, period," he says. "But it was not a mistake in judgment. I could not judge what I could not see, and I never saw the kid. But I still think after watching the film so often that the guy was not going to catch the ball. Tony Tarasco had reached the peak as far as height; he was not going any higher. He is on his toes and done right there. Now we have a problem, fan interference. Even if I call the play right, it was going be controversial. If I call it an out, a double, or the way I called it, I am in the shithouse with somebody. The play was destined to get somebody in trouble."

After the game, Tarasco disputed Garcia's view. He had time on such a high drive to position himself to make a leap. But he didn't. He moved into a stationary position and just waited. His body language, Tarasco reasoned, expressed what he thought: The ball was coming straight down to him. He never wavered. He was going to make the catch for the second out of the bottom of the eighth inning.

Garcia did not see it that way. Davey Johnson was ejected from the game and lodged a formal protest. He knew he could not protest a judgment call by an umpire, so he was not making his case against Garcia but, rather, the failure by the Yankees to provide what was promised: enough security in the outfield corners to cope with this kind of issue.

"That is pretty ironic, that we discussed just this kind of play before Game 1, and it happened, and the umpires still got it wrong," Orioles assistant GM Kevin Malone recalls. "[General Manager] Pat [Gillick] and I were flabbergasted. We had gone over it, the umpires were looking for it, and they missed it anyway. That is mind-boggling."

Just as stunning was how quickly celebrity was created for a child still a month shy of his 13th birthday (Maier celebrated his bar mitzvah early because

240 BIRTH OF A DYNASTY

of scheduling conflicts with the hall). Maier was a seventh grader who attended the game by cutting his last class with a note from his mother, claiming he had an appointment with his orthodontist. Maier considered it a blessing just to be there. If Game 1 had been played as scheduled the previous night, someone else would have used the ticket purchased by Bob and Fern Altman, friends of the Maier family. But the rainout had made this ticket available.

Within minutes of the controversial play, the media swarmed Maier to learn his life story and gain insights into his most famous play. Within an hour, his mother, Jane Maier, had accepted an invitation for Jeffrey to appear on *Good Morning America* the next day and fielded calls from shows hosted by David Letterman and Rosie O'Donnell. Oriole personnel were irate that a kid who broke the rules and should have been ejected from the stadium was instead feted as a hero.

"Let me put it this way," Bobby Bonilla said at the time. "If that were a home run for us, Steinbrenner would have him hanging from the Throgs Neck Bridge."

Maier said: "I didn't mean to do anything bad. I'm just a 12-year-old kid trying to catch a ball."

Rather than being four outs away from winning Game 1 on the road, the Orioles were locked in a 4–4 tie. Maier did not even see the conclusion of this game live. In a few hours he would be at the Plaza Hotel for his *Good Morning America* gig. For now he was doing interviews in the bowels of Yankee Stadium as the on-field heroes of Game 1 emerged.

Jeter's controversial homer had removed the possibility of a save situation for the Yankees, so Joe Torre decided to use John Wetteland to pitch with the score tied in the ninth inning. With the rainout having reconfigured the schedule so that the first five games were to be played in 5 days, Torre hoped Wetteland could work one inning, and the Yankees could score and win in the bottom of the ninth, preserving Mariano Rivera for the tough upcoming stretch. But neither team scored in the ninth, so Torre called for Rivera to open the 10th inning.

Amid Rivera's indomitable season, he experienced more difficulties against one opponent than any other. The Orioles were the lone club to score multiple runs twice off Rivera in 1996, and they inflicted two of his three losses (both at Yankee Stadium) and produced his only homer against (by Rafael Palmeiro). Baltimore hitters had demonstrated a discipline to lay off Rivera's high fastball. The Orioles averaged just 4.8 strikeouts per nine innings and batted .250 against Rivera, while all other teams averaged 11.4 strikeouts and batted just .182. Baltimore players hardly talked of Rivera in reverent tones or expressed any level of intimidation.

In the 10th inning, Palmeiro and Eddie Murray both singled, but Rivera escaped. In the 11th inning, Todd Zeile singled with two out. That brought up Alomar. The crowd of 56,495 had been meanly serenading Alomar all day, and he played as if unnerved. His second-inning error had created an unearned run, and he had struck out with the go-ahead run on second base in the ninth inning. Now, in the 11th, Alomar moved the count full. He had been the eighth-hardest player to strike out in the AL that year, but he could not check his swing quickly enough on yet one more high fastball. Rivera completed two shutout innings with a strikeout. He had bettered the Orioles. But it took 44 pitches, a total that meant Torre could not send Rivera out for the 12th inning and probably did not have him now for Game 2 the next afternoon. That only intensified the imperative for the Yankees to win Game 1 and win it quickly.

The weak underbelly of the bullpen—Brian Boehringer, Graeme Lloyd, and David Weathers—had pitched well in the Division Series. Still, Torre did not want to put this opener in their hands. He had used Wetteland and Rivera. Because of that, in his mind, the Yankees had to win. This was the Yankee Formula for success: getting Torre's two best relievers the ball. The Yankees lost only twice all year in games in which Rivera and Wetteland both appeared. Now Torre understood that he had no more pitches coming from either.

Wetteland, Rivera, and Jeffrey Maier gave the Yankees their best efforts. Yet the Yankees still needed another star turn.

Bernie Williams was different. No one who had played with him would dispute that. "Bernie is Bernie," Mariano Rivera explains. "How else can you put it? He is in his own world. There is only one of him." Williams was quiet, shy, and predisposed to internalize life. He was nice but not overly friendly. He was bright yet often projected flightiness. He seemed almost to travel in a dream state. Billy Masse played right field next to Williams at Triple-A Columbus, and it was a running joke how often, Masse recalls, "I'd never get a warmup throw because Bernie was in his own world. The center fielder was supposed to bring the ball, and Bernie would just forget."

Williams had been a 3.9 student at the private Escuela Libre de Musica High School in San Juan. Sitting off alone in a corner, strumming his guitar, was heaven for Williams. "He was an artist" in an athlete's world, Don Mattingly recalls. He was not hardwired like a ballplayer. He even admitted how difficult the game was for him, that his full concentration was needed to do even the most repetitive, routine act on a field. It frustrated teammates, coaches, and management through the minors and, especially, once he arrived in the majors in 1991. "The best thing that happened to me was that when I came up, we were not a very good team, so I was given time to work through my issues," Williams says. "If we had been a good team, I would have been traded."

Then GM Gene Michael persistently resisted George Steinbrenner's impetuous calls to trade Williams. Even as late as 1995, Williams hit just .198 through the Yankees' first 31 games, and the Boss wanted his center fielder unloaded. He heard San Francisco's Darren Lewis was available. Michael was not ready to give up on Williams's talent, so he lied to Steinbrenner about Lewis's availability and reported no team was inquiring about a player in such a horrid slump. "Stick had a way of getting lost so George could not find him every time

[Steinbrenner] wanted to trade Bernie," then hitting coach Rick Down says. Ultimately, Williams rebounded for his best regular season and batted .429 with two doubles, two homers, and seven walks against Seattle in the Division Series.

Still, the Yankees did not believe Williams should be paid akin to an elite player. An uncomfortable negotiation had left Williams bitter in 1995, when the Yankees renewed his contract at only $400,000. In 1996, his first year of arbitration eligibility, Williams submitted a request for $3 million, and the Yankees countered at $2.555 million. Normally, with such a relatively small differential, the sides negotiated an agreement around the midpoint. But Williams would not relent. The Yankees had made him mad with the renewal and all of their counteroffers to multiyear proposals that stacked him beside players he felt were inferior. To prove a point, Williams went to arbitration and won his $2.6 million raise in salary, which further irritated Steinbrenner. But the Boss missed the point with Williams, as so many often did. Beneath the surface, Williams was far tougher and fiercer than he let on. You just had to pay attention to appreciate it.

Williams slept on every minor league bus ride, whether it was 5 minutes or 5 hours. But what his teammates noticed was that when the game began, Williams was instantly explosive. Though he was pitching coach for the Indians' Double-A affiliate, Canton-Akron, in 1989 and 1990, Will George says his strongest memory of the Eastern League occurred an hour after each game at the Yankees' Albany-Colonie facility. By then, all the Albany players would be gone as George headed to the team bus—all the players except one solitary figure working out hard in the weight room. "There, in a soaked T-shirt and shorts, was always Bernie Williams," George says.

In early June 1996, Williams's 5-year-old son, Bernie Jr., developed a bone infection behind his left ear. Williams left the team for a day to fly to Puerto Rico, returning when it seemed under control. He even hit two homers in a game June 8 at Tiger Stadium before being notified that his son had taken a turn for the worse and was in the midst of lifesaving surgery to remove a bone and drain the infection to relieve pressure near the brain. Again, he missed only one game and returned just in time on June 10 in Toronto to get two hits. "I always had to prove I could play," Williams says. "They all saw me and always thought I was too mild, that I wasn't tough enough, that I didn't care, that my mind was not into baseball. But none of that was true."

All the hours in the weight room had strengthened Williams to hit 29 homers in 1996, the most by a Yankee center fielder since Bobby Murcer hit 33 in 1972. During the season, Joe Torre recognized that Williams performed best when his significance to the team was reinforced. So Torre might privately encourage a wise teammate such as David Cone to stress Williams's relevance to the Yankee cause in the media in such a way that Williams was sure to hear about it. For the playoffs, Torre sent his message to Williams symbolically, stationing the switch-hitter exclusively third or fourth in the batting order, spots of honor, after using him mostly as a second- or sixth-place hitter during the year.

Williams began to recognize something about himself the past two successful Octobers: that the need to concentrate so hard every day helped him in the postseason. "Because I am aware of the shortcoming, it means I know how to really focus in hyperpressure situations," Williams says. So as soon as second-place hitter Wade Boggs popped out to end the 10th inning of Game 1, the third-place-hitting Williams began honing in on a single thought for what would be his leadoff at-bat in the 11th inning: "Do not let Baltimore closer Randy Myers beat me with a slider." From a lefty such as Myers, that meant a pitch breaking hard and in toward a righty batter's legs.

With a 1–1 count, Myers tried to deliver just that pitch but hung it. Williams launched a drive to deep left. The only question was whether the ball would hook foul. But Williams knew it would not. By concentrating so ferociously on the slider, Williams did not open up on the pitch. He kept his hands inside the ball on his swing, and, therefore, the ball did not have an exaggerated hook. It landed deep in the left-field stands. No fans needed to assist the ball into the crowd; they only had to stand to applaud and admire it.

The walk-off home run made the final score 5–4 in 4 hours and 23 minutes, another Oriole-Yankee marathon. The front page of the next morning's *New York Post* read "Angel in the Outfield." It was in honor of Jeffrey Maier. But with the Yankees having taken Game 1 of the ALCS, the honor just as easily could have belonged to Bernie Williams.

David Cone was in trouble in Game 2. The score was 2–2, the bases were loaded in the sixth inning, and 50-homer man Brady Anderson was due up. Cone had just walked his fifth Oriole, ninth-place-hitting Chris Hoiles, the kind of righty hitter on whom Cone routinely feasted when he was throwing with command. He already reached a season-high 128 pitches when Joe Torre, not pitching coach Mel Stottlemyre, went to the mound.

"What do you think?" Torre quizzed. Cone met his manager's stare, never flinched. "I can get this guy," he told his manager. There was only one pitcher on the Yankees for whom Torre would have this kind of conference, only one pitcher he so intrinsically trusted to participate in a managerial decision. Torre was an easy convert. He indeed did not have Mariano Rivera available after that 44-pitch Game 1, making Graeme Lloyd the other option. Besides, Torre believed that a starter of Cone's ilk had earned the right to win or lose his own games. "If you don't get this guy out," Torre said in good humor as he turned to leave Cone, "I'm going to tell all the writers that you talked me into it, and it's your fault." Cone justified his manager's faith by getting Anderson to fly out to left on a 2–2 splitter. But now his workday was really done at 133 pitches, and, without Rivera, Torre turned to Jeff Nelson. For the first time in these playoffs, the Yankee bullpen faltered. Nelson faced nine batters and allowed three runs on five hits, including another homer by Palmeiro.

That made a winner of David Wells, furthering his Yankee killer status. On this day, even the presence of Jeffrey Maier could not rescue the Yankees. Maier had completed a whirlwind day of talk-show interviews, limousine service, free meals, and chants of his name at the ballpark by sitting behind the home dugout, where he could not aid the Yankees in another rally. Jeter singled and Williams walked with one out in the ninth inning to knock out Randy Myers. But Benitez entered to induce both Cecil Fielder and Tino Martinez to pop out to end the longest nine-inning ALCS game ever, 4 hours and 13 minutes. Tony Tarasco, fittingly, caught the last out in right field, and he never did relinquish the ball. The Orioles' 5–3 victory enabled them to wrest the home-field edge from the Yankees. The next three games were at Camden Yards.

Going to Baltimore was not the Yankees' big problem. They were 6–0 at Camden Yards in the regular season. The Yankees were bedeviled by a lack of consistent production from anybody in the lineup other than Jeter and Williams, who had combined for 10 hits in the ALCS, compared with 12 for all the other hitters. For the postseason, Jeter and Williams had teamed to bat .488 while the rest of the club batted .201. Tino Martinez had yet to drive in a run in the playoffs. Wade Boggs doubled in his first at-bat of the Division Series before going hitless in his next 16. Paul O'Neill was going so badly (2 hits in 18 at-bats) that Torre had been forced to pinch-hit for him in four straight playoff games. Boggs had a bad back, and O'Neill was limping around on a damaged hamstring. Martinez, who had driven in more runs (117) than any Yankee in a decade, did not have as ready-made an excuse to explain his offensive malaise.

Torre benched Boggs and O'Neill for Game 3, yet Mike Mussina extended the Yankee funk through seven innings. Mussina was from a small town in Pennsylvania and had hated New York, so he was glad to be moved back to start in Camden Yards. He also had particular difficulty against the Yankees. From 1994 to 1996, Mussina established himself as one of the majors' finest pitchers, yet he went 0–6 in seven starts against the Yankees, compared with 54–19 against all other AL teams. He had tried and failed four times during the regular season to win his 20th game. He had started the only Division Series game the week before, in which the Indians had beaten the Orioles. Overall, this had created enough of a pattern that Mussina's big-game fortitude was beginning to be questioned. But Mussina was overwhelming the Yankees with the deception of his knuckle-curveball and the precision of his fastball, allowing just one run on four singles as the eighth inning began. That the Yankees were still in the game, trailing just 2–1, was because of a pitcher whose fortitude was beyond question.

Jimmy Key's eyelids always seemed on the verge of closing; he spoke in an unhurried, benign Southern twang; and his clubhouse persona was unobtrusive. It was a great disguise. On the mound, Jimmy Key was an executioner, killing batters softly. Key had been a good hitter in college at Clemson and, Oriole B. J. Surhoff says that "allowed him to understand the psyche of hitters." Key climbed into the mind of his opponents; he knew hitters never wanted to look foolish by letting one of his oh-so-hittable fastballs pass. That left them susceptible to his devastating changeup. His first Yankee manager, Buck Showalter, marveled at the guts Key displayed to throw a pitch that delectably slow two, three, four times in a row to a hitter. Al Leiter, a Blue Jays teammate of Key's, recalls that Key walked hitters with certain pitches early in an outing, "just so he could get them out with the same pitch later in the game."

It took a certain kind of moxie and intellect to commit to such strategies. When it came to repertoire, Kenny Rogers was, in many ways, a carbon copy of Key, except he probably had a little more life on his fastball. But Key had gall. New York did not bother him. Big games did not bother him. You got the feeling Jimmy Key would pitch the same game in downtown Beirut during shelling as in County Stadium in May with 5,000 people in the crowd. That was why the Yankees were so worried early in the season about the lefty. Key had undergone rotator cuff surgery on July 5, 1995, his fourth left-arm operation, the third on his shoulder, and the most extensive one. While he recuperated in August 1995, he served as an analyst for the Little League World Series, joined by another baseball man who recently found himself out of work: Joe Torre.

The television work was just a momentary distraction. Key was working hard at his rehabilitation, though the odds were against him. Doctors were more and more able to get pitchers who underwent elbow surgery back to performing well. The shoulder, though, was a more complex region with a poorer success rate. Key was pretty much in uncharted territory with a trio of procedures. In October 1994, he had undergone an arthroscopy designed to relieve inflammation and rotator cuff tendinitis, but he followed that by lasting just five starts in 1995. Obviously, a more thorough repair was necessary. James Andrews, MD, had to forgo the arthroscopy and perform full surgery on the shoulder this last time, which by its sheer invasiveness diminished the chances for a complete return to form, even though the tear was fixed. Because of this, Key made a mental deal with himself not to try to rush again but, rather, to build toward usefulness in the second half, to help in a push for a title. However, he pitched so well in spring training that all timetables were scrapped, and he made the rotation.

Early in the season, though, it was evident that he was not Jimmy Key, and not just because he fell to 1–5 with a 7.14 ERA the night after Dwight Gooden no-hit the Mariners in May. More frightening to the Yankees was that the best poker face on the team was so obviously flustered. Key simply could not get the ball to obey his command as it always had. The sport finally discovered what could bring overt anguish to Jimmy Key: on-field failure that made his baseball mortality more real than ever.

The Yankees stopped counting on him. There was a feeling that Key had developed some mental scars to go along with the 3-inch reddish scar atop his left shoulder. He was 35, and there wasn't Gooden's 12-step program or Cone's radical surgery to make him as good as new—which is why Key's return ended up being such a triumph of determination. As he thought initially, Key needed time. Over his final nine regular-season starts, his arm strength improved, and Key went 3–2 with a 3.52 ERA. He generated the Yankees' best start of the Division Series. But it was more than the numbers. Jimmy Key was back to being Jimmy Key. His pitches were following orders, so he was again imperturbable, a trait that was absolutely necessary in ALCS Game 3.

Brady Anderson opened the Oriole first with a line single, and Todd Zeile followed by whipping a curveball into the left-field corner for a home run. Five pitches into his outing, Key put the Yankees behind 2–0. Zeile circled the bases, and a crowd of 48,365 roared. It could have been an unnerving moment, but not for Key. He used it as a blessing, a bit of extra time to walk to the back of the mound and recalibrate. One decision was easy; he had a bad curveball and scrapped it on the spot. Key then convinced himself to go forward as if the game were just beginning. For him, it really was. Surhoff singled in the second, the Orioles' last hit off Key. Eddie Murray walked in the fifth and was erased on a double play, the last base runner against Key.

Key was back to his old self, feathering the outside corner with changeup after changeup against just the kind of team most susceptible to his wiles. The all-or-nothing Orioles lived by the home run. They were brutish hitters who would not evolve. Hitting a changeup like Key's demanded a willingness to bend and drive the ball to the opposite field. The Orioles, however, took one mighty, futile wallop after another as Key's seductive pitches floated beyond their menace. The machismo of the Orioles was an ally for Key.

With Kenny Rogers scheduled to start the next day, the Yankees desperately needed length and excellence from Key, who responded with his best game in 2 years. He was the main reason the Yankees were still within 2–1 as Mussina quickly retired the first two Yankee batters in the eighth inning. Mussina had put down 10 straight and was cruising. But he had returned to the land mine of the Yankee order, and the wonderboys, Derek Jeter and Bernie Williams, struck. Jeter doubled and Williams socked the next pitch for an RBI single. The score was tied 2–2. And the player most closely associated with Joe Torre was just about to change the outcome of Game 3, and he was not even a Yankee.

Todd Zeile was in the midst of his first full major league season with St. Louis, in 1990, when Torre was named Cardinals manager in August. Zeile was a catcher before reluctantly making the switch in 1991 from behind home plate to third base to allow Tom Pagnozzi to become the Cardinals' full-time receiver. Torre was an ideal person to shepherd the move, for he had made it himself in

1971, also for the Cardinals, and won the National League Most Valuable Player award in his first season as a third baseman. But the link was far stronger than that. In August 1994, when the players' strike hit, St. Louis owner August Busch III made the Cardinals the only team that did not fly its players back home from the road. Zeile, the Cardinals' player rep, chartered a plane for the players and families, and Busch III was lambasted in the St. Louis media for his pettiness. He did not forget or forgive. When camps reopened the following spring, the Cardinals reached an oral agreement on a 3-year, $12 million deal with Zeile. No contract was officially signed, however, and in late May the Cardinals pulled the offer, largely because of his union involvement, Zeile believes.

Due to labor-related disruptions, arbitration hearings were held *during* the 1995 season, and Zeile had a hearing scheduled for June 16. Zeile asked for $4.2 million, and the Cardinals wanted to avoid arbitration so much that they eventually offered as much as $4.1 million. But Zeile told the Cardinals they could arbitrate, resurrect the 3-year contract in full, or trade him. He would not settle. Zeile and Torre grew closer during this process, partly because Torre—17 years after being traded due, in part, to his union work—counseled Zeile like a father rather than browbeat him or ignore him. "I know what the organization offered you," Torre told Zeile. "I know you're going to stick by your principles. I can understand your position. I wish you the best, and you should know I am on your side."

At midnight, as June 15, 1995, turned to June 16, St. Louis traded Zeile to the Cubs when he agreed to accept a 1-year, $3.7 million contract with Chicago and waive any right to file a grievance against the Cardinals. What the Cardinals did not know was that Zeile had been backgrounding a reporter from the *St. Louis Post-Dispatch* about all the broken promises and dubious negotiating strategies, with the understanding the story could be written only if Zeile either went to arbitration or was traded. So that morning the major newspaper in town flayed the Cardinals, which emboldened talk-radio hosts to make it open season on St. Louis management. There had been no plans to fire Torre. GM Walt Jocketty had given Torre a public vote of confidence the week before. And Torre said his bosses would never have kept him in the Busch Stadium offices until midnight to help decide what to do about Zeile if he were going to be canned.

But wanting a distraction away from the Zeile matter, Busch and team president Mark Lamping ordered Jocketty to fire Torre. Lamping cited Torre's lack of dugout animation. At an organizational brunch after the firing, Busch III made a toast to getting rid of the bad energy surrounding the team, lumping Torre in with Zeile. "It was a smokescreen," Zeile recalls.

So Torre was central to Zeile's vagabond baseball life, from catcher to third base, and from the Cardinals to the Cubs, which led to the Phillies and, on August 29, 1996, a trade to the Orioles. Torre could have cursed the day he steered Zeile to third base, because by playing that position for Baltimore, he resolved so many of the Orioles' season-long issues. The disruptive talk of Cal Ripken shifting over from shortstop was gone. With Zeile at third and Eddie Murray as the designated hitter, Bobby Bonilla received his full-time wish to be the right fielder and excelled down the regular-season stretch.

Torre good-naturedly appealed to Zeile when their paths crossed before Game 3. "You're still young," Torre had told the 31-year-old Zeile. "You'll get a chance to put a ring on your finger. I'm an old man."

Zeile nevertheless homered for a second straight game. But now in the eighth inning, Jeter and Williams blunted the impact of Zeile's blast by tying the score. Pitching coach Pat Dobson visited the mound, and lefty Jesse Orosco was ready. But Davey Johnson stuck with Mussina, and Tino Martinez followed with the Yankees' third straight hit to the opposite field, a double into the left-field corner. Surhoff fielded and threw to third, too late to get the sliding Williams. Zeile whirled toward second and began to throw but did not. Why? "What people don't know is that I was legitimately going to throw to second, but Robby [Alomar] was on the way to the bag," Zeile explains, nearly a decade later. "So because he was on the move, I decided to hold it instead, and it slipped from my fingers."

Zeile looked like a quarterback spiking a football to stop the clock, only this was unintentional. Zeile remembers it feeling like slow motion; *surreal* is the word he uses. The ball trickled slowly toward shortstop. But something moved fast and decisively for the Yankees—the long-indecisive Bernie Williams. Third-base coach Willie Randolph was yelling, "Go, go, go," but Williams could not hear him above the din; besides, he had already made up his mind, popping up from his slide and racing home. Ripken fielded the ball and his side-arm fling arrived high to catcher Chris Hoiles and a moment too late to nab Williams, sliding again. Williams leaped in exhilaration as the Yankees poured off the bench to mob him as he neared the dugout. The Yankees were now ahead 3–2. The Orioles would never lead in the series again. Zeile says, "It added to the whole allure that another strange play after the Maier play had changed a game around in favor of the Yankees."

Still, Johnson stayed with Mussina. Cecil Fielder had just six hits in 39 lifetime at-bats against the righty and was hitless in three at-bats with two strike-outs so far in this Game 3. In his dire moment in the first inning, Jimmy Key had found the poise to gather himself. Mussina admittedly could not find that place. Mussina was orderly, Rain Man–like, and any disturbance of his normal patterns discombobulated him. Zeile's misplay was way beyond a normal on-field occurrence. Mussina had been four outs away from finally winning that elusive 20th game of 1996, four outs away from a masterpiece that would have moved the Orioles ahead in this series, with Kenny Rogers up next for the Yankees. But now he had lost his lead and his composure, and because of that, with the count 1–0, he hung his signature pitch, a knuckle-curve, and Fielder crushed it deep into the left-field stands.

The Yankees were ahead 5–2. Key finished his bravura effort with a perfect eighth to become the first Yankee starter to win in the playoffs. John Wetteland retired the Orioles in order in the ninth, and the Yankees had their fifth victory of the postseason, all comeback triumphs, four of the rallies occurring in the eighth inning or later. All of those late-game rallies had something in common: the magic touch of the youngest Yankee. Jeter had instigated the nail-biting surges that won Games 2 and 3 over Texas in the Division Series; he had homered with the assistance of Jeffrey Maier to tie the ALCS opener; and now his two-out, eighth-inning double had positioned the Yankees to tie the score and force extra innings. "How do you explain it?" Torre says in recollection. "Some players are just special, and Derek was special from the beginning."

And the Orioles also learned, as they had expected, that their protest of Game 2 was denied. They could not beat the Yankees when it counted on or off the field. "During the playoffs, they had an intangible quality that was tough to beat," Zeile says. "It felt like an extra force on the field. I don't believe in destiny, but if that ever was apparent anyplace, it was apparent with that team."

In Game 4, Torre reinserted Paul O'Neill into the lineup because, he said, there must be loyalty to the men who had lugged you to that point with their skill and mettle. O'Neill hit a two-run homer. Torre stuck with Darryl Strawberry for a second straight game because Torre liked how much life was in his body and, especially, his hands in Game 3. Strawberry moved from right field to left field in place of Tim Raines and homered twice, the second one to left-center field against a 97 mph Armando Benitez fastball. Bernie Williams homered yet again, a two-run shot to give the Yankees a first-inning lead. And Torre once more did not leave Rogers around to spoil the good work of others. The Yankees took a 2–0 lead in the first; Rogers gave one back in the bottom half. The Yankees went ahead 3–1 in the second; Rogers allowed a Hoiles homer in the third. The Yankees built a 5–2 lead in the top of the fourth, and Rogers opened the bottom half by allowing a walk and a single. Torre simply could not watch the defeatist body language, stalling, and indecisiveness any longer. Rogers had faced 16 Orioles, and his fear of the challenge was illustrated by going to at least three balls on nine of them. Rogers simply could not mimic Key's ability to take a shot, shake it off, and refocus. Every failure ate at his fragile ego, reiterated to him that he was so desperately not what he so badly wanted to be: a full member of this tough-minded group.

In relief of Rogers, David Weathers worked another $2\frac{2}{3}$ shutout innings. Graeme Lloyd induced Brady Anderson to pop out with the tying run on base in the sixth. That maligned relief duo had now combined for $10\frac{2}{3}$ playoff innings of shutout relief. In the eighth inning, with the Yankees ahead by four runs, the Orioles loaded the bases with none out against Mariano Rivera. It was as if Rivera were building a challenge for himself, showing the Orioles who was really the master of whom. Against the tying run, Rivera struck out Chris Hoiles and Anderson and got Zeile to pop out. The Yankees still needed one more win, but that felt like the last gasp of the 1996 season for an Oriole team known in some circles of the Baltimore media as the Tin Men: They lacked a heart, especially compared to the steadfast Yankees.

Torre made all of the right decisions and now stood nine winning innings away from the prize that had evaded him: the World Series. Once again, Bob Watson inappropriately imposed himself onto what should have been a great moment. He picked the hours before Game 5 to publicly reveal what had been whispered all year, that Mike Stanley had not been retained because David Cone had told Yankee officials he would not re-sign if there were not a change to a more defensive-oriented catcher. Cone, then and now, denied that was the case. In addition, Watson explained he was ordered to mislead the media by George Steinbrenner, saying, "There was a script handed to me, and I had to follow the script. You have to understand the position I am in." Steinbrenner denied ever having told Watson to lie, though other officials said it was the Boss's common practice to warn that if certain information escaped to reporters, he would fire the offender.

The game ultimately dulled the relevance of Watson's ill-timed complaints. Jim Leyritz, Fielder, and Strawberry all homered off of Scott Erickson in the third inning, enabling the Yankees to take a 6–0 lead by outdoing the Orioles at their own long-ball style. They were the Bronx Bombers, just as Steinbrenner had dreamed when Strawberry and Fielder were added. The Yankees outhomered the Orioles 10–9, the 10 homers an ALCS record for five games. But the Yankees won in every phase. They committed just one error in the series, compared with two by Gold Glover Roberto Alomar. The second one by Alomar came on what should have been an inning-ending double play in the third that instead permitted Fielder and Strawberry to bat and break the game open.

But at that point, the Yankees were done scoring, and what felt like an interminable wait within his interminable wait began for Torre. The final six innings seemed like a season. How many times can you go to the bathroom, get up for water, stretch your legs? Andy Pettitte pitched brilliantly, allowing just a Zeile homer in the sixth inning and an Eddie Murray homer in the eighth. Torre wondered if the torment would ever end. Bobby Bonilla, who had no hits in his first 20 at-bats in the series, lifted a two-run homer off John Wetteland with two outs in the bottom of the ninth inning. One more base runner would bring the tying run to the plate. But Cal Ripken grounded a ball to the shortstop hole. At 36, Ripken had spent the ALCS no longer having the range or arm necessary to consistently make just this kind of play. But the Yankee shortstop was 22, and, in what felt like a changing of the guard, Derek Jeter backhanded in the hole and fired across the diamond. Tino Martinez scooped the ball as Ripken dived into first. The time was 7:20 p.m. on October 13, 1996. It was the time of Joe Torre's life.

In the morning, before a pitch had been thrown in Game 5, Torre had made his now-routine daily call to Room 156 on the sixth floor of the Millstein Building at Columbia-Presbyterian Medical Center. His brother Frank, who had moved to first in line for the next available heart, told him, "One more." He was talking about wins to the World Series, not his place on the heart list. Torre cried for the first time that day. Now, as his players converged on the field in euphoria and his coaches hugged him in the dugout, Torre hung back to soak it all in and shed a few more tears as a country welled up with him. The enormous stage of the postseason had provided a forum for a nation to become fully aware of a good man's story of tragedy and now, finally, triumph. For years he had shut off the television when the celebrations began. But now, after 4,284 games as a player and manager, regular season and postseason, it was not somebody else going to the World Series. It was not somebody else's time to celebrate. In this year of personal anguish involving his older brothers, Torre was having the season of his dreams; the Yankees' 34th pennant was his first. At the victory podium, Torre dedicated this series win to the memory of one brother and the hopes of another, and then snuck away to make a phone call again to Room 156 and cry some more.

As it turned out, Game 5 had played as a microcosm of Orioles-Yankees. The Yankees broke out to a big lead, and the Orioles charged but couldn't catch them. The Yankees went into first place on April 30 playing the longest nine-inning game in major league history and winning in Camden Yards for the first time in 1996. They finished 9–0 in the Orioles' home and were now 5–0 on the road in the postseason. These Yankees had grit.

"The strange thing is, we felt we were better, yet they knew they were going to beat us," Kevin Malone remembers. "They had our number. We were uncomfortable playing them. They were reflective of Joe Torre. They played under control. They did little things. Whatever they needed to do, they did it against us. Maybe they did it against everybody."

In Game 5, 28-year-old Bernie Williams stamped this as his time with a single and double. He was like the ever-climbing Dow Jones, which was just about to close over 6,000 for the first time. Williams was also soaring, finishing with 9 hits in 19 at-bats and the ALCS MVP award. A scout who had been watching the playoffs said, "Forget that border on superstar thing. This guy has crossed the border." But Williams stayed grounded, refusing to separate himself within the clubhouse. "The real MVP," he said, "is this team." He was right. Torre had used 13 of the 15 position players on the roster, and all 13 produced at least one hit. Luis Sojo, a late-season waiver claim, played defense at second base for Mariano Duncan in the ninth inning of Game 3, furthering Todd Zeile's misery by robbing him of a hit not long after the unintentional spike. "Nice move, Skip," Duncan told Torre. "I couldn't have made that play."

That embodied this team, and Torre adored it. He used a lot of parts, and those who were not playing submerged their egos and cheered for their teammates. Williams, Jeter, Pettitte, and Rivera were young, but none of the success was changing them. Darryl Strawberry was older and wiser, recommending to Torre, at times, that he should sit and Tim Raines or Cecil Fielder should play.

Still, Torre found enough at-bats for Strawberry to set an ALCS record for slugging percentage. Uplifted by a chance at a ring, Fielder had abandoned his go-for-the-fences approach, delivering meaningful hits to the opposite field. The accomplished David Cone had encouraged the concept of the young Pettitte starting the ALCS opener. All six members of the bullpen had contributed huge moments during the first nine playoff games.

But what Torre admired most was the ability of his players to embrace the suffocating pressure and perform. He had always wondered how he would handle this atmosphere as a player, a question that would go forever unanswered. But his confidence and calm as a manager had been like a season-long intravenous drip into his players' bloodstream. They were him now, and he was them. On the flight home to New York, Torre got on the intercom and told his jubilant team: "This is Joe Torre, manager of the Yankees. I just wanted to congratulate everyone for winning the AL title, and tell you all that you can enjoy tomorrow off and be ready to return to work Tuesday."

Torre let a few beats go by. "By the way," he then continued. "I just wanted to tell you I love you all."

A plane full of men stood and applauded.

13 | THE PERFECT GAMES

"Atlanta's my town. We'll take three games there and win it back here on Saturday."
—*Joe Torre bracing George Steinbrenner before what he expected to be a Game 2 loss and a two-game deficit in the World Series*

The World Series turned bad for the Yankees before a single pitch was thrown, and there was nothing they could do about it. By winning the American League Championship Series in five games, the Yankees assured themselves five off days before the World Series opener. A fine line exists for players between rest and too much rest. No matter the physical wear, players' bodies are attuned to performing daily, and every day that passed in the valley between winning the pennant and the Fall Classic saw the Yankees lose sharpness and have their momentum seep away.

In that period, the Yankees also received an eyeful of the awesome machine that they were about to encounter. The Cardinals had raced to a three-games-to-one advantage in the National League Championship Series, and Torre looked as if he would get to face the team that had fired him as manager during the previous season. Instead, St. Louis stirred sleeping giants, and Torre wound up preparing for the organization that had fired him after the 1984 season. The defending World Series champion Braves—behind the imposing rotation work of John Smoltz, Greg Maddux, and Tom Glavine—captured the final three games of the NLCS and the pennant by a combined score of 32–1.

The World Series opener was then rained out, allowing Braves manager Bobby Cox to push scheduled Game 2 starter Denny Neagle back to Game 4 and start Smoltz, Maddux, and Glavine on full rest over the first three games. It was a pitching Murderers' Row. Glavine had won the National League Cy

Young Award in 1991, and Maddux had won the next four. And with a major league-high 24 victories, six more than any other NL pitcher, Smoltz was destined to take the baton in 1996. Members of the Yankees with NL lineage such as Mariano Duncan, Paul O'Neill, and Darryl Strawberry had faced the Big Three, but what insights could they truly offer? Yankee hitters were a lifetime 119-for-567 (.210) against the Braves' trio of aces.

Meanwhile, as with the previous series, a Game 1 postponement scrapped the scheduled off-day between Games 2 and 3, eliminating Torre's chance to avoid using Rogers as a fourth starter again. And the rainout added a sixth off day for the Yankees before the World Series opened, further robbing their game of energy and acuity.

"It's simple," Torre said of the postponement. "This benefits the Braves."

The positives derived by the Braves from the rainout merely compounded a sense of inevitability about this World Series. Before the Fall Classic started, the *Toronto Sun* ran a poll of 25 baseball writers and only one—a reporter from New York—did not select the Braves to win it all. The recommended line put out by Las Vegas Sports Consultants to casinos also had Atlanta as a substantial favorite; a gambler would have to bet $175 on the Braves to win $100.

Then the series began, and all the prognostications were seemingly validated. Smoltz and Maddux dominated the first two games, combining to hold the Yankees to one run on eight hits over 14 innings. The Braves won the opener as 19-year-old Andruw Jones became the youngest player to hit a World Series homer, removing Mickey Mantle's name from the record books. Mantle was 20 when he homered in the 1952 World Series. Jones, who had opened the season at Single-A, also homered in his second at-bat. Andy Pettitte, unable to keep his pitches down, recorded just seven outs and surrendered seven runs in the Braves' 12–1 rout.

Game 2 was the lowest-rated televised prime-time World Series game in history as a lack of competition drove viewers away. Maddux needed just 82 pitches to work eight shutout innings, treating the Yankees more like a junior varsity team than the AL champs. He produced 19 outs on the ground, including five comebackers. Yankees hitters were mesmerized, feeling as if Maddux could read their minds and work accordingly to their weaknesses. Wade Boggs called Maddux "a master illusionist." The lefty hitters were dazzled by Maddux's ability to throw his two-seam fastball at their front knee and have it break back over the plate for a strike. The righty hitters managed just two soft singles in 11 at-bats. Fred McGriff, traded by the Yankees as a farmhand in 1982, drove in three runs to give him five RBIs for the first two games. The final score was 4–0, and the Braves' tally was now 16–1 in the World Series and 48–2 in their last five games.

George Steinbrenner was his usual panicked self. He had initially thought making the World Series was an incredible stand-alone achievement, but that quickly evaporated. Now he was worried that a humiliating World Series sweep would eradicate all the positives of this heartwarming season. The Yankees had recaptured New York's imagination with their great stories while other teams in the city floundered. The Mets had finished 20 games under .500. The football season in New York was going miserably. With Dave Brown at quarterback, the Giants were 2–5. The Jets, coached by Rich Kotite, were even worse at 0–8. The hockey and basketball campaigns were just starting. New York was a Yankee town again, and Steinbrenner was quite intimate with how the goodwill engendered by playoff success had, for example, helped the Mariners get Seattle to agree to build them a stadium just a year earlier. Now his eyes were still on Manhattan's West Side, and he could not have his club tank in the playoffs and squander the citywide benevolence.

Not for a second did Steinbrenner believe Torre's pre–Game 2 assessment that the Yankees would go into the Heart of Dixie and return the following weekend leading the World Series. Frank Torre recalls, "George called me in the hospital after Joe had said Atlanta was lucky for him, and I agreed with George—my brother was nuts. Atlanta had a great ball club. George would have been happy to win one game after the Yankees were so overmatched in the first two games." In fact, in Steinbrenner's mind, this was 1976 all over again, when the first Yankee team during his ownership reached the World Series and was swept by the Big Red Machine. Cincinnati won a second straight title along with recognition as one of the greatest teams ever. The Braves now felt as if they were playing for all of that as well. They had represented the NL in four of the last five World Series and were defending champs. They were well on their way to being the Team of the 1990s—and maybe much more than that.

When Yankees personnel awoke in Atlanta on October 22, they slowly became aware of Mark Bradley's column titled "'27 Yankees Might Lose to These Guys" in that day's *Atlanta Journal and Constitution*. The piece began, "That the Braves are going to win this World Series is apparent. It is also, in the grand scheme, secondary. No longer is this team playing against the overmatched Yankees. The Braves are playing against history." Bradley ranked these Braves as the greatest team of the post–free agency era, even better than the Big Red Machine that had devastated the Yankees 2 decades earlier. The column ended, "We are no longer watching a competition. We are witnessing a coronation." Word circulated within the Yankee family about the column, but the players were already heated. The pitcher who had learned at Budd Park in Kansas City as a boy how to create a chip on his shoulder now made sure every other Yankee had one as well.

With the off day between Games 2 and 3 lost to the rainout, David Cone was scheduled to take a 4 p.m. flight October 21 to Atlanta so he could rest for his Game 3 start the next night. But his plane developed mechanical problems and sat on the tarmac for an hour before Cone pleaded with the pilots in the cockpit to let him off. He returned to Yankee Stadium to watch Game 2. Cone was a night owl anyway; it wasn't like he would sleep in Atlanta. He did not care that he would be arriving at his hotel room about 4 a.m., 14 hours before his start. He was happier supporting his teammates than stewing by himself. As Game 2 transpired, Cone watched the celebrating on the Atlanta bench and grew more and more irate. Was it greater than normal? Maybe, maybe not. But in David

Cone's mind, it was excessive and crossed the line into bad sportsmanship, and he made sure to circulate his feelings among his fellow Yankees: Look at how the Braves came into our house and disrespected us.

Torre had started Andy Pettitte and Jimmy Key in the two games at Yankee Stadium because the team's scouts had told him the Braves were weaker against lefty pitching. But Pettitte and Key had managed one strikeout against 16 hits in 8⅓ combined innings. Atlanta hitters hardly looked fooled by southpaws. But Torre also set up his rotation in this fashion because he wanted Cone starting Game 3. Torre determined that the third game of a series was the most important because you could break a tie, take a commanding lead, or prevent the opponent from taking it. Torre, it turned out, needed Cone to prevent the Braves from going up three games to none and reducing the rest of the series to a formality.

Torre also started Cone because of his NL roots. Cone had more familiarity than any Yankee starter with Atlanta-Fulton County Stadium. His last start there was Game 6 of the 1992 World Series, which his Blue Jays won to clinch a title. He also experienced his most embarrassing on-field moment there on April 30, 1990, when he argued a call with first-base ump Charlie Williams with his back turned to the infield as Dale Murphy and Ernie Whitt scored. Still, Torre liked that Cone was comfortable with everything from the slope of the mound to hitting in an NL park to the Tomahawk Chop frenzy in the crowd. In retrospect, Torre called preserving Cone until Game 3 his most important decision of the 92nd World Series.

Working on 11 days' rest, Cone carried what might have been his best fastball and so much more to the mound that night. This was the man who had not left his apartment for weeks after his personal and team devastation in Game 5 at the Kingdome the previous October. He felt he had let a team and a city down. He signed the largest per annum pitching contract in history and ached that he was not earning his money due to missing 4 months following his surgery. Through the first two rounds of the playoffs, the Yankees had lost just twice, and it was in the games Cone had started. Cone, a lead dog throughout his career, was miserable, believing that the Yankees were winning to this point either in spite of him or regardless of him. No one in his clubhouse felt that way. But, again, David Cone needed to mentally make it him against a world of doubters.

Facing an offense that entered with 48 runs in its past 43 innings, Cone shut out the Braves through five innings. He took a 2–0 lead and a three-hitter into the bottom of the sixth. With his starter excelling also, Atlanta manager Bobby Cox permitted Tom Glavine to bat and, ominously, Cone walked the Braves' starting pitcher after being ahead 1–2. Cone briefly looked toward center field with exasperation, and Mel Stottlemyre called the bullpen to order Mariano Rivera and Graeme Lloyd to warm up. A clock began ticking against the Yankees. This was an inning too early. Torre had thought all day about Cone handing a lead to Rivera after six innings to trigger the Formula: two innings from Rivera and one from John Wetteland. Cone was due up third in the top of the seventh inning. Perfect. He could be pinch-hit for then. But Torre knew he could not wait for the ideal situation if Cone faltered badly here. This was a must-win game, and if Rivera had to be pushed for three innings, so be it.

Cone was one of the great put-away pitchers of the era because he had so many weapons to confuse and deceive hitters, especially righty hitters, when ahead in the count. So when Marquis Grissom fell behind 0–2 before poking a single in front of a lunging Tim Raines in left on a 1–2 pitch, the signs were more worrisome. That was two consecutive batters that Cone had lost at 1–2. Mark Lemke popped out to Cecil Fielder on a sacrifice bunt attempt before Cone missed badly on a 3–1 pitch to walk Chipper Jones to fill the bases with the go-ahead runs—the runs that would almost certainly finish off the Yankees in the 1996 World Series. To a background of Tomahawk Chops and warlike chanting, Torre jogged toward the mound.

It was Torre again, not Mel Stottlemyre. Just like in the ALCS, he was going out to confer with the only pitcher on his staff he respected enough to help make a decision. Running out was a signal by Torre to the pitcher that he was not stalling to get more time for the relievers to ready themselves; the visit was a consultation, not necessarily a hook. Cone immediately told Torre, "I'm all right." The manager was not interested in that. Torre grabbed his starter by the hips and moved close, so close it was as if this were a movie and two actors were readying to kiss. Joe Girardi peered in from one side, Mariano Duncan from the other. But the two main principles had blinders on, locked on one another. Torre did not want a rote answer from the warrior in Cone; he wanted the truth. Even Stottlemyre, standing on the top step of the dugout, waiting for a gesture to let him know whether to get Lloyd into the game, did not know what his manager would do.

Lloyd's improbable Yankee renaissance had continued in the losing Game 2 when he had relieved Key and struck out the only two batters he faced, Chipper Jones and Fred McGriff. Now McGriff was readying to hit, already the owner of the record for RBIs in a single postseason with 15. Lloyd would at least provide the Yankees a lefty-lefty matchup. But in his baseball soul, Torre did not want to take the ball away from Cone. Torre's decision was the same as Buck Showalter's a year earlier in the Kingdome when Cone lost his stuff, a lead, and ultimately Showalter's job. In the eighth inning of that Division Series game, Cone had put the tying run in place by going walk, single, walk, with Rivera warming up—same as here. But Showalter stuck with Cone all the way through Doug Strange, through 147 pitches, because he believed so mightily not just in Cone's arm but also in Cone's heart.

"This is very important," Torre said, staring into Cone's gray-blue eyes, searching for honesty. "I need the truth. How do you feel?" Again Cone told his manager he was fine and revealed that his slider had abandoned him, but he had enough other choices. With all the John Wayne–ish conviction he could muster, Cone locked on his manager and said, "I'll get this guy for you."

That was not enough for Torre, who appealed one more time for the truth. "Don't bullshit me," he said.

Cone still did not flinch, never losing eye contact. "I can get him. I can get out of this inning."

Satisfied, Torre responded, "Okay, go get 'em." Torre jogged back to the dugout, the greatest relief pitcher in the world and Graeme Lloyd still warming in the bullpen down the left-field line. As it turned out, Cone was Marlon Brando with a splitter. He had virtually nothing left.

"It was a lie," Cone says of his side of the conversation with Torre. "But you have to trick yourself into believing you can get Fred McGriff out in that situation. Because if you don't believe it, what are you doing out there?"

With Don Zimmer's arm around his neck, Torre watched as McGriff skied a pop up to Derek Jeter in shallow center. Two out. Torre chewed hard on a piece of gum, his raccoon eyes fixed intently on the mound as the count went full to Ryan Klesko. Cone unleashed a fastball to the upper and inner regions of the strike zone. It was a borderline call either way, and home-plate umpire Tim Welke did nothing, meaning ball 4. Cone raised his hands to his side in protest and disbelief, saying, "Come on, Tim," as Glavine crossed with Atlanta's first run. Zimmer yelled, "You fucking stink" toward Welke and was joined in angry screams by Torre. Zimmer never did stop his screaming. But Cone quickly dispatched it all. He still had the lead, 2–1, and Torre never wavered; he was going to let Cone face righty-hitting Javy Lopez as well. For the second straight postseason, a manager had decided that a game—a season—belonged to Cone until a lead was gone. Sometimes destiny does not smile upon you. Sometimes it does.

David Cone, who 5 months earlier did not know if he would even pitch again as doctors performed a risky surgery on his right shoulder, threw a high 0–1 slider to Javy Lopez, his 97th pitch of Game 3, his final pitch of a trying 1996. He had badgered himself for nearly 2 weeks that the season could not go this way. He was outpitched in October by John Burkett and essentially held to a draw by David Wells. He needed to contribute; no, more than that, he needed to make a difference. On this night he stopped the rampaging Braves, turned the 1996 World Series into a contest, and honored Torre's commitments to start him in the pivotal Game 3 and also stick with him through a sixth inning lived on the cliff's edge. Cone would remember that slider as perhaps his worst pitch of Game 3, the kind that hangs and turns games. Sometimes destiny does not smile upon you. Sometimes it does.

Javy Lopez popped out to Girardi. The Yankees still had their lead. Glavine returned to the mound, thinking, "We have just opened a door for them."

Sticking with Cone was not the only difficult decision Torre had to make for Game 3. He again benched Wade Boggs against a lefty, starting Charlie Hayes. Paul O'Neill had one hit lifetime in 20 at-bats against Glavine, so Torre once more rested O'Neill's damaged left hamstring and instead started another lefty, Darryl Strawberry. Strawberry had fractured his right big toe fouling a pitch off of it in the ALCS finale and had to wear a specially designed cleat and tape the toe heavily. But Torre's most anguishing decision was to bench Tino Martinez, whom he considered part of the glue of this team. In April, Torre stuck religiously with Martinez as he worked through his issues with the ghost of Don Mattingly. But it was October now, and Torre felt it was unfair to the team's goals to ignore zero RBI production for the playoffs any longer, especially because in the NL stadium, no designated hitter would be used. So Cecil Fielder started.

Strategically, Torre returned to his NL roots in the first inning, when he had Derek Jeter follow a Tim Raines leadoff single with a bunt. Torre thought it was important for the Yankees to lead for the first time in this World Series. Bernie Williams supplied that edge with an RBI single, his first World Series hit after going hitless for Smoltz/Maddux. Strawberry came up with Williams on second and one out in the fourth inning. A decade earlier, the Mets had lost the first two games of the World Series at home to the Red Sox before rallying to win the title in seven memorable games. Strawberry played right field for a New York team known for its bawdy, strutting, arrogant behavior, and no one defined those qualities better than Strawberry. In Jeff Pearlman's book *The Bad Guys*

Won! about those 1986 champions, Strawberry's Mets teammate Ed Hearn called the team's cleanup hitter "as big an asshole as I've ever met."

The feeling around the 1996 Yankees was the polar opposite; Strawberry was beloved, having evolved from a petulant man-child to an elder statesman. Strawberry, more than any other Yankee, pepped up his teammates to believe a comeback in this World Series was possible, since he had already lived through one just like it. Strawberry also evolved as a hitter. He did not simply stand and whale at every pitch, hoping to crush 800-foot homers. Glavine, trying to avoid that power, pitched the ball away to Strawberry, who defeated the Braves' shift to the right side with a single to left. Strawberry's RBI single made it 2–0 for Cone, who was acquired by the Mets in 1987 from Kansas City for a backup catcher named Ed Hearn.

In the seventh inning, to protect Cone's 2–1 lead, Torre inserted Luis Sojo to play defense for Duncan. With two outs, Luis Polonia tried to steal second to move the tying run into scoring position. Joe Girardi's throw bounced, but even in Sojo's short time with the Yankees, Derek Jeter had noticed something about him: "softest hands I've ever seen." Could Duncan's less friendly hands have controlled the short hop? We will never know, but Sojo hauled in the peg and in the same motion slapped a tag on Polonia for the final out. Polonia had pinch-hit for Glavine, so the lefty was now out of Game 3, and the Yankees had what their whole psyche and style were built around: a battle of the bullpens.

Greg McMichael came on, and Jeter led off the eighth with an infield single. McMichael then hung a 1–0 changeup to Bernie Williams, and, batting from the left side for the first time in Game 3, Williams walloped a deep homer to right. Williams's record-tying sixth homer of the postseason was accomplished with Girardi's bat. Off in Bernie World, Williams had actually forgotten to pack his bats for a World Series road trip. Fielder doubled and scored on a single by Sojo. The lead was 5–1, seemingly safe with the Yankee bullpen. But for the first time in October, Mariano Rivera stumbled in the eighth. Marquis Grissom tripled and scored on Mark Lemke's single. Chipper Jones struck out, and with lefty mashers McGriff and Klesko again due, Torre did what would have been unthinkable 2 weeks earlier and even at this moment was still highly dubious. He summoned the man who was going to get Bob Watson fired to replace the man most responsible for the Yankees playing in October.

But Graeme Lloyd's elbow was feeling much better and, more important, so was his head. He had resolved that the playoffs were a chance to start anew, to erase all the bad pitches and ill will that had stacked up against him late in the regular season. And because Cone convinced Torre that he could finish the sixth inning against the Braves lefty hitters, Torre still had his only southpaw reliever available. Lloyd got McGriff to fly to center. There were two outs. Atlanta manager Bobby Cox could have pinch-hit righty-swinging Jermaine Dye, but if he did, Torre would have countered with the now warming John Wetteland. Cox still preferred the lefty-lefty matchup of Lloyd versus Ryan Klesko. However, Klesko did not. Klesko, who had led the Braves in homers with 34, demonstrated what he thought of Lloyd's improved stuff by trying to bunt for a hit and fouling it off. Lloyd threw two more sliders that Klesko missed by half a foot. The Braves' last real chance of Game 3 was done.

Torre managed brilliantly, being rewarded for faith in an NL style, as well as players such as Fielder, Strawberry, Sojo, Lloyd, and, especially, Cone. The Yankees had become the first team ever to win six straight postseason games on the road. It felt like a World Series again, and then Kenny Rogers went out in Game 4 and showed an aversion to the strike zone, fear in every offering. Steinbrenner had taken to regularly challenging Rogers not only in the media but face-to-face. He went as far as to lobby Torre to start Andy Pettitte on 2 days' rest rather than use Rogers. Even if Torre started Pettitte in Game 4, the Yankees would be playing Game 5 (their fifth game in 5 days) in 24 hours. Under those circumstances, Torre knew he would have to use Rogers in Game 5 anyway. So why wait, he figured.

On the same day opening statements were given in the O. J. Simpson civil trial, Rogers never recorded an out in the third inning, leaving the Yankees behind 5–0. In uniform though he was disabled, Pat Kelly turned to his friend

Jim Leyritz in the downcast Yankee dugout and said, "Well, thankfully, we won yesterday, so we won't get swept." Leyritz nodded knowingly in agreement.

There had been 541 World Series games played before October 23, 1996, and only twice had a team that trailed by as many as six runs rallied to win. The first time occurred October 12, 1929, when the Philadelphia Athletics used a 10-run seventh inning to eliminate an 8-run deficit, winning Game 4 by 10–8 over the Cubs. A's manager Connie Mack had a 3-4-5 in his order of Hall of Famers Mickey Cochrane, Al Simmons, and Jimmie Foxx. The second big comeback came October 5, 1956, when the Dodgers rallied from 6–0 in the second inning to beat the Yankees 13–8. That Brooklyn team had four Hall of Famers— Pee Wee Reese, Duke Snider, Jackie Robinson, and Roy Campanella—in their lineup that day. Joe Torre did not believe he had that kind of firepower available, so when the Yankees came to the bench down 6–0 to begin the sixth inning, he told his players not to try to be heroes but to put some runs on the board and make the Braves start thinking the worst.

"That is what Joe always has done," Bernie Williams says, looking back. "Take small bites."

Denny Neagle had allowed just two singles to that point. His presence on the mound exemplified the genius of Braves GM John Schuerholz, though it had as much to do with a mistake by Bob Watson. To be traded after July 31, a player must either pass through waivers or be traded to a team that claims the player on waivers. Most claims are registered merely to block a player from going anyplace else, and the Yankees were one of the most aggressive claimers for the purpose of blocking in the majors. One of then assistant GM Brian Cashman's tasks in 1996 was to recommend which players to block. He noticed in early August that the Pirates had put their top starter, Neagle, on waivers and suggested the Yankees claim the lefty.

Watson, however, assured his assistant that he had been in regular contact with Pirates GM Cam Bonifay and that the Pirates were not dealing their ace. But Cashman worried that new Pirates ownership might want to strip down payroll and rebuild more seriously. At $2.3 million for 1996 and $3.5 million for 1997, Neagle was Pittsburgh's most expensive pitcher and most attractive asset to lure young talent. So Cashman asked his boss, "What if they have a financial situation?" to which Watson replied, "That ain't happening." So Neagle went unclaimed, meaning any team could now deal for him, and while the rest of baseball napped, Schuerholz swooped in on August 28 and obtained Neagle to go along with Glavine, Maddux, and Smoltz. It felt as if someone owning ABC, CBS, and NBC had just added FOX. To this day, Cashman has never told George Steinbrenner about how Neagle evaded the Yankees.

Now here were Neagle and the Braves 12 outs away from a three-games-to-one lead in the World Series, with Atlanta having Smoltz, Maddux, and Glavine available for Game 5 and, if necessary, 6 and 7. Derek Jeter led off the sixth by popping a ball into foul territory near the right-field line. Right-field ump Tim Welke, who had so annoyed David Cone 24 hours earlier behind the plate, turned his back to the field to watch the path of the ball. Right fielder Jermaine Dye chased with his head up looking at the pop. Ump and player never saw each other, and Dye bumped into Welke and could not recover in time to catch the ball. Rather than one out, none on, Jeter again capitalized this postseason on an issue involving a right-field umpire by flipping a single into right field. "I was going to catch it," Dye says, looking back. "I was running, and the ump must have been unsure where I was going because he never got out of the way. It cost us the game, I think."

Of course, even with the mishap, the Braves were still leading 6–0, and just one man was on. But Neagle had some Kenny Rogers in him; despite a big lead, he was nibbling and walked Bernie Williams. Neagle got ahead of Cecil Fielder 0–2 but could not put him away. Fielder darted a single to right and Dye, trying to shoestring the ball, missed it. Rather than one run scoring, both Jeter and

Williams came home, and Fielder moved to second. The reason Watson had stayed in touch with Cam Bonifay and thought he knew Neagle's status was because he was talking regularly to the Pirates GM about Charlie Hayes. Three days after Atlanta obtained Neagle, the Yankees acquired Hayes. Here Hayes ended Neagle's season with a single to right that scored Fielder and made the score 6–3.

Darryl Strawberry drew a walk off reliever Terrell Wade, but Mike Bielecki relieved to whiff Mariano Duncan, as well as pinch-hitters Paul O'Neill and Tino Martinez. It was frustrating because all three strikeout victims were the tying run. But the Yankees had met Torre's mandate to chip away, and they had worked into the Braves' suspect bullpen. And there was one other thing: O'Neill had pinch-hit for Joe Girardi, which meant the Yankees had to send their backup catcher, Jim Leyritz, into the game.

Not getting drafted hardly dimmed Jim Leyritz's opinion of himself. From the moment he began playing in the Yankee minor leagues in 1986, Leyritz started gabbing, and no one can quite remember him ever stopping. "Jim was the exact opposite of Bernie," says Andy Stankiewicz, Leyritz's teammate from his first year in pro ball all the way up to the Yankees. "He would always be talking in the clubhouse. Even in [Single-A] Lauderdale, he was talking about playing in the majors. Everyone else at A-ball is trying to figure out life. Jimmy had it all figured out. Even in the minors, Jimmy had swagger, and he always wanted to be up there with the game on the line."

Leyritz was another farmhand the Yankees tried to teach to switch-hit, but Leyritz was also attempting to learn to catch that first pro season and had a run-in with his Single-A manager, Bucky Dent, who wanted him to keep working on his lefty stroke. Leyritz was demoted to Rookie League Oneonta because of the dispute. It was hardly the last time Leyritz had difficulties with Yankee authority. Buck Showalter managed Leyritz at three minor league levels and again in the majors and thought Leyritz was the antithesis of all the Yankees were trying to instill. Unlike Williams, Derek Jeter, Andy Pettitte, and Mariano Rivera, Leyritz lacked modesty and dignity and would never let his bat do all of his talking for him. Even his exaggerated bat wiggle was perceived as obnoxious.

Leyritz did not know his place. The first time on the Yankee team plane, he saw the beer in the back where the veterans congregated, and he naturally thought this was his place to be. "Rookie, get the hell out of here," Dave Righetti told him. When superstars gathered on the field, Leyritz was the sore thumb, making himself more overt by talking the most and loudest and laughing inappropriately. Don Mattingly nicknamed him "The King" and others called him "Jumbo Jimmy." Leyritz not only did not mind—he loved it. He was aware of his reputation and reveled in it. "You could tell Jim Leyritz to shut the fuck up and it wouldn't bother him," says Rick Down, both a minor league manager and major league hitting coach for Leyritz. Few adored the big-league life like Jumbo Jimmy. Leyritz stayed out too late and was a clubhouse lawyer, but most stunning was that he would plead guilty to the charges with a smile. "Everything was more important than the game to Jim," Down remembers. "He forgot what got him to the majors. Buck didn't like it because he was very ordered and totally about the game. Jim's life was about everything but the game. He was squandered talent."

Torre was generally more tolerant than Showalter, but he shared Showalter's dislike of Leyritz's antics. Leyritz did not fit the professional profile that Torre wanted his Yankees to project. Leyritz defied weight mandates, which annoyed George Steinbrenner and, therefore, became Torre's problem. And Leyritz, as always, was never satisfied with his status as a reserve. Jim Leyritz looked in the mirror and saw a star. "Joe made it clear as the season went along that you did it his way," Leyritz recalls. "You had to buy into the team concept. He always considered me a pain in the ass because I wanted to play more."

Leyritz had two attributes as a major leaguer that saved him to the point where, amazingly, he was the senior Yankee. He could really hit a fastball, and,

because he imagined himself a star, he craved pressure situations when the spotlight belonged exclusively to him. He loved being Jumbo Jimmy.

Mike Bielecki, who had to all but beg for even an invitation to a major league
camp while spring training was under way, had settled down the game for the
Braves with two hitless innings in which he struck out four men. Bielecki had
thrown just 34 overpowering pitches. Cox could have stuck with him further or
brought in Brad Clontz. However, there was an uneasiness about the Braves
now. Torre had been right, that by nibbling at the lead, the Yankees had the
Braves worried about the impact of blowing such a large advantage. So Cox
turned to his closer, Mark Wohlers, to try for a six-out save, figuring this was
the chance to drop the hammer on the Yankees.

Wohlers had graduated to become the Braves' closer the previous year,
and—after Tom Glavine had assured his World Series Most Valuable Player
award with eight one-hit innings in Game 6 against Cleveland—recorded the
final three outs of the 1995 Fall Classic to bring the city of Atlanta its first major
sports championship. Wohlers threw even harder than Baltimore's Armando
Benitez, touching 100 miles per hour on occasion. During the 1996 regular
season, he struck out 100 batters in 77$\frac{1}{3}$ innings while registering 39 saves. The
dominance extended into the playoffs. In the first two rounds against Los
Angeles and St. Louis, Wohlers had pitched 6$\frac{1}{3}$ innings and yielded one hit
while striking out eight in going five-for-five in save chances. In his only appearance of this World Series, he had struck out the side in Game 2. Wohlers
was fully rested and pitching great.

But one of Cox's strongest managerial attributes was his knack for putting
players in spots in which they could thrive. Wohlers had been requested to pitch
two innings just once in all of 1996, and in his second inning on September 6
against the Mets, he permitted two runs to blow a save for Neagle. There was
an unspoken message of dread being sent out of the Atlanta dugout before

Charlie Hayes topped the first pitch of the eighth inning down the third-base line. Normally a ball that begins that close to the line spins foul, but Wohlers and third baseman Chipper Jones watched and watched, and the ball never deviated from a straight line. It was a bizarre single. Torre had decided to start Fielder, Hayes, and Strawberry for a second consecutive game. Fielder and Hayes had both had huge hits in the Yankees' three-run sixth inning, and now Strawberry again went to the opposite field to produce a single. It was first and second, with no outs.

Cox had sent Rafael Belliard in to play shortstop for defensive purposes an inning earlier, replacing Jeff Blauser. And Mariano Duncan hit a routine double-play ball at Belliard, but the shortstop bobbled and was only able to get the force out at second. So rather than two out and a runner on third, Leyritz was coming up as the tying run. Leyritz was Andy Pettitte's personal catcher, so he knew he would be starting Game 5 against John Smoltz the next night. He had just two game bats remaining and, having seen Smoltz's hard and harder repertoire in Game 1, realized he might need them both. So even with the World Series in the balance, he oddly did not want to risk breaking a game bat against Wohlers's heat. So he grabbed one of Darryl Strawberry's bats, which were 35 inches and 33 ounces, just like his, but had thinner handles. That was fine with Leyritz. He thought a thin handle enabled him to whip the bat quicker through the strike zone, an asset he definitely needed here.

Leyritz had yet to take a swing in Game 4 and nevertheless fouled Wohlers's first pitch, a 98 mph fastball, straight back, usually a sign that a hitter has the pitch timed. Nothing had changed. Jim Leyritz could hit a fastball. So Wohlers came back with two straight sliders, both high, to fall behind in the count. Wohlers's best pitch was his fastball; his second best, a splitter, he threw mainly to lefty swingers. On the FOX broadcast, analyst Tim McCarver said, "I think Wohlers is going to the breaking ball too much. . . . If you get beat, you want to get beat with your best pitch, not your third-best pitch." And, indeed, Wohlers returned to his fastball, this one 99 mph, and Leyritz again fouled it straight back, again seemingly showing that he could time the heat. Even if it was his third-best pitch, Wohlers's slider was no ordinary slider. He threw it in the high 80s, faster than the two starters in Game 4, Rogers and Neagle, delivered their fastballs, and Leyritz barely tapped an 86 mph slider down the third-base line to stay alive.

The duel had now reached its sixth pitch. Leyritz mentally dismissed the slider. Wohlers threw too hard to sit on a breaking ball with two strikes. If Wohlers came with a slider, Leyritz decided, he would react the best he could, like he just had on a 2–2 slider. But the advantage clearly belonged to Wohlers, who had held hitters to a .117 average with 1 homer in 154 at bats during the regular season when he reached two strikes, such was the potency of his arsenal.

"I called a fastball, but Wohlers said no," Braves catcher Eddie Perez recalls. "And I was good with that. I really wanted a slider, too, but a good slider. I wanted the slider down and away. Wohlers wanted to throw the slider because he thought he was going to throw a better slider."

Smoltz was sitting in the TV room adjacent to the Braves dugout, watching the game on a monitor to study the Yankee hitters for the following day. He saw Perez switch to the slider sign and cringed. "Baseball gets confusing when it looks like guys are on pitches, but they aren't," he says, looking back. "It seemed like Leyritz was locked in on the heater because he was fouling it back. But he really wasn't on the heater." Glavine remembers, "Watching that at-bat, I thought to myself that the only pitch Leyritz would be able to hit was a slider." The theory of the two Braves starters was that Leyritz would never be able to generate enough bat speed to hit Wohlers's fastball fair with authority, but by having to ready for that pitch, it made him extra quick with his swing should something slower come along—something like a slider.

Wohlers had bounced up and down from the minors early in his career because, in jams, he always tried to throw harder and harder still. It was not until he began to master and trust his secondary stuff that he stuck full-time with the Braves. Mike Aldrete, who had yet to bat in the postseason, was on deck, but Wohlers was focused only on Leyritz. He did not want to mess around and put the tying run on base with a walk. Perez squatted with half his body off home plate on the outside corner and his glove perched at knee level. Leyritz initiated his high front-leg kick even before Wohlers had released the ball. It was Leyritz's timing mechanism, and he knew that with Wohlers he had to start early. In his attempt to throw an even better slider than the last one, Wohlers muscled up. His 86 mph pitch did not break as he wanted, down and away, but rather stayed up and headed in the opposite direction, backing up toward the middle of the plate. Leyritz recognized that he was not getting heat and was able to keep his hands back just long enough to drive a belt-high pitch toward left field. Just as Smoltz had fretted when he saw the sign for the slider, Leyritz's bat had sped up, and the head of the bat was out in front of the hitting zone, where he could drive a pitch. Fulton County Stadium was known as the Launching Pad for the frequency of long balls, but Leyritz had not been able to get his full body into driving the pitch. The ball was hit so high that a stadium full of spectators and players rose to watch its flight with uncertainty. But somebody in the Yankee dugout knew where the ball was going.

The first homer ever hit in Fulton County Stadium was on April 12, 1966, with one out in the fifth inning, to essentially this same spot. Joe Torre, who would play three seasons as a Brave in this facility, had hit it off of Bob Veale, and he knew that balls carried particularly well to that area. So Torre recognized Game 4 of the 1996 World Series—the next-to-last game scheduled at Fulton County Stadium, which was being torn down, with Turner Field soon to become the Braves' home—was going to be tied. But for a few seconds, the outcome was a mystery to just about everyone else. Andruw Jones would go on to become one of the greatest center fielders ever, but with Marquis Grissom manning that position in 1996, the young, athletic Jones was in left field. He leaped and tried essentially to walk his way up the wall to take a stab, but the ball struck a restraining wall beyond the left-field fence. The noise drained out of the stadium. Eddie Perez remembers just one sound: "the Yankee wives screaming."

It was Leyritz's second career postseason homer. His first had come in the rain in Game 2 of the 1995 Division Series, a two-run blast in the 15th inning that put the Yankees within one triumph of advancing to the ALCS. The Yankees never won again, and because of that, Leyritz's memories of that home run are not overly fond. It was one of his first thoughts here after he returned to the bench: how badly he wanted this home run to be not a footnote but a turning point. He knew that Game 4 was tied but not the World Series.

In truth, everything had changed. Tim Welke's inadvertent pick on Jermaine Dye, Hayes's groundball hugging the third-base line, and Belliard's bobble on the double-play ball had furthered the sense that the Yankees were enjoying an inexplicable magic in this postseason. Leyritz's homer merely galvanized the growing feeling that the 1996 Yankees were special. When asked nearly a decade later what he remembers best about this World Series, Chipper Jones stares with an incredulous grin at the inquirer for nearly 10 seconds before saying, "What do you think?" Jones then adds, "We're up 6–3. If we get Jim Leyritz out, we're out of that inning, and I am pretty certain we win that game 6–3. Then we have Smoltzy going in Game 5. I believe we win one of the last three games in that series if we win Game 4. The momentum swung on one swing of the bat. It was enough to lift them to another level. The last 2½ games they played like a different team. From the Leyritz homer on, they were riding confidence and momentum."

The momentum certainly was on the Yankees' side. Still, there was that little bit of unfinished business. They had to win Game 4.

Torre badly did not want to use Mariano Rivera. The lithe righty had thrown 15 pitches in Game 2, 35 more in Game 3. Rivera was feeling pain in the back of his shoulder that he thought was defusing the late kick on his fastball. But, shockingly, the score of Game 4 was now tied, so Torre reluctantly summoned Rivera for a third straight day. In the ninth inning, Rivera's second frame of work, the Braves put two men on with one out. Torre understood he had a tired reliever who needed out. Torre also recognized he had an asset now in Graeme

Lloyd, who for the second straight game was called upon to bail out Rivera. Lloyd, who was such an unlikely candidate to even make the roster that the Yankee media-relations department did not put his biography in the team's postseason media guide, provoked an inning-ending double play from Fred McGriff.

Steve Avery entered to pitch the 10th inning. There was a time in the early 1990s when it was easy to believe Avery would be the best Braves starter of them all. He won 18 games as a 21-year-old in 1991 and again won 18 in 1993. But Avery began to lose his fastball young, and 1996 was an injury-plagued season that motivated the Braves to obtain Neagle, reducing Avery to a mop-up man. Game 4 was his first appearance in a close game this postseason. Avery retired two Yankees quickly; one of them was Lloyd. Torre had only Wetteland left in his bullpen, so he felt he could not pinch-hit. Avery then lost the plate, walking Tim Raines on four pitches before Jeter singled to put runners at first and second. Bernie Williams was up next, and righty Brad Clontz was ready to relieve. But Cox made an unorthodox and fateful decision. Though only third base was open, Cox ordered Williams walked. The judgment spoke to the new-found respect for Williams, especially as a righty hitter. But mostly it was strategic. The lefty-swinging rookie Andy Fox was on deck, and he had not batted in a game since the regular-season finale nearly a month earlier. The only other position player remaining for Torre was also a lefty, Wade Boggs, whose great bat had gone dormant. During the first two playoff rounds, Boggs had endured the longest hitless streak of his career, 22 at-bats, and had started neither of the games in Atlanta.

Boggs had come to the Yankees on a 3-year, $11 million free-agent contract on December 15, 1992, against the wishes of then GM Gene Michael and manager Buck Showalter. They were concerned he was on the decline, having batted just .259 in 1992 after hitting .300 every year dating back to Single-A Winston-Salem in 1977. Michael and Showalter also worried about Boggs's self-absorption with his hitting statistics and bizarre behavior as a Red Sox that included, among other things, talking on prime time with Barbara Walters about his 4-year affair with a woman named Margo Adams. But Boggs was from Tampa, as was the Yankees' owner in exile. Commissioner Fay Vincent had lifted George Steinbrenner's banishment agreement, effective March 1, 1993. But every instrumental executive in New York believed Steinbrenner, wanting to make sure he had a team that could win upon his return, had ordered the signing of Boggs. The irony, in retrospect, was that Boggs had been recruited because the Yankees had miscalculated and lost Charlie Hayes in the expansion draft to the Colorado Rockies. Now Hayes had returned to make the struggling Boggs a part-time player in the postseason.

Boggs surprisingly elated the Yankees by being a good teammate. He was indeed obsessed with his numbers, especially staying on track for 3,000 hits. He was filled with idiosyncrasies, repeating as many as 70 to 100 superstitions daily. Ultimately, Boggs melted into the Yankees' professional clubhouse, adoring the work-oriented structure created by Showalter, for Boggs was nothing if not a workhorse. He had taken hundreds of groundballs daily to evolve from a nonprospect, due to his fielding, to the oldest nonpitcher to win a Gold Glove in 1994 at age 36. He toiled endlessly to keep his swing a metronome, looking as if he were taking a tennis backhand and lobbing it over the shortstop's head over and over. He batted .320 from 1993 to 1995 as a Yankee, making third-base prospect Russ Davis expendable in the deal for Tino Martinez.

But Boggs's greatest gift to the Yankees went beyond his glove and line drives. No Yankee was more influential in the mid-1990s in fostering the patient plate style that became the organization's offensive staple. He hardly ever swung at the first pitch and was not afraid to hit with two strikes. Boggs was 6 feet, 2 inches tall but not overly powerful. He was agile but not an elite athlete. Yet he was going to the Hall of Fame because he knew what a strike was, and that resonated with teammates who saw him make the most of what he had because of that skill. From 1993 to 1996, Boggs's first four seasons, the Yankees drew more walks than any team. In the 4 years before he arrived, the Yankees drew the fifth-fewest walks in the majors. Yes, they had better players in the Boggs era, but some of those players, notably Paul O'Neill, derived much from watching Boggs translate ordinary talents into greatness due to his keen strike-zone awareness.

That's what made his postseason to this point so strange; Boggs had just one walk in 37 plate appearances. He was swinging early in counts, having lost confidence in the talent that defined him—his hitting eye. Yet Torre could not stick with the rookie Fox, who had been sent in to run for Fielder an inning earlier. By walking Williams, Cox had put the skittish Avery in a position where he had to throw strikes, and the Yankees had the player up who best knew what a strike looked like. In this chess game, Torre had been holding and holding Boggs, trying to find the ideal spot to use him. Here it was. The most patient Yankee had patiently waited nearly 4 hours in the dugout for this moment.

"You look at their bench and you go, 'Oh my God,'" Chipper Jones recalls. "They've got Martinez, O'Neill, and Boggs because they are playing Strawberry, Raines, Fielder, and Hayes."

Boggs drew the Hebrew symbol for life, chai, in the dirt—one of his superstitions—and Jeter clapped overhead from second base for encouragement. Boggs immediately fell behind 1–2, but he then checked his swing on a slider that missed being strike 3 by millimeters. That was an incredibly encouraging indicator for the Yankees. To not swing at that pitch meant Boggs was honed in despite his recent travails. It meant he was the usual Wade Boggs, unconcerned about operating with two strikes. In 1996, only Rickey Henderson and Edgar Martinez swung at a lower percentage of pitches than Boggs. Another slider missed away. The last two sliders had both broken late and just off the plate, and a vast majority of lefty hitters would have lacked the discipline to avoid swinging at one or the other, especially with two strikes. But this was Wade Boggs, to whom swinging at a pitch out of the strike zone was blasphemy. So those pitches were merely balls 2 and 3. It was a full count, two outs.

Ten years earlier, Boggs had been one strike away from being a champion, but then the 1986 World Series went horribly wrong for the Red Sox. A ball went through Bill Buckner's legs in Game 6, Strawberry hit a big homer in

Game 7, and the Mets completed their improbable recovery to a title. Boggs was on the wrong end of that rally from two games lost at home — the same situation that Strawberry had described to encourage his Yankee teammates earlier in this World Series.

But that wasn't why Boggs had cried in a Shea Stadium dugout at the conclusion of the 1986 series. He had been in the Yankee Stadium visiting clubhouse on June 17, 1986, when his cousin called to tell him his mother, Sue, had been killed instantly in a collision between her car and a cement truck in downtown Tampa, the day before her 63rd birthday. The guy operating the cement truck was a prisoner on work detail who had strayed 50 miles off course. He ran a red light trying to make up time when he broadsided Sue Boggs's vehicle. Wade Boggs cried in the dugout 4 months later because he could no longer hide within the batter's box; he instead had to go home and grieve the loss of the woman who first took him to play Little League.

Now, at age 38, Boggs was back in the World Series for the first time since then, still chasing a first championship. Avery threw a fastball, up and in, not even close. For the 1,296th time in his career, including the postseason, Boggs had drawn a walk. But he had never drawn one as important as this. He trotted to first, Tim Raines came home, and the Yankees led 7–6. Cox now turned to Clontz to face Hayes and double-switched Ryan Klesko into the game at first base so that his last position player could lead off the bottom of the inning. Klesko had played just two games at first all year. Another destiny moment had arrived. On the first pitch from Clontz, Hayes was jammed and blooped a ball toward first. Klesko squatted, losing the ball in the lights. It went off his glove for a run-scoring error.

"He," Bernie Williams said years later looking skyward, "was a Yankee fan back then."

The Yankees had now scored eight straight runs and led 8–6. And since Klesko was in the game, Torre could stick with Lloyd for one batter. Lloyd struck out Klesko. Wetteland, of course, went out on the tightrope again. He allowed an Andruw Jones single before Jermaine Dye flied out to the warning track in left as the tying run. Terry Pendleton then shot a ball even deeper to the warning track in left, and Tim Raines made the catch tumbling to the ground, ending the longest World Series game in history at 4 hours and 17 minutes. The Yankees had won Game 4. The World Series was tied, but the tenor had turned to the Yankees' favor.

Game 4 had expressed all the Yankee strengths: bullpen, depth, and resiliency.

One-to-15, the Braves had a superior roster to the Yankees. But rosters had 25 men, and it was in the length of the team that the Yankees held superiority. Because they had so many quality players, the Yankees were more prepared to play a National League–style game with pinch-hitters and double-switches than the NL champions. The Braves finished this game hitless in 18 pinch-hit at-bats in the 1996 postseason. Leyritz and Boggs had come off the Yankee bench to provide huge moments, and Boggs's influence was as strong as ever. His 10th-inning base on balls marked the ninth drawn by the Yankees in this game. Atlanta's bullpen had yielded five runs in five innings. The uncelebrated trio of Brian Boehringer, Jeff Nelson, and Lloyd had been instrumental in the Yankee pen, permitting just one run in eight innings in relief of Rogers. The Yankees, in fact, were 3–0 in Rogers's postseason starts, though he had a 14.14 ERA, because of the work of their relievers.

The Yankees had forgotten to pack lineup cards before making this trip and had to use those left over from the regular season by the Cincinnati Reds. When Torre looked at his card after 10 innings, he noticed that he had used 22 of his 25 players. Only starting pitchers David Cone, Jimmy Key, and Andy Pettitte had not played, and Torre had asked Cone to be ready to bat for another pitcher and Key to be ready to pinch-run. The game ended at 12:36 a.m., with Cone and Key both wearing spikes.

"We went back to the clubhouse and we were all, 'I can't believe this and that.' We were so down," Atlanta's Eddie Perez remembers. "I looked in everyone's faces and thought we lost the series."

14 | THE PERFECT
ENDING/BEGINNING

"I feel like we lost to destiny—with all the stuff with Joe Torre. I feel they finished off an incredible story. Unfortunately, we were on the other end of it."
—*John Smoltz*

No player on the Yankees derived more from the stunning Game 4 victory than Game 5 starter Andy Pettitte. The World Series was now assured to return to New York, regardless of the outcome of Game 5, and that fact brought Pettitte great peace. "I was sitting all game when it was 6–0 [in Game 4] and thinking, *It's all on me,*" Pettitte recalls. "And then, boom, the pressure was gone." All of the Yankees felt that way. They had won Game 4 with Rogers pitching appallingly the night before. They had surged from a two-game deficit to halt all of the premature eulogies for their season and all the glorified odes to the magnitude of the Braves. They had once again reached down and found not only their talent but also the resilience that had accompanied their season.

Still, with all that had happened positively for the Yankees over the previous 48 hours, the baseball analysts on the Fox pregame show, Dave Winfield and Steve Lyons, both said the Braves would win this World Series in six games; such was the specter of invincibility projected by John Smoltz, Greg Maddux, and Tom Glavine. Smoltz took the mound in Game 5 as arguably the greatest big-game pitcher of the generation. He was 9–1 overall in his postseason career, 4–0 with a 1.20 ERA in these playoffs, including his overwhelming effort in the opener against the Yankees. His only postseason loss had come on October 10, 1993, in Game 4 of the National League Championship Series against Philadelphia, and both runs against him in a 2–1 loss were unearned. Smoltz had won 24 games during the regular season, started and won the All-Star Game, and won all four of his October starts. So a victory here meant 30 wins in 1996. The only question was how he would handle starting on 3 days' rest. The answer came as quickly as his pitches. He threw 17 first-inning pitches—16 were fastballs in the mid-90s—and struck out Derek Jeter, Charlie Hayes, and Bernie Williams in order.

So it was simple for the Yankees: To win Game 5 of the 1996 World Series, Pettitte was going to have to pitch the game of his life.

Pettitte had been annoyed by how nervous he had been in Game 1 and how that had derailed his energy and attentiveness. "I wanted to win so badly," he says, looking back. "And because of that, my ball was up and my focus was not where it needed to be. I immediately thought to myself, *No matter what, that ain't happening again.* I just prayed so much from the moment I came out of Game 1 to get another chance. After the way we lost those first two games, I was convinced I wasn't going to get the chance."

So it was a blessing to Pettitte to be locked up again with John Smoltz, a battle of the pitchers with the most wins in their respective leagues in 1996. Pettitte had committed to himself before throwing a pitch that, no matter what negative event occurred in Game 5, he would not lose composure and concentration. This was the second chance for which he had prayed, and no way was he going to sully the opportunity.

Pettitte walked a batter and allowed a stolen base in both the second and third innings, but relying on curveballs and sinkers and peppering the outside corner consistently—all tactics he had not deployed with any regularity in Game 1—he worked out of trouble. That allowed him to match zeroes with Smoltz, who remained overpowering by striking out six of the first nine batters he faced. So Game 5 was scoreless when Charlie Hayes led off the fourth inning. In Games 3 and 4, Torre had started Hayes at third and Cecil Fielder at first for the slumping Wade Boggs and Tino Martinez. But that was against lefty starters

Tom Glavine and Denny Neagle. Against the righty Smoltz, Torre continued to heed his gut, which told him the righty hitters were swinging much better.

Torre shunned convention and stuck with Hayes and Fielder. Boggs and Martinez appreciated that Torre kept holding face-to-face meetings to explain his thinking, but they were annoyed nevertheless that they could be so vital from spring training forward and be bench players now; Martinez, in particular, was devastated. But a key to the success of the 1996 Yankees was that the players mostly internalized their anger, not allowing it to metastasize across the clubhouse and create teamwide discord. Martinez made sure that no one cheered louder for Fielder than he did. "Guys were not happy with sitting," Joe Girardi remembers, "but guys did not lose sight of the goal."

Hayes drove a deep fly to right-center, almost perfectly to the middle of Marquis Grissom and Jermaine Dye and nearly to the warning track. David Justice was the Braves' regular right fielder. He had homered off lefty reliever Jim Poole in the sixth inning of Game 6 of the 1995 World Series, providing the lone run in Atlanta's title-clinching 1–0 victory over Cleveland. But on May 15, 1996, Justice took a violent swing against a Pittsburgh starter named Denny Neagle and dislocated his right shoulder. He was lost for the season. His replacement, Dye, was a wonderful athlete but just 22 years old. He made a youthful mistake as he converged at full speed toward the ball with Grissom. Grissom called for the ball, but rather than ducking away, Dye stepped in front of Grissom, who momentarily lost sight of the fly and had the ball kick off his attempt at a last-second basket catch.

Dye had been the player involved in the unintentional pick play in right created by umpire Tim Welke. That had helped the Yankees toward three sixth-inning runs in Game 4, triggering their improbable comeback. Game by game now, it felt as if all the little breaks and mistakes were flowing favorably one way. This one led to Grissom, just about to win his fourth straight Gold Glove, being charged with an error that left Hayes on second. Bernie Williams grounded to second on a 3–0 pitch to move Hayes to third. Realizing the premium on runs, the Braves brought the infield in against Fielder. Atlanta pitchers lived on the outer half, a style favored by pitching coach Leo Mazzone. But Fielder had thwarted that strategy by producing all five of his hits in the first four games to either center or right field.

When Fielder had first returned from Japan to the majors in 1990, he was not just a burly masher but also a thoughtful hitter, willing to use the whole field. But as the Tigers worsened and Fielder's lineup protection vanished, he saw fewer and fewer hittable pitches. He took it upon himself to be the power source and became pull conscious and homer crazed. Even initially as a Yankee, Fielder wanted to justify his acquisition and was shooting for homers. But playing for a championship had Fielder thinking more like a hitter again, and his former Tiger manager, Sparky Anderson, noticed during the World Series that Fielder "was back to his old ways."

Smoltz had noticed as well. He was the one Atlanta starter who threw hard enough to consistently challenge hitters on the inner third of the plate, and he decided to surprise Fielder by working toward the big man's hands. Fielder thwarted that strategy, too, and made Torre's hunch to keep playing him look inspired. Anticipating that Smoltz would try to get him to roll over an inside pitch because the infield was in, Fielder was quick enough to drill a one-hop drive off the wall in the left-field corner for a run-scoring double and his team-best 14th RBI of this postseason. It was a smart and necessary bit of hitting because the Yankees would have 16 at-bats in Game 5 with runners on base, and this would be the lone hit.

It was an unearned run, the first against Smoltz in the postseason since Game 4 of the 1993 NLCS, which was his only previous playoff loss. It also emphasized the defensive advantage the Yankees were enjoying in the World Series. In the bottom of the fourth, the rotund Fielder went into a split to catch a low peg from Derek Jeter to complete an inning-ending double play. Andruw Jones led off the Braves fifth with a single, but Pettitte used the majors' best pickoff move to nab Jones. Pettitte had led baseball with 11 pickoffs during the season, and, as Bernie Williams remembers, "it was only Andy's second season.

The pickoff was still fresh, people didn't know all about it yet. It was a huge weapon."

Pettitte was far from done helping himself.

Pettitte's sixth inning began miserably. He allowed a single to the opposing starter, Smoltz, and another single to Grissom when ahead in the count 1–2. That put runners on first and second with no out in a one-run game, a classic sacrifice situation. And the Braves just happened to have Mark Lemke coming up. He had led Atlanta position players in sacrifice bunts in each of the past 3 years. Pitching coach Mel Stottlemyre came out to remind Pettitte that he had coverage toward third base. But Pettitte was 6 foot, 5 inches and not an agile athlete like any of Atlanta's Big Three starters. Gene Michael, in fact, called Smoltz the best athlete among pitchers he had ever seen. Smoltz actually had three postseason steals. So the Braves had an excellent bunter and speed on the bases; they could not have been set up more ideally. In addition, Pettitte was the pitcher all the Yankees good-naturedly taunted during fielding practice in spring training because of his awkwardness.

Lemke, though, did not steer a bunt toward third base; rather, he tapped a two-hopper back toward the mound. Pettitte came forward and leaned his big body down to barehand the ball just before it took a third bounce. There were 51,881 fans screaming. To simply field the ball cleanly with a bare hand exemplified poise and defied Pettitte's athletic reputation. Jim Leyritz had ripped off his mask and from about 30 feet away was screaming for Pettitte to throw to third. Because of all the noise, Pettitte did not hear his catcher. "It was the craziest thing I ever did," Pettitte recalls. "I just went on my internal clock and believed I had a play at third base."

He did, but it was going to be a bang-bang play, necessitating now an accurate throw executed in one smooth motion off of the scoop of the bunt. The sliding Smoltz's right foot was perhaps 2 feet from the bag when Hayes caught Pettitte's peg with a backhand. The Yankees had cut down the lead runner.

"I still don't believe he made that play," Smoltz says, nearly a decade later. Jorge Posada, who had played in the minors with Pettitte and was watching from the visitor's bench as an inactive player that night, asks, "Do you know how gutsy it is to pick up a bunt in that situation barehanded and throw to third base?"

It fit Pettitte's mind-set for this game, his promise to himself that after his disastrous Game 1, he would not lose his poise, no matter what the circumstances in Game 5. Even after making his startling defensive gem, Pettitte recognized his job was not over. It was still first and second and only one out and the Braves' RBI leader, Chipper Jones, at bat. Pettitte pinpointed a two-seamer away that Jones hit weakly off the end of the bat back to Pettitte, who turned and fired to Mariano Duncan to initiate an inning-ending double play. In two pitches, Pettitte had recorded three outs to escape this jam, belying his reputation as an ordinary fielder on both plays. The Yankees still led 1–0.

Yet the Yankees had a problem. Because Kenny Rogers had given them so little the night before and this was the fifth game in 5 days, the bullpen was exhausted. No one was more drained than Mariano Rivera, so Torre could not turn to his Formula of six innings from a starter, two innings from Rivera and one from Wetteland. On this night, Pettitte needed to be his own setup man. He pitched around a leadoff error by Jeter in the seventh inning. Jeff Blauser opened the eighth inning with a drive to deep left field. In his younger days, Darryl Strawberry had been the most indifferent of outfielders. But here, operating on the fractured right big toe, he raced back, reached with a backhand, and extended his 6-foot-6 body to catch the ball before crashing into the wall and holding on. Even he smiled thinking about it: Darryl Strawberry, defensive star. Grissom singled with two out, but Pettitte induced Lemke to ground out.

Smoltz, as advertised, was brilliant, striking out 10—stained by just the unearned run. The only way to have outdone him was to allow no runs. Pettitte had needed the game of his life—and had produced. He was not as dominant as Smoltz, allowing at least one base runner in every inning except the first. But he honored his vow not to lose focus. However, his manager was not yet done investing in Pettitte's gumption. The Yankees generated first and third with two outs in the ninth against Mark Wohlers. The pitcher's spot was due. Torre wanted to stick with Pettitte for Chipper Jones and Fred McGriff in the bottom of the inning. He favored that over pinch-hitting with either Wade Boggs or Tim Raines, two patient batters who would make the shaky Wohlers work. It meant Torre was pretty much conceding the chance to open up the lead further.

"I thought I was done," Pettitte admits years later. "Joe and Zim [Don Zimmer] called me over to the bench while I was in the on-deck circle, and they were joking to me to hit a home run off Wohlers." Pettitte flied out instead, and Jones opened the Braves ninth with a double. The tying run was in scoring position with none out. A McGriff groundout to first advanced Jones to third. Now Torre removed his starter.

Usually John Wetteland got himself in and out of trouble; now he was being beckoned to clean up someone else's mess and to save not just a game but Torre. If the Braves won, Torre was going to be second-guessed mightily for not pinch-hitting for Pettitte in the top of the ninth.

Wetteland fit the caricature of a closer—he threw hard and had a bizarre streak. He had broken his toe kicking a pitching screen in 1993 because he was mad at himself for hanging a curveball in, of all things, batting practice. He never changed hats during the season, no matter how grimy and discolored from sweat his became. He reasoned that the hat had come that far with him and deserved to make the whole journey. He admitted to a past of drugs and drink, and one member of the Dodgers organization says that Los Angeles dealt him to Cincinnati in November 1991 because then Dodgers manager Tommy Lasorda "thought he was high maintenance" and littered with off-field issues.

But by then Wetteland had begun to reconstitute his life. He had found both his future wife, Michelle, and Jesus. That settled him down off the field, where he began quoting scripture. On the field, though, he only began to show some semblance of control when put into the role for which he was best suited, late-inning reliever, with the Expos in 1992. Wetteland was too intense to distribute his energy over nine innings. He was built for one inning, to give everything he had emotionally, physically, and spiritually in a short burst. With Wetteland as its closer, Montreal forged the majors' best record before the strike prematurely ended the 1994 season. When the strike was settled, the Expos decided they could not afford to retain their outstanding team. Initially, Wetteland was part of a group of players that was given service time during the strike and became free agents. If that decision had been upheld, Wetteland would have signed with the Red Sox. Instead, service time was not granted, and the Expos traded Wetteland to the Yankees on April 5, 1995, choosing a prospect named Fernando Seguignol over Russ Davis.

Wetteland's time in New York was not totally pleasant. He had encountered his salary fight with George Steinbrenner that nearly went to arbitration. Buck Showalter had left him frozen in the bullpen as the Mariners clinched the 1995 Division Series against Jack McDowell. Wetteland also rebelled initially against the team's leadership. Pitching coach Mel Stottlemyre says that Wetteland was "difficult to work with at first because he was so set in his ways." Joe Girardi, another religious man, slowly gained Wetteland's trust and convinced the closer to use his slider more and stop trying to throw harder and harder in times of difficulty. Mainly, though, Wetteland found comfort in being relied upon, in being the back end of the Yankee one-two Formula. Because even his greatest detractors would agree that Wetteland loved being accountable and craved the ball fearlessly in the big moments. As his minor league pitching coach, Dave Wallace, recalls, "John always had big nuts." Stottlemyre says more tactfully, "John was very competitive and liked being the guy with the game on the line."

Now here he was with a chance to save his third game in as many days and sixth of the playoffs. The Yankees were two outs from taking a three-games-to-two lead, and Chipper Jones was 90 feet away from tying the score. The in-field played in, and Javy Lopez smacked the first pitch on the ground right at Charlie Hayes, who threw to first for the second out with Jones holding at third. Pettitte wrapped his head in a towel, unable to watch as Torre went to the mound. The decision was made to walk Ryan Klesko, who was pinch-hitting for Andruw Jones. It was intrepid and extremely risky. Torre again was rejecting convention by putting the go-ahead run on base. He was making another choice that would make the Yankees winners or losers in Game 5—and make him either a genius or a fool.

Luis Polonia was sent to pinch-hit for Dye. He was ideal for this situation. He could bunt for a hit and beat out an infield single, and he struck out infrequently. But he was ideal for another reason: No Brave wanted to damage the Yankees quite as much as Polonia. The Yankees had acquired Polonia in June 1989 as part of the package for Rickey Henderson, who went on to help the A's win a title that year. Polonia was arrested less than 2 months later and ultimately convicted of having sex with an underage girl while the Yankees were in Milwaukee. The Yankees dumped him the following year before re-signing him to be their leadoff hitter after the 1993 season. When George Steinbrenner's personal project, Darryl Strawberry, was promoted in early August 1995, the Yankees cleared roster space by trading Polonia to the Braves. Polonia was bitter about both Yankee experiences.

Wetteland fired six straight fastballs to Polonia, and the little lefty hitter fouled off each one, all either straight back or to the opposite field. On the fourth foul, Yankee first-base coach Jose Cardenal determined that Polonia would have difficulty pulling the ball and certainly would not drive a ball down the right-field line. Cardenal was also in charge of positioning the outfield, and he waved for Strawberry to move closer to the left-field line, Bernie Williams to shade more toward left-center, and O'Neill to take about seven steps toward right-center. That O'Neill was even in right field was somewhat of a surprise. Torre had decided to bench not only Boggs and Martinez for a third straight game but O'Neill as well. His original design had Tim Raines in left field and

Darryl Strawberry in right. But O'Neill had reacted so gloomily to Torre's face-to-face meeting to break this news that Torre altered his plan. Unlike Martinez, Torre felt O'Neill would become useless as a player if he did not start in a third straight game, so he reconfigured his lineup to put Strawberry in left and O'Neill in right. Raines was 10 inches shorter than Strawberry and probably would not have had the length to catch Blauser's drive in the eighth inning.

O'Neill had suffered a severely strained left hamstring on August 24, legging out a double against Oakland's Buddy Groom. He needed a month off and would not get it until the off-season. As far back as Game 4 of the American League Championship Series, Torre had second-guessed himself for leaving O'Neill in as he watched a potentially critical eighth-inning single by Baltimore's B. J. Surhoff fall in front of the right fielder. Strawberry had won his World Series in 1986, in part because Red Sox manager John McNamara's loyalty to Bill Buckner kept the hobbled first baseman on the field to celebrate a championship, rather than his usual defensive replacement, Dave Stapleton. O'Neill was only in the lineup due to Torre's loyalty and remained in only because the team's best defensive outfielder, Ruben Rivera, was deactivated for the World Series because he could no longer play through a right shoulder strain incurred making a throw against Milwaukee on September 25. A limping O'Neill, Torre surmised, was his best option.

For the seventh pitch of the sequence to Polonia, both Wetteland and Leyritz considered a breaking ball, since the sheer surprise might catch Polonia looking at a called third strike. But two factors worked against it: Wetteland was liable to bounce a breaking pitch, and, with a runner on third base, the risk was too great of a run-scoring wild pitch. More important, Leyritz was still thinking about how Mark Wohlers had gained infamy the previous night by going with his third-best pitch in a game-deciding situation. Wetteland's best pitch was his fastball up in the zone, and Polonia was a low-ball hitter. So Leyritz called for a seventh straight fastball, Wetteland concurred, and Polonia drove it deep to the gap in right-center to about the same area in which the miscommunication between Grissom and Dye had helped produce the lone run in this game.

Had he not been repositioned by Cardenal, O'Neill would have had no shot whatsoever on the ball. Even while running as hard as he could on unsure legs, O'Neill was not certain he would catch up. As he ran, the phrase "oh my God" kept racing through his mind because it seemed to him that this ball had extra carry. O'Neill was 6 feet, 4 inches and, because he was a lefty thrower, his glove was on the right hand, the hand he could stretch farther into the right-center gap. If the ball landed, not only would Chipper Jones walk home from third with the tying run but Klesko almost certainly would score from first with the winning run. Instead, O'Neill fully extended his glove, and the ball stuck in the webbing before he took a few more steps and slammed both hands into the fence in elation. O'Neill came limping back to the infield, chaperoned by Williams. The Yankees led the World Series.

"You say, 'Oh my gosh, how does he make that play on a bad leg?'" Tom Glavine says. "It is two runs and the game if he doesn't make the play. Suddenly, he makes the play, and you don't like our chances." Eddie Perez recalls, "I still don't know how he caught that ball. I thought, *It's not our series.*"

The Yankees had won Game 5 because one outfielder with a fractured toe made a terrific catch and another outfielder with a damaged hamstring outdid him. They had won because their worst fielding starting pitcher made a play that no one on his own bench thought possible. That pitcher, Andy Pettitte, had redeemed himself from a Game 1 brutalization by registering $8\frac{1}{3}$ shutout innings to outduel Smoltz at his best. The Yankees, who just a year earlier had been swept out of the playoffs because they could not win one of three games on the road in Seattle, had just completed a three-game sweep in Atlanta to improve to an inconceivable 8–0 on the road in the playoffs.

Torre's bold proclamation to Steinbrenner had been fulfilled. The Yankees had indeed gone into Atlanta and won the final three games ever in Fulton County Stadium before the Braves moved across the street to Turner Field. They were, as Torre had vowed to Steinbrenner, coming home not to pack up their lockers but to pack Yankee Stadium at least one more time with a chance to win a World Series. To Joe Torre, it all felt like a miracle.

He hadn't seen anything yet.

Early on the evening of October 24, just about the time the Yankees were beginning Game 5 in Atlanta, a 28-year-old Bronx man died of a herniated brain at Montefiore Medical Center. The family of the dead man consented that his kidneys, lungs, liver, pancreas, and heart be donated. The New York Regional Transplant Program used a computer program to match blood and tissue type, and the size and weight of his heart, to find the most ideal candidate on the waiting list. The most perfect match belonged to a 64-year-old man who had been lying in Room 156 of the Millstein Building at Columbia-Presbyterian Medical Center for 11 weeks. At 3 a.m., less than 4 hours after gimpy-legged Paul O'Neill had corralled Luis Polonia's long fly to right-center, Frank Torre was awakened and told a heart had been located for him.

Frank Torre had suffered three heart attacks in his life and had ischemic cardiomyopathy, essentially congestive heart failure. Medicines were keeping his heart beating, but that was growing more tenuous. "He had class IV heart failure, which meant he could essentially do nothing; he had no quality of life," recalls Donna Mancini, MD, medical director of the heart-transplant program at Columbia-Presbyterian. "He was really at the end." One of Frank Torre's surgeons, Mehmet Oz, MD, looks back more tersely: "Without a new heart fast, Frank was a dead man watching his last World Series."

At 5:45 a.m. on October 25, about half an hour after he returned to his Westchester home following a flight from Atlanta, Joe Torre answered the phone to be informed his brother was being prepped for surgery. Eric Rose, MD, and Dr. Oz performed the 4-hour procedure that began at 8:30 a.m. and watched as the old patient and the new heart immediately took to each other. By midafternoon, all of New York was growing aware of this lifesaving surgery, and the city celebrated. The Torres had evolved into the first family of New York during this postseason. There was one of Joe's sisters, Rae, who served as the family matriarch and still lived in the same brick row house on Avenue T in Brooklyn that Joe had grown up in. His other sister, a nun, Sister Marguerite, was the principal at the Nativity of the Blessed Virgin Mary Elementary School in Ozone Park, and Joe's office was full of schoolchildren's art, wishing him well. The city knew about the heartbreak of Rocco Torre dying suddenly in June and had followed the drama of Frank Torre awaiting a new heart. And, of course, there was Joe, a baseball lifer finally drinking full the glories of October.

Joe Torre had been a mistake child, the youngest of five siblings. The next youngest, Frank, was 8 years older. Frank was Joe's tormentor and defender. He belittled his younger brother for being overweight, but he was more father to Joe than was their actual abusive father. He paid for Joe's high school tuition to St. Francis Prep and insisted that his heavyset brother be moved to catcher as a teenager while playing with his traveling sandlot team. It was that transition that got Joe signed to a professional contract and led to him outdoing his brother on the field in all but one way.

The last time the Braves and Yankees had played in the World Series was 1957 and 1958, and at that time the Braves called Milwaukee home. Frank Torre was the first baseman for those clubs. The Braves had won the title in 1957 in seven games and lost in seven games in 1958. Frank Torre presented his 1958 league championship ring to his mother, who did not wear it and eventually gave it to Joe. While Joe Torre was staying at the Omni Hotel in New York in 1972 to ratify a new collective-bargaining agreement and end a players' strike, the ring was stolen from his room. Frank Torre told Joe that to make amends, he had to win a championship ring of his own and present it to Frank's son. Frankie Torre was 20 years old now and still ringless. But Joe Torre was closer to getting that jewelry than ever before, all because he had taken the job his brother was initially adamant against him accepting.

"Are you crazy?" Frank Torre had said to Joe 12 months earlier, when Joe told him he was mulling over the Yankee managerial position. "I knew George and

his track record. I figured with that stage, why would you even think about it,"
Frank Torre remembers. "He said, 'I still want to get into a World Series. I still
need that chance.' That being the case, I thought, *George is tough to work for, but
he won't hesitate to spend what is needed.* Also, I thought he was coming in at a
good time. They were in a 17-year slump, and George was hungering to win. I
gave it my blessing."

The decision essentially saved Frank Torre. First, it put Joe back in New York,
where he could pull the necessary strings to get his brother into probably the
world's best cardiac-care program; also, it gave baseball back to Frank Torre.
Baseball gave him something to look forward to every day in the hospital, something to live for. He anticipated the daily phone calls with his brother to discuss
strategy and provide his input on the lineup. "I think it helped him enormously,"
Dr. Mancini says. "Every day he talked to Joe multiple times. He was like a bench
coach. He was always watching the game. It was a wonderful distraction for him."

Even deathly sick, Frank Torre was hardheaded and opinionated, still net-
tling his brother, but now about batting orders and pitching changes, not weight
issues. The Panasonic television in the corner of the room had become a lifeline
to the game and the brother he loved, a way to share something with Joe. For
years Frank had been his brother's most ardent defender, stressing that Joe belonged in the Hall of Fame as a player and deserved a better lot than managing
bad, and/or underfunded rosters. Now he was able to find happiness in that dis-
eased heart because after all these years, Joe Torre was finally on this championship stage. "The baseball kept my spirits up and my mind off of what I was
going through," he says.

Joe Torre was both exhausted and exhilarated when he arrived at the hospital late the afternoon of the transplant, entering as his brother awoke from
the anesthesia. He was tired, but not so tired that he did not see the miracle in
all of this. This was the same hospital where David Cone had undergone his
risky aneurysm surgery. The hospital was 2½ miles from Yankee Stadium. One
of the lead surgeons who had performed the operation was born and raised in
the Bronx as a Yankee fan (Rose) and the other surgeon's last name was, of all

things, Oz. And here was Joe Torre on the brink in his lifelong crusade to win a World Series. "All the transplants are like little miracles," says Dr. Mancini, who coordinated Frank Torre's pre- and postoperative care. "But this really was like a fairy tale."

Dr. Oz adds, "Joe had been told by Frank's doctors in Florida that his brother was dying, and there was nothing he could do about it. Joe got him into the program in New York. For all of this to happen, it would be like being down 2–0 in the World Series and winning. It was all like a dream."

Joe Torre felt each and every one of these blessings, as well as one other on the calendar. Game 6 was the next day. The rainout before Game 1 meant that October 25 was the only day during the World Series in which a game was not played.

"You can tell my brother is a baseball person," Joe Torre said. "He waited to the off day to have surgery."

Heart. New life. The metaphors seemed all too easy for these Yankees. Yet how could you ignore the obvious? This team that had very good talent had great heart. This team left for dead 6 days earlier in a one-two Braves punch of Maddux and Smoltz was the talk of the town. New York wrapped its arms around the club that just did not know how to go away. "I do believe it," Tino Martinez says, looking back. "I think we were special."

Still, aware the Braves had been prematurely anointed champs earlier in the series, Joe Torre had concerns about losing now when his team was finally supposed to win. Atlanta, after all, had crawled out of a three-games-to-one hole in the NLCS by storming the Cardinals 32–1 over the final three games. The pitching matchup of Greg Maddux versus Jimmy Key favored the Braves. No one knew that better than the Yankees. When they had a chance to get both, they had greatly favored Maddux.

Following the 1992 season, then Yankee general manager Gene Michael wanted to add two starting pitchers and prioritized Maddux above all others. Michael had managed the Cubs in 1986 and 1987, when Maddux first broke in and recognized his pitching intellect, serenity, and athleticism, even as the righty struggled as a youngster. From 1988 to 1992, only Roger Clemens pitched more innings and won more often than Maddux, who culminated that run in 1992 with his first 20-win season and National League Cy Young Award. Maddux did not particularly want to be a Yankee, but with George Steinbrenner due back from his suspension in March 1993, Michael suddenly had more money to assemble a better team. Michael escorted Maddux around the New Jersey suburbs to show Maddux and his wife that there was a peaceful life just a few miles outside of New York City. Michael went lowbrow in restaurant choices, taking Maddux to Charlie Brown's, but there was nothing low about the Yankees' 5-year, $34 million offer, which would make Maddux the highest-paid pitcher ever. Before leaving for his home in Las Vegas, Maddux told his agent, Scott Boras, to make the deal.

"When he got on the plane, truthfully, I thought he was with us," recalls then Yankee co-assistant GM Tim McCleary. But while Maddux was in the air, Boras received a call from Braves GM John Schuerholz. The team could move starting pitcher Charlie Leibrandt and his $2.5 million 1993 salary to Texas, which would give them money to offer Maddux a 5-year, $29 million deal. Would he accept? Since he did not really want to play in New York or the AL, Maddux left money on the table and chose Atlanta.

The Yankees then turned to David Cone at the Winter Meetings in Louisville, Kentucky. But Cone was offended by how disorganized the Yankees were in pursuing him and instead accepted a $9 million signing bonus to return home to play for Kansas City. That left a pool of six free-agent starters featuring Key, Chris Bosio, Jose Guzman, Doug Drabek, John Smiley, and Greg Swindell. At this point, the Yankees were ready to complete a deal with whichever above-average starter would take their money. The Blue Jays had a policy under their general manager at the time, Pat Gillick, not to give 4-year contracts to pitchers, and Key wanted 4 years. He was the winningest lefty in

team history and had just won the clinching game of the World Series in relief. What Toronto refused to do, the Yankees were now desperate enough to
offer. Key's then wife, Cindy, served as his agent, and while on a Caribbean
cruise, the couple finalized a 4-year, $17 million deal with the Yankees.

"There were eight free-agent starters on our list, and Key was the eighth
guy," says the other co-assistant GM at the time, Brian Cashman. "We came out
of Louisville feeling like we failed."

Key defied that assessment. He won 35 games between 1993 and 1994, tying
with Glavine for the second most in the majors. Only Maddux won more at
36. Key's unflinching persona rubbed off on a clubhouse as surely as Wade
Boggs's plate discipline. Eighth choice or not, Key had been a great signing by
the Yankees, even if he did miss almost all of the 1995 season. He was one of
the essential players in professionalizing the clubhouse culture. Now, in what
would be the final game on his 4-year contract, Key had to try to outdo the
Yankees' first choice from the 1992–93 off-season.

Neither starter allowed a hit through the first two innings, Key helped by another fine defensive play in left field by Darryl Strawberry. Key then worked
through a scoreless top of the third, aided by Joe Girardi throwing out Terry
Pendleton trying to steal. That defensive acumen was just why Torre and
Zimmer had lobbied to bring Girardi to New York against the wishes of just
about every fan and member of the media. Torre and Zimmer got what they
wanted. Girardi got misery.

It was strange. Torre had replaced Buck Showalter and Tino Martinez had
stepped in for Don Mattingly, and life was certainly difficult for both new
Yankees in succeeding extremely popular figures. But nobody was more abused
than Girardi. "Fans do not relate to managers like they do players, and Don
Mattingly was retiring; someone had to replace him," Girardi says, looking back.
"But the perception was that I pushed Mike Stanley out of town."

Stanley had arrived to the Yankees for the 1992 season after having been released in consecutive years by the Rangers. He built himself up from a nonroster player to an All-Star in 4 years. He was another one of those team-oriented guys who flourished under Buck Showalter and helped create a championship fabric that ultimately Torre would inherit and benefit from. His navigation from scrub to core member of a playoff team endeared him to the Yankee fan base. But Torre had watched tapes of Stanley after taking the job, and he felt that the team needed a more skilled player behind the plate. Stanley's strength was offense. He was serious about his catching but not smooth at it. He also had made an enemy of George Steinbrenner favorite Billy Connors because, one member of the organization from that time period says, "he didn't believe in any of Billy's bullshit." Another member of the organization says, "Billy Connors always pushed Leyritz, who he liked, as a much better catcher than Stanley."

Torre, Zimmer, Mel Stottlemyre, and Bob Watson had all just come from the NL, and each admired how Girardi worked a game. But Girardi's attributes were understated and difficult to sell. He had 18 career homers, as many as Stanley had the previous season. What Girardi did was harder to quantify, and, because of that, he was lacerated more in the media and among the Yankee faithful. At the Yankees' annual Fan Festival on February 4 at the New York Coliseum, the mere announcement of his name drew loud booing, as it did at the club's Welcome Home Dinner and home opener.

Girardi was devastated. He struggled early in the regular season with just two RBIs in the team's first 21 games. Over and over, the powerful all-sports station in town, WFAN, would play a tape from a previous season of Girardi grounding out weakly to Mets starting pitcher Bobby Jones as a way of defining him as a powder-puff performer. The station also mockingly played a song parody "Joe, Joe, Girardi-o" played to the same cadence of the deifying "Joe, Joe DiMaggio" performed by Les Brown in 1941. Girardi heeded the counsel of David Cone and Cone's business manager, Andrew Levy, to call the station unsolicited and display a sense of humor about the whole thing, surmising that would humanize Girardi. It definitely helped. So did Zimmer's advice a month into the season to stop trying to be Mike Stanley.

But time was Girardi's greatest ally. Only time would allow all of his attributes to be seen. Over time, the fans saw the sincerity with which he played. His hustle never waned. If the pitchers had a good day, he did too, even if he went hitless in five at-bats. The scoreboard provided Girardi's final grade; if the Yankees won, he was satisfied. He was serious and bright. The pitchers loved pitching to him; Dwight Gooden gushed over and over again about Girardi's game calling, counsel, and framing of pitches during his no-hitter, and that was a big turning point with the fans as well. Girardi was low maintenance and high energy. He had the look of a Marine. He was muscular, with a crew cut and a square jaw. And he had an attitude to match. Slowly the fans adopted him, just as they had Stanley. "It was a growing experience for me," Girardi says. "What I learned is the New York fans were loyal fans, so they were loyal to Mike Stanley. I had to play awhile for them to become loyal to me."

Girardi won them over by the time he batted in the third inning with his cribbage partner, Paul O'Neill, on third base with one out. Bobby Cox ordered his infield in. Girardi was a ninth-place batter without a hit in his last 12 post-season at-bats. In Game 2 against Maddux, Girardi failed to get the ball out of the infield in three at-bats. Girardi led the Yankees in sacrifice bunts in 1996 with 11, and when he looked down to third-base coach Willie Randolph, he was sure he was going to see the sign for a safety squeeze. He did not. Instead, it was him against a man he knew all too well. In his second major league game in 1989, Girardi had caught Maddux, and he was the starting catcher in 43 of Maddux's Cubs starts from 1989 to 1992. Girardi knew Maddux would attack a weak hitter to get an out, so he guessed first-pitch fastball and concentrated solely on driving the ball to the outfield for a sacrifice fly. The Yankees had not scored in Game 2 against Maddux, so it was important in Girardi's mind to break that hex.

Maddux threw a first-pitch fastball but did not execute. He wanted it down near Girardi's knees to induce a groundball. But it was waist high and Girardi pounced, clobbering a ball perhaps as far as he could hit it to straightaway center. Marquis Grissom was playing shallow, and he could not catch up as the ball hit the lip of the warning track and bounced against the fence. O'Neill scored, and Girardi chugged into third with a pop-up slide.

An electricity had been building over the past 48 hours in New York, ever since the Yankees closed out the Braves in Game 5. Frank Torre's heart transplant had added more poignancy, drama, and excitement. City life revolved around Game 6 on the night of October 26. Five hundred extra police had been assigned to Yankee Stadium, and even 5 hours before the game there was a bustle outside the stadium, a cocktail of anticipation and euphoria. The Yankees had returned 8-year-old Christina Lynn Skleros to sing "The Star Spangled Banner." She was dubbed the Yankees' "Angel in the Infield" because the team had rallied to win the three previous times she had performed the national anthem, including Game 2 of the Division Series. She was not even halfway done when the crowd already was in full froth, growing louder with each inning and seemingly building toward the moment when Girardi slid into third. The stands in the stadium literally shook as 56,375 folks saw just how loud they could yell, how high they could jump in joy. Those who were there still talk about that sound, a sound so different from what Joe Girardi had experienced at the other end of the season.

"I don't want to get too mushy, but I was almost in tears at third base," Girardi recalls. "What I went through in April . . . I never thought a moment like this was coming. It was the happiest moment of my career, and the biggest regret of my career was that I could not stop and listen, because everything happens so fast in the game of baseball. I was so happy that I lost the ability to hear what was going on around me. You know what I wish? I wish I could go back and listen to it all, and then just return and go on with my life."

By the time the third inning was over, Derek Jeter and Bernie Williams—bigger stars than anybody this October—had each lined an RBI single to center. The

Yankees led 3–0. And then Game 6 of the World Series mimicked Game 5 of the ALCS. The Yankees had scored all their runs in that contest in the third inning, as well, then waited and waited for the game to end. The interminable wait for a championship began now in Game 6 of the 1996 World Series.

One thing did happen quickly: Key gave a run back to the Braves in the fourth inning. With one out, he allowed a walk and two singles before walking Jermaine Dye to force in a run. Key, in many ways, resembled a Braves starter. He pitched with precision to the outside corner and slowly expanded to seduce overanxious hitters to chase pitches not in the strike zone. Even with the bases filled with the go-ahead runs, Key refused to abandon his style. He was the best guy to have pitching in an amped-up stadium. Key was imperturbable. How cool was he? Just before he had left for perhaps the most important start of his career, Key proposed to his girlfriend, Karin Kane. He gave away one ring around 1 p.m., and now he needed one more big moment in the hunt for another.

David Weathers was warming up as Key fell behind Terry Pendleton 3–1. One more ball and Weathers was going to enter the game. Still, Key had determined that he had to stay away and change speeds on these Atlanta hitters, even if it meant pitching from behind, as he had been. So he threw yet another changeup, risking ball 4. But Pendleton was too frisky, chopping the ball to Jeter, who stepped on second and fired to first for an inning-ending double play. Key survived the fifth inning when second-base ump Terry Tata incorrectly called Grissom out trying to advance to second on a ball that dribbled a few feet away from Girardi. Braves manager Bobby Cox, at his boiling point, argued with Tata and then, unprovoked, lit into third-base ump Tim Welke, whom he was still mad at for getting in Jermaine Dye's way in Game 4. Cox was ejected and returned to the clubhouse to watch the rest of this World Series.

A double by Chipper Jones and a groundout by McGriff put a runner on third with one out, and finally Torre had seen enough. Key was chagrined, but he soaked in a standing ovation that made a third shoulder surgery and all the taxing rehab worthwhile. He put on a warmup jacket, wrapped a towel around his neck, and watched Weathers fan Javy Lopez on three pitches. Andruw Jones walked, and Ryan Klesko was sent up to pinch-hit for Dye. It was time again for Graeme Lloyd, who for the third time in this World Series baffled Klesko, who popped to second to end the sixth inning. Weathers had pitched 11 postseason innings and permitted one run. Lloyd had worked 5⅓ innings and yielded one hit. Together, Weathers and Lloyd had redeemed themselves from their miserable regular season, and on the night of October 26, they had teamed for what Torre thought was the most important facet of the game: They had bridged the gap from Key to the Formula.

Mariano Rivera walked Pendleton to open the seventh on four straight pitches and then retired six straight Braves. Rivera believed that with two outs in the eighth inning there was one out left in his season. So when he got ahead 1–2 on Javy Lopez, he reached back one last time to find all the energy in his skinny body. He reached back to Panama and days as a nonprospect and career-threatening elbow surgery. He darted a ball belt high to the outside corner. Lopez, like so many in 1996, had no chance, swinging through 95 miles per hour of menace. Rivera returned to the dugout to a thunderous ovation, having completed a postseason in which he permitted one run in 14⅓ innings. His ERA for the whole year, regular and postseason, was 1.92, and he had 140 strikeouts against just one homer in 122 innings. But the numbers did not fully explain the magic. This was a season of offense and squalid middle relief. Rivera was a one-man fortress against the trend. "When I think of 1996," Girardi says, looking back, "I think of Mariano Rivera."

Rivera had taken the Yankees to within three outs of a title. But first Wetteland had to negotiate another ninth inning as only he could, which meant testing everyone's heart, old and new. One of Frank Torre's surgeons, Dr. Rose, had given his blessing for his patient to watch Game 6 because "we think he is much better off with this heart than the old heart, and we let him watch the games with the old one." So Frank Torre was among the television audience who sat rapt as Wetteland sandwiched two strikeouts around two singles before

Grissom singled in a run to make it 3–2. The tying run was on second. The go-ahead run was on first. Mark Lemke was the batter.

George Steinbrenner paced in the press-box pathway, muttering in anguish and encouragement. Joe Torre worked a piece of gum on the bench in the middle of what had become the Yankee Mount Rushmore during the season, Don Zimmer to his right and Mel Stottlemyre to his left. Wetteland went to a full count; of course he did. He was John Wetteland. Lemke lifted a fastball toward the third-base stands. Charlie Hayes fell into the Braves dugout, trying and failing to make the catch.

At 10:56 p.m., Lemke popped foul again to this area, just a little farther down the line. Hayes drifted toward the stands and Jeter came over as well. This time Hayes stopped, his right leg perhaps a foot from the railing. The ball was in the air long enough that he could repeat over and over in his head, *Squeeze it, squeeze it*, and for Torre to have one more long wait in a career built around the long wait. Girardi jogged down the line, staring at the ball, yelling, "Stay in, stay in." It did. Jeter threw his arms in the air in celebration the instant before the ball rested in Hayes's mitt. Wetteland jumped into Girardi's arms, a single index finger raised overhead as his teammates swarmed the mound. Once again the old stadium swayed in noise and joy.

In the dugout, Torre was swallowed by a group hug from his coaches. With the last ounce of strength in his damaged hamstring, O'Neill finished a sprint from right field by leaping high into the on-field pile and flipping over in a somersault. Wetteland was screaming, part in elation, part because he thought his ankle was going to break beneath the mass of humanity. Always an analytical catcher, Girardi was already plotting not to get caught under the next championship pile because he could not catch his breath now.

Before Game 6, Zimmer had suggested that if the Yankees won the World Series, they should take a victory lap, and Torre gathered his team to do a loop as Frank Sinatra's "New York, New York" morphed into Queen's "We Are the Champions." Wade Boggs, despite a lifelong aversion to horses, was so overwhelmed by bliss that he climbed on back of a horse ridden by a police officer. It was the greatest party in New York, and no one wanted to leave. The champagne flowed in the clubhouse, but recovering addicts Dwight Gooden and Darryl Strawberry did not drink.

Over and over, the members of this team hugged and looked at each other full of pride, but also full of amazement at this unfathomable journey. They had come from the depths of addiction, from the Northern League, from last place in Detroit and Pittsburgh, from aneurysm surgery, from replacing legends and fan favorites, from Clyde King's disapproval, from an unlikely confluence of events in Panama, from being stashed in a Connecticut baseball academy, from the misery of the Seattle Division Series the year before, from retirement, and from nearly 4 decades futilely pursuing a World Series. They had united to win the Yankees' 23rd title, tying them with the Montreal Canadiens for the most in team sports. They had come together to thrill a city. They had bonded to create a way in which the organization would play—and win—for years. They had put aside personal agendas, found strength in the group, and given birth to a dynasty.

EPILOGUE

"That one [World Series] eats at me. With that team, I felt we had the best team in baseball. Every other year since then, I felt we were beaten by a team that was either better than us or playing better at the time. No disrespect to the Yankees, but I thought we had the best team."

— *Chipper Jones*

Some estimates had as many as 3½ million screaming, jumping, and jubilant spectators lining the Canyon of Heroes as the Yankees paraded up lower Broadway. A snowstorm of confetti blanketed the route from Battery Park to City Hall on October 29. Fans came from all over the tri-state area to celebrate a storybook come to life. Young women held up signs offering themselves to Derek Jeter. Kenny Rogers, a champion on the backs of others, climbed to the top of a float, waved a Yankee flag, and carried on more outlandishly than any of his teammates. Cecil Fielder filmed the proceedings. David Cone alternated pumping his fist and applauding those who were applauding him.

Block after block, along the route that once hailed Charles Lindbergh and the Apollo astronauts, a city lovingly told the Yankees how it felt about a championship that was part opera and part Oprah, a mixture of hardball and cornball, and a blend of a season on the brink and a season in the sun.

The last time a baseball team had traveled this path was a decade earlier, when New York saluted the 1986 Mets. Millions attended that parade, but what is most remembered is who did not. Dwight Gooden admitted years later that he was in no shape to partake in the festivities following a night of heavy drinking; there were already plenty of whispers about his rampant cocaine use.

Gooden and Strawberry, the stars of that Mets team, succumbed to addiction, and an organization spiraled downward, never to win another championship.

These Yankees, however, were just starting. They won three consecutive titles from 1998 to 2000. Young stars such as Derek Jeter, Andy Pettitte, Mariano Rivera, and Bernie Williams possessed the discipline and maturity that Gooden and Strawberry had lacked. Their heads never swelled, and the lurking evils that accompany success, especially in New York, never derailed them. For good measure, Gooden and Strawberry were around these Yankees as cautionary tales, happy passengers in this parade. The presence of such fallen stars was another bit of blessed fortune that cloaked the 1996 Yankees. The chapter titles of this book play off the word *perfect* because with all of the financial advantages the Yankees have had over the years, they still needed a perfect storm of events to create an unlikely champion in 1996 and an enduring one thereafter. The 1996 club came together almost by magic, through hundreds, if not thousands, of decisions and events, both planned and capricious. Jim Leyritz took the most meaningful and memorable swing of the season. Yet if Jorge Posada had not broken his ankle blocking the plate in a July 1994 Triple-A game, he almost certainly would have been the backup catcher in 1996, allowing the Yankees' front office to do what it longed to do for years—trade the unpopular Leyritz.

Instead, with his progress stunted, Posada was on the bench in a warmup jacket as an inactive player when Mark Wohlers threw one slider too many. He was a witness to a championship season filled with plots both sappy and maudlin, yet unscripted and unpredictable. When the year began, Joe Torre was among baseball's all-time losers, Jeter was an untested rookie, and Rivera was a failed starter. In 1996, they took their first meaningful steps toward being baseball giants.

It was a Yankee season full of redemption and rebirth, a season in which the most famous sports organization in the world got its groove back. The 1996 Yankees paved a path for years of pinstriped greatness that led to four championships in 5 years. Those titles were won with an offensive philosophy built more on plate discipline than on Bronx Bomberism, with a bullpen centered around the great Rivera that neutralized the opposition and made stirring late comebacks feasible, and with a stout confidence in each other that deepened the resolve of the group. All of those characteristics first flourished in full for the Yankees in 1996.

That is why that club stands distinct and why, with the perspective of a decade gone by, it seems the right time to set the record straight on that team and fully honor those Yankees for how they were assembled and what they meant to baseball history. They were the building blocks for arguably the greatest run by a major league team ever.

Unfortunately for the legacy of this group, the success of these Yankees coincided with a powerful push by central baseball to convince fans that the disparity between the financial haves and have-nots was destroying the competitive balance of the sport. The Yankees came to embody the big-market superpowers. They were demonized for buying championships. They were cast as villains by a Commissioner's Office that saw the advantages of portraying them as a prop in a strategy to win salary concessions from the players in collective bargaining. Thus, the Yankees of this era do not receive near the credit they deserve for what they accomplished.

Those Yankee teams certainly benefited from financial might, but most of it was expressed in retaining the players they shrewdly developed or acquired in trades. The only major free-agent signings to significantly help the Yankees in 1996 were those of Wade Boggs and Jimmy Key, who both had joined the Yankees 4 years earlier. In addition, there were many teams within payroll proximity to those championship Yankees. Coincidence or not, the Yankees stopped winning titles when they started to monetarily dust the field. If anything, the latter financial monsters who failed to reach the Canyon of Heroes accentuate just how extraordinary the championship Yankees were. It would be difficult for an All-Star team to win three rounds of playoffs as regularly as the Yankees did from 1996 to 2000. The first 20 times a Yankee team captured a title, it simply had to win one playoff round: the World Series. In 1977 and 1978, the Yankees won two rounds. How many of those record 22 overall titles would they have won if they had to survive three rounds?

Besides, despite the long-held propaganda, Torre did not have All-Star teams at his disposal. Go around the diamond. Only Jeter and Williams were constantly among the best players at their positions. In the four championship years, a Yankee player received a total of three first-place votes for the MVP, all by Jeter. This team won because it had a lot of very good players. But it also won because of harder-to-define elements. The Yankees of this era drew confidence simply from being around one another. They had an indefatigable belief in what the group could accomplish, which diminished the pressure on individuals and, in particular, allowed Yankee players to perform with such grace in the crucible of October.

Again, time lumps that first champion of the Torre era with all the others, as simply a group of well-paid stars overwhelming the field. But Mariano Rivera was 12th in the American League Most Valuable Player voting in 1996, the highest of any Yankee. The 1996 Yankees finished ninth in the AL in runs and fifth in ERA. No World Series winner in history had ever ranked so low in its league in both categories. All of the previous 22 Yankee championship teams finished either first or second in runs in the AL, except in 1923 (third) and in 1977 and 1978 (fourth both times). Every previous Yankee champion had wound up in the top three in ERA. The 1996 Yankees ranked 11th in the AL in homers. The only time a Yankee champion previously failed to finish in the top three was 1978, when the Yankees ranked sixth.

So these Yankees were hardly an overwhelming force. Multiple players from the 1996 Rangers, Orioles, and Braves all said they thought they were better than the Yankees and went into their postseason series believing they would win. That they didn't, these players almost universally agree, owed to something more than the Yankees' talent.

"That one series haunts me more than any other," John Smoltz says, "because we had it won. We won the first two games in New York, and we didn't win another game. It's kind of hard to believe still that we didn't win it. What sticks to my mind is that it was a fluke. If we play that series 10 more times, we win it all 10 times. But the one time we had to win it, we didn't."

Maybe Smoltz is right. Maybe the Yankees were fortunate to win a series in which they seemed so clearly overmatched and that began so ominously. Or, perhaps, those Yankees were just exhibiting a tenacity and mettle that would come to define them. The Yankees lost the opener of that World Series 12–1, The 11-run differential in a loss was worse than the Yankees had ever endured in 187 previous Fall Classic games. The Yankees then had a string of 65 straight postseason games without being shutout end the next night, when they lost 4–0 to fall behind two games to none, with the series shifting to Atlanta. At that moment, the Braves were defending champions, playing in the World Series for the fourth time in 6 years. Smoltz, Tom Glavine, and Greg Maddux were all 30 years old or younger. Andruw Jones was 19; Chipper Jones, 24. It is hard to believe the dynasty being born was that of the Yankees. The idea that the Yankees would end up being the team of the decade was absurd.

"Maybe if we didn't let that one get away, it would have changed the whole mind-set of the organization from top to bottom," Glavine says. "We would have had the confidence of winning back-to-back World Series. Maybe we would have won a lot more." The Yankees rallied in that World Series by relying on assets that would buoy their championship run. For example, they lost Game 4 of the 2000 Division Series by 10 runs, 11–1, to the A's, yet stayed focused enough to fly cross-country to Oakland to win a decisive fifth game the next day, en route to a third straight championship.

The Yankees closed out the 1996 World Series with a 3–2 win, making them 5–0 in the 1996 postseason in one-run games. In the championship years of 1996 and 1998 to 2000, the Yankees were 12–0 in one-run games in the playoffs. Think about that; they won all 12 times a one-run game could have gone one way or another. After losing all three Division Series games in Seattle to get eliminated from the 1995 Division Series, the Yankees won all three in Atlanta and finished 8–0 on the road in the 1996 postseason, kick-starting what would be a 24–5 road record in the championship years, including 9–1 in the World Series. The Yankees' season ended in extra innings in 1995. A year later they won an extra-inning game in all three rounds of the postseason, most memorably in Game 4 of the World Series after Jim Leyritz's three-run homer off Mark Wohlers tied the score. The Yankees were 6–1 in postseason extra-inning games during their championship years.

Game 4 of the World Series was one of six times in the 1996 postseason that the Yankees scored the go-ahead run in the seventh inning or later. Of the 44 wins they produced in their four championship years, in a staggering 16 (36.4 percent), they scored the go-ahead run from the seventh inning onward. They won four times in their final at-bat in the 1996 postseason and nine times overall during the championship years.

All of the close wins, all of the late-game comebacks, were tributes to the superiority of the Yankee bullpen. In 1995, that phase of the game—more than any other—had betrayed Buck Showalter. But one October later, Yankee relievers would go 6–1, produce seven saves in seven tries, and post a 1.81 ERA. In 1995, Showalter did not know just what a great weapon he had in his pen, shunning Rivera over and over again in the critical eighth inning of the decisive Game 5 at the Kingdome until it was too late. Torre, however, knew what he had. He used Rivera eight times in the 1996 postseason, and the Yankees went 7–1 in his appearances. Later, as a closer himself, Rivera was a frequent sight as early as the eighth inning, shortening the games and the playoff lives of opponents. An amazing 27 of the 33 postseason saves Rivera amassed from 1997 to 2005 were more than one inning. The calm he had revealed that so impressed his peers in the minors and again as a novice in the Kingdome was no act; it was a trait that enabled Rivera to pinpoint more critical October pitches than anybody in history. During the championship years, Rivera remained the weapon no other organization could match.

The other on-field trait that sustained the Yankees during the championship run was their unrelenting offensive discipline. Years after World Series Game 5, John Smoltz still could not comprehend how he could allow just one unearned run in eight innings and yet be made to throw 136 pitches. "How is that possible?" Smoltz says incredulously. "That was the Yankees. They were the team that wouldn't swing."

Still, in the 1996 World Series, the Braves outscored the Yankees (26–18), outhit them (.254–.216), and outhomered them (4–2). To win, the Yankees needed more than Rivera and plate discipline. They had lost 919 players' days to the disabled list during the season, the fifth most in the majors. The four teams ahead of them did not make the playoffs. The Yankees did more than that. They won a championship. They were mentally tough, and that enabled them to rally from what felt like an insurmountable deficit. The Yankees won four straight games over Atlanta, triggering what would be a major league record 14 consecutive World Series victories.

But something else was hatched in these playoffs. Never again under Torre would the Yankees be viewed as an underdog. As the years passed and the stresses, expectations, and payrolls swelled, Torre would wistfully look back to 1996, a time when simply reaching the World Series was considered such a great achievement for him and his team. The sense of vulnerability evaporated, quickly replaced, in part, by a culture of celebrity. Torre was on the *Late Show with David Letterman* 2 days after the World Series triumph, getting doused in champagne by several of his players who'd been lurking offstage. Derek Jeter became a corporation. The Yankees morphed into a brand as much as a baseball organization. What passed for the Age of Innocence for the Yankees was swept away with the confetti.

In its place, the pressure around the Yankees magnified and patience disintegrated. Bernie Williams would acknowledge that had he come along after the championship, the organization would not have let him work through his issues and flourish as a star. "I came at the perfect time," Williams says. "After a while, we stopped letting players like [Alfonso] Soriano and [Nick] Johnson mature. We just traded them. That would have been me."

Reality and change intruded on the championship Yankees as well. John Wetteland, the World Series MVP, left for free agency and was replaced as the closer for 1997 by Rivera. Jimmy Key signed with the Orioles because the Yankees would not guarantee a 2-year contract, and the Yankees countered by signing David Wells away from Baltimore. Leyritz was finally traded, to the Angels, and Posada became Joe Girardi's backup. However, a core group headed by Jeter, Rivera, Pettitte, Williams, Tino Martinez, Paul O'Neill, and David Cone stayed through the championships, nurturing those around them with their talent and poise. Torre remained the glue. The Yankees had bickered to titles in 1977 and 1978. But with all the stresses around the clubhouse, Torre marvelously inoculated his players from, among other things, the harrying spirit of George Steinbrenner. That would help the Yankees earn three more trips up the Canyon of Heroes.

But never again would it feel like that first time. The 1996 Yankees had won more than a championship. They had won hearts, admiration, and their place in history.

Acknowledgments

I kept tabling and tabling writing the acknowledgments for this book because, in many ways, I found it more formidable than the book itself. How do you thank so many who have come to your aid so often? I finally succumbed, but I make my own acknowledgment that it will fall far short of my true gratitude.

For starters, I want to thank the leadership of the *New York Post* sports section. Greg Gallo and Dick Klayman graciously allowed me to pursue this project and for years have opened space in our newspaper for me to joyfully expound on baseball, which gave me the footing to write this book. Our Yankees and Mets beat writers, George King and Mark Hale, were the best teammates in baseball this past year, when I was distracted thinking about 1996 rather than the current state of the New York clubs. Mostly, though, I would like to express gratitude to *New York Post* columnist Mike Vaccaro. He encouraged me to become an author, introduced me to his agents, and read various versions of this project. His counsel and insights were invaluable. I am blessed to call him friend.

I was further blessed that the two hardest-working, most able people at the *Post* were allies of this project. Laura Harris, who runs the library department, always found the time and resources I needed. Her competence is matched only by her kindness. Charles Wenzelberg helped make the daunting process of going through reams of photos at the *Post* bearable and productive. To this day, I have never seen anyone more tireless or diligent than Charlie was at the 1996 Summer Olympics, and he did it lugging around 50 pounds of equipment and laughing at all my dumb jokes.

Lou Rabito was the best copy editor I ever worked with when we were at NYU together in the early 1980s, and nothing has changed. He also read chapters as I went along and earned more saves than Mariano Rivera, catching mistakes, fixing grammar, and—as always—offering honest appraisal, knowing our friendship is based on that and not gratuitous backslapping. Ken Rosenthal of Foxsports.com read portions of the manuscript, which was both kind and helpful, but not nearly as helpful as reading a year's worth of his insightful, fearless work from 1996 in the *Baltimore Sun*.

Mike Bonner of the Yankees, Pat Courtney at Major League Baseball, Bobby Mills of the MSG-Network, and John Filipelli at the YES Network supplied tapes of games that were simply invaluable. The New York Yankee media relations department of Rick Cerrone, Jason Zillo, and Ben Tuliebitz helped with stats, phone numbers, and remembrances. Bob Waterman and, especially, John Labombarda of the Elias Sports Bureau kindly checked and double-checked many of the statistics in this book.

So many colleagues who shared jokes, beers, compassion, and expertise over my years, first as a Yankee beat writer and later as a baseball columnist, assisted in this book. But I would be remiss if I did not cite two. Jack Curry of the *Times* and Jon Heyman of *Newsday* made me a better newspaperman by performing their jobs so expertly and morally that, in competition, I was dragged up by their skills and character. More important, they made me a better man by being such wonderful friends in what can so often be a snake-pit business.

I learned during this process that many celebrity forewords are not actually written by the celebrities, many of whom simply offer their names. But know this: David Cone wrote the foreword to this book, proving his gifts stray well beyond a pitcher's mound.

My agents, Greg Dinkin and Frank Scatoni, helped a first-time author navigate from the germ of an idea to finished product. I thank them for always having my best interests and my back.

Stephanie Peterkin and, especially, Lorna Linton took such amazing care of my children, creating pockets of time to work on this project that otherwise would not have existed.

It feels wholly inadequate to thank my wife, Jillian Schwedler, for her contributions to this book. Her love, encouragement, decency, honesty, and intel-

lect have inspired every good occurrence in my life for 2 decades. How lucky are
you when the best person you have ever known also happens to be your wife?
Jill, too, became an author this year with the release of her book, *Faith in*
Moderation, Islamist Parties in Jordan and Yemen (Cambridge), and 18 months
ago she gave birth to our dynasty, my wonderful boys, Jake and Nick.

A Note on Sources

In many ways I have been preparing to write this book for much of my professional life. I began covering the Yankees as a beat in 1989, starting an education that would inform nearly every page of this project. I became a columnist in 1996, which made it a special year for me as well. However, so many folks involved in baseball were good enough to be interviewed for this book, a good deal of them on numerous occasions. The following were interviewed specifically for this book:

Sandy Alderson, Marty Appel, Gord Ash, Brad Ausmus, Gene Bennett, Gordon Blakeley, John Blundell, Scott Boras, Mike Borzello, Jim Bowden, Clete Boyer, Brian Butterfield, Josh Byrnes, Jose Cardenal, Brian Cashman, Tony Clark, Casey Close, David Cone, Pat Courtney, Bobby Cox, Lou Cucuzza, Rob Cucuzza, Jack Curry, Mike DeJean, Carlos Delgado, Gary Denbo, Steve Donohue, Rick Down, Jim Duquette, Jermaine Dye, Kevin Elfering, Bill Evers, Steve Fehr, Fred Ferreira, Rich Garcia, Will George, Bob Geren, Steve Greenberg, Jack Gillis, Joe Girardi, Tom Glavine, Marvin Goldklang, Wayne Graham, Dick Groch, Alan Hendricks, Chico Heron, Stuart Hershon, Trey Hillman, Jay Horwitz, Reggie Jackson, Derek Jeter, Davey Johnson, Randy Johnson, Sandy Johnson, Chipper Jones, Joe Klein, Jim Krivacs, Dave LaPoint, Ricky Ledee, Andrew Levy, Jim Leyritz, Rick Licht, Bill Livesey, Mitch Lukevics, Kevin Maas, Ken Macha, Jeffrey Maier, Kevin Malone, Donna Mancini, Tino Martinez, Don Mattingly, Tim McCleary, Michael McGorry, Mark McLemore, Jim Mecir, Doug Melvin, Gene Michael, Omar Minaya, Julian Mock, Gene Monahan, Mike Mussina, Ray Negron, Phil Nevin, Mark Newman, Gary Nickels, Dan O'Brien, Dan O'Dowd, Darren Oliver, Paul O'Neill, Mehmet Oz, Les Parker, Terry Pendleton, Eddie Perez, Sam Perlozzo, Andy Pettitte, Tom Pettitte, Lou Piniella, Jorge Posada, Nick Priore, Paul

Quantrill, Tim Raines, Willie Randolph, Herb Raybourn, J. P. Ricciardi, Arthur Richman, Mariano Rivera, Alex Rodriguez, Ross Sapp, Steve Sax, Mark Shapiro, Glenn Sherlock, Buck Showalter, Ruben Sierra, Randy Smith, Tal Smith, John Smoltz, Luis Sojo, Mike Stanton, Mel Stottlemyre, B. J. Surhoff, David Sussman, Rob Thomson, Carlos Tosca, Ali Torre, Frank Torre, Joe Torre, Bobby Valentine, Robin Ventura, Fay Vincent, Jerry Walker, Dave Wallace, Bob Watson, David Weathers, Mark Weidenmaier, Bernie Williams, Gerald Williams, Mickey White, Charlie Wonsowicz, Bill Wood, Frank Wren, and Don Zimmer.

Seven people, almost all former employees of the Yankees, were interviewed but asked not to be identified over concerns of retribution.

George Steinbrenner was one of about a dozen people who refused to be interviewed for this book.

Sources

Newspapers and Periodicals

The Atlanta Journal Constitution
The Baltimore Sun
The Bergen Record
The Dallas Morning News
Fort Worth Star-Telegram
Newsday
New York Daily News
The New Yorker
New York Magazine
The New York Post
The New York Times
Sports Illustrated
The Washington Post
The Washington Times

Books

Angell, Roger. *A Pitcher's Story: Innings with David Cone*. New York: Warner Books, 2001.

Harper, John, and Bob Klapisch. *Champions! The Saga of the 1996 New York Yankees*. New York: Villard, 1996.

Jeter, Derek, with Jack Curry. *The Life You Imagine: Life Lessons for Achieving Your Dreams*. New York: Three Rivers Press, 2000.

Olney, Buster. *The Last Night of the Yankee Dynasty: The Game, the Team, and the Cost of Greatness*. New York: HarperCollins, 2004.

Pearlman, Jeff. *The Bad Guys Won! A Season of Brawling, Boozing, Bimbo*

Chasing, and Championship Baseball with Straw, Doc, Mookie, Nails, the Kid, and the Rest of the 1986 Mets, the Rowdiest Team Ever to Put on a New York Uniform — and Maybe the Best. New York: HarperCollins, 2004.

Torre, Joe, with Tom Verducci. *Chasing the Dream: My Lifelong Journey to the World Series.* New York: Bantam Books, 1997.

Vincent, Fay. *The Last Commissioner: A Baseball Valentine.* New York: Simon & Schuster, 2002.

Index